WORKING ALLIANCES
POLITICS of DIFFEREN

WORKING ALLIANCES AND THE POLITICS OF DIFFERENCE

Diversity and Feminist Ethics

JANET R. JAKOBSEN

Indiana University Press
Bloomington and Indianapolis

The paper used in this publication meets the minimum require-
ments of American National Standard for Information Sciences—
Permanence of Paper for Printed Library Materials,
ANSI Z39.48-1984.

Manufactured in the United States of America

Library of Congress Cataloging-in-Publication Data

Jakobsen, Janet R., date
    Working alliances and the politics of difference : diversity and
feminist ethics / Janet R. Jakobsen.
        p.   cm.
    Includes bibliographical references and index.
    ISBN 0-253-33357-1 (cloth : alk. paper). — ISBN 0-253-21165-4
(pbk. : alk. paper)
    1. Feminist theory.   2. Social movements.   3. Feminist ethics.
4. Pluralism (Social sciences).
    HQ1190.J356   1998
    305.42—dc21   97-22852

1 2 3 4 5   03 02 01 00 99 98

*This book is dedicated with love to
Carrie Jane Singleton.*

Contents

Contents

Acknowledgments

THIS BOOK IS, in large part, based on a political education I gained working at the Washington Office on Africa from 1982 through the passage of the anti-apartheid economic sanctions bill in 1985. I am indebted to my colleagues at W.O.A. who taught me the sometimes difficult, but always rewarding, lessons of alliance politics: Jean Sindab (who is missed), Kenneth Zinn, Jacqueline Wilson Asheeke, Lisa Crooms, and Randy Nunalee. I am also thankful to the various members of the African National Congress with whom I traveled the United States; they taught me that an alternative understanding of democracy was possible.

Three mentors in particular have encouraged my intellectual development from the time when I began to think that intellectual life might be a worthy (and fun) endeavor. The advice and support of my M.A. advisor Ann Taves meant that I could change my life through engagement with feminist movement. Perhaps most importantly, she taught me to read primary texts in my first history class, and so I dedicate the readings of the first chapter to her. Beverly Harrison, who made possible the very existence of a field called "feminist ethics" in religious studies, convinced me to pursue that field by giving (as I have said on a number of occasions) "the best damn speech I ever heard" at the Women's Interseminary Conference in Denver in 1986. As with so many of us in the field she helped to foster, she has been generous to me with her friendship and support. Her emphasis on "making the connections" is the starting point for my work. Elizabeth Castelli was at this time and remains today my model for how to be a "smart girl." I am similarly grateful to my mentors at Emory University, particularly the members of my dissertation committee: Angelika Bammer, Robert Franklin, Jon Gunnemann, Hortense Spillers, and Steven Tipton. My director, Rebecca Chopp, remains an inspiration in both her intellectual integrity and her continuing ability to negotiate gracefully the multiple roles of friend, colleague, and advisor. I would like to thank the American Association of University Women for an American Fellowship in the final year of dissertation writing.

My true colleagues at Emory were my fellow graduate students, and I am grateful to those women who participated in the various reading, writing, and political groups that made it possible for me to live and work at Emory:

Gwendolyn Dean, Amanda Gable, Martha Henn, Kathy Jones, Vicki Kirsch, Kim Loudermilk, Ami Mattison, Fabienne McPhail, Annie Merrill, Maria Pramaggiore, Rosetta Ross, Donna Smith, Kim Whitehead, and Julie Wilson. Alicia Mitchell and Susan Dolan-Henderson, who traveled with me through that strange social formation known as the "Ethics and Society" program, remain close to my heart. Finally, daily telephonic support and input from two friends made writing possible: Laura Levitt, who over the course of our years together has become my sister in some literal sense, is also mother to Bleiben, the original dog, and godmother to Sophie dog. Juliana Kubala remains an unwavering friend and ally.

I would like to thank my students at the University of Arizona for their instruction of my thinking, especially the students of "Contemporary Feminist Theories" in spring 1994, who taught me how to finish this book, and the fall 1995 "Contemporary Theories of Cultural Studies: Queer Theories," who pushed me to think beyond the ending. During my first year, a few students in particular taught me that intellectual exchange could make a difference, and, in so doing, they gave me hope: Katie Boudreau, Judy Freeman, Jodi Kelber, and Caren Zimmerman. I owe a special debt of gratitude to my original partner in crime in Arizona, Robert Kaplan.

My colleagues in the Women's Studies program, Karen Anderson, Myra Dinnerstein, Janice Monk, and Judy Temple, and the Director of the Religious Studies program, Fr. Robert Burns, have made Arizona a surprisingly open place for me to pursue my diverse interests. Women's Studies staff member Mary Contreras will always have a special place in my heart. The arrival of a new wave of junior colleagues made me feel as if my academic location could also be a site of movement; thanks to Julia Balén, Susan Craddock, Adrienne Estill, Kari McBride, Ranu Samantrai, Banu Subramanium, and particularly Miranda Joseph, who took up with me the project of constructing (and performing) queer studies at Arizona. I would also like to thank Maureen Fitzgerald, Leisa Meyer, and Beverly Seckinger for their love and support from the time I arrived in the state. Leisa was a particularly important ally as Coordinator of the Committee for Lesbian, Gay, and Bisexual Studies in 1993–94. A spring 1995 fellowship at the Udall Center for Public Policy at the University of Arizona provided me with the realization that I could only write ethics through social movement.

For the particular materialization of my thoughts and activities that this book has become, I am indebted to the generosity of those who read all or part of the manuscript in one of its many forms and offered me both encouragement and criticism: Laura Berry, Katie Cannon, Jehanne Gheith, Ada María Isasi-Díaz, Beth Mitchnek, Katherine Morrissey, Carrie Jane Singleton, and David Harrington Watt. I am especially grateful to Juliana Kubala, whose reading of the entire manuscript enabled my completion of the final edits during a difficult time. I did what she told me to. Walter Johnson and Maria Grazia Lolla offered me generously supportive friendship during the year the book was in production.

The place of honor is Carrie Jane Singleton's, the importance of whose material commitment, intellectual companionship, love, and affection over the course of more than a decade I cannot adequately articulate. For once words fail me.

WORKING ALLIANCES AND THE POLITICS OF DIFFERENCE

Introduction

W HAT MAKES ALLIANCES work? This question has become central in many of the debates in feminist ethics and politics.[1] As the practice of feminist politics has demonstrated, the moral commitments of feminism to resist domination and enable the well-being of women refer not to a simple or singular category, but rather to a diverse and complex group of persons with varying interests, needs, and desires. This diversity and complexity implies that feminism, rather than being constituted through the practice of a single movement, depends on a series of alliances among and across a spectrum of issues and movements. The past several decades have seen repeated challenges to dominative feminist theories and practices which would deny the diversity and complexity of those women who are the subject of feminist movement(s).[2] Women of color, lesbians, poor and working-class women, Jewish women, "third world women," sex radicals, disabled women . . . (this list can never be completed) have repeatedly challenged theoretical and political practices which would narrow the focus of feminism and reinscribe social structural dominations along the lines of race, sexuality, class, religion, ability . . . (Beck 1982, Moraga and Anzaldúa 1981, Lorde 1984, Samois 1987, Zandy 1990, Mohanty et al. 1991, Eiesland 1994). These challenges have established a recognition that any feminist undertaking is the site of complicated alliance politics and further that any woman is herself the subject of diversity and complexity, living in the midst of (sometimes contradictory) alliances and divisions (de Lauretis 1986).

The recognition that diversity and complexity are the subject of feminist movement(s) has raised further questions about contemporary democratic politics. Feminist movements challenge public spaces which exclude or subordinate women, and they raise the question of whether democracy itself depends on alliance formation in and among public spheres. Why, for example, have the modern democratic promises of liberty and justice for all remained unfulfilled for the majority of persons? Put in terms of ethical theory, why have the enlightenment moral claims which supposedly ground democratic politics, particularly the claim to universal respect for all persons, been persistently accompanied by historical dominations? And, what of the social movements which have over the past two centuries been dedicated to addressing and redressing inadequate democratization—women's movements, anti-racist movements, anti-colonialist movements, labor movements, Marxist movements? Why have the achievements of social movements in extending democratic participation remained partial? Have counter-public social movements been fully democratic themselves? How can the constitution of radically democratic alliances within and among social movements contribute to the constitution of democratic public spheres?

Despite the current emphasis on alliances in feminist theories and practices, the production of alliances has proven difficult, often with significant consequences. Feminist movements have sometimes broken down over the failure to form alliances, while right-wing groups seem at times to be more effective at alliance politics than do feminists; hence, the urgency of the question, How do alliances work? The challenges of alliance politics can be more usefully addressed, however, by focusing on the activities and processes of alliances building, thus, reversing the question, How do alliances work? to How do we work—in, with, through—alliances? How can we make alliances work? This shift toward the active unsettles some of the assumptions which have proven problematic for alliance formation, assumptions, for example, that women share some commonality prior to the activity of movement or that unitary, pregiven selves and communities are the building blocks of alliances. A focus on the activities and processes of alliance building brings to the fore questions of constitution: How do women become a movement? How are various women's movements related? How do they interact?

Through this shift in focus, the "we" that turns the question of alliances from the passive to the active voice—that turns How do alliances work? to How do we work alliances?—is recognized as the active site of alliance formation. "We" is a term which has been the subject of much criticism because of its tendency to assume as already existent the very relationships which it constitutes. Naming and claiming a "we" can establish a group of diverse and complex persons as a collectivity or even a movement. Yet, this act of naming a particular "we" can establish a series of exclusions, inclusions, and marginalizations, while also obscuring the action of constructing these relational locations, making both inclusion and exclusion appear pregiven or natural. Naming a particular "we" creates a "they" which is not part of "us," while it can also falsely include persons who do not recognize themselves within a particular movement or who may be included only on the margins with little influence in structuring the relationships implied in "we." The temptation to give up on the "we" (as both linguistic term and social location) is countered by the possibility that such a denial will once again erase the operations of social construction, hiding the particular activities which form social relationships and, thereby, removing them from potential criticism. Thus, the task of alliance politics is to constitute the term "we," while simultaneously questioning it and pushing its limits.

A further question is raised by asking how we work in and through alliances: the question of how "we" become allies. The term "alliance" usefully includes a reference to a subject position within the context of alliance, that of the "ally." How does working in solidarity also work to create persons who can be allies? Persons or groups do not necessarily come to alliances with predetermined needs and interests, or even selves and communities.[3] Rather, the processes of interaction which are alliance formation constitute both persons and groups. Chela Sandoval's (1990, 1991) analysis of "oppositional consciousness" as a site of alliance among "women of color" or "third world women" is a salient example of this type of self- and alliance-constitution. There is no necessarily shared interest among the groups of women named by Sandoval. In fact, much of dominative U.S. politics is dedicated to creating divisions among these groups. Thus, only by creating a joint position (as Sandoval argues was done, for example, in certain struggles within the National Women's Studies Association in the early 1980s) could the "oppositional" subject position of women as allies over against the power structures of enforced separation become a site of political activity. Sandoval further argues that positions of alliance across difference must continually shift, be constantly re-created, as the differences among women "give us access to ever new and dynamic tactics for intervening in the systems which oppress us—tactics which are capable of changing to confront the ever-changing movements of power" (1990, 67). Focusing on the question of how we not only create alliances, but how we also create ourselves as allies, denaturalizes both the "we" and the "I" who are the subjects of moral agency.

In raising issues of moral agency I am engaging a field of contemporary feminist theorizing which has been constituted around questions of "agency." Debates over modern or postmodern theories, for example, frequently revolve around the question of whether modern theories constrain, or postmodern theories undercut, possibilities for agency.[4] In these arguments agency means variously ethical agency or political agency or simply human action. Given that the possibility of agency, of action, is seen as central to the possibility of human subjectivity, agency and subjectivity are frequently intertwined.[5] I will argue that the subject of agency is constituted in and through activity, recognizing that social power relations both enable and constrain, but don't simply determine, this constitution. As anthropologist Anna Lowenhaupt Tsing points out, "[p]eople play with, pervert, stretch, and oppose the very matrix of power that gives them the ability to act" (1993, 232). Alliances and moral agency will be read as interactively constituted within fields of social power. I undertake this study as an ethics in order to address these questions of agency directly, but in so doing I also challenge the boundaries which have traditionally contained the ethical, reconnecting ethics to both politics and subjectivity. The purpose of my analysis is to consider how feminist movements think and do "agency," and how we might think and do agency "differently." Thus, I use ethical theory as a prism for rethinking issues of difference, in part because ethics has served as a central site for the constitution of the coherent, modern subject in relation to the normal/normative. I argue, however, that ethical spaces can be constituted as places of required contestation, thus, subverting the supposedly coherent subject of agency.[6] This move marks the ethical as a space of both diversity and complexity, even as it marks agency as a space of alliances.

The Problem of Diversity

Contemporary challenges to modern moral reasoning from a number of perspectives have led to a recognition that moral claims are made within a social world of moral multiplicity.[7] This world is marked by diversity and complexity—diversity created by differences within and among persons and a correlative complexity created by multiple criss-crossing power relations and resulting contradictions. Challenges to modern moral reasoning have also incited a passionate debate as to whether morality can be sustained at all in the face of moral diversity. Political theorist Arlene Saxonhouse (1992) traces the fear of diversity in western thought to the pre-Socratics, and yet, she argues that even in classical thought unity and diversity are most often intertwined, the question being not how to establish either unity or diversity alone, but how to establish the relationship between the two. Modern moral reasoning was supposed to provide precisely this type of coherent relationship between unity and diversity. The promise of enlightenment ethics was that conflict, specifically the interreligious conflict sparked by the Reformation, could be resolved while maintaining universal respect for diversity. The light of reason, a reason supposedly universal to all humanity, was to fulfill this promise. Thus, reason was thought to provide the key to maintaining a unified moral framework which could both respect and contain diversity.

This modern moral tradition, however, has also been widely criticized by feminists, among others, as reinscribing biases which block rather than facilitate emancipatory politics and the recognition of diversity, and, thus, the modern promise of emancipation remains unfulfilled (Eisenstein 1981 and Jaggar 1983). Enlightenment ideals of respect, freedom, and equality have been accompanied by gender domination and a historical period of western domination in the form of colonialism and imperialism; furthermore the institution of the liberal state maintains persistent underrepresentation.[8] Similar problems have carried over into feminist ethics and politics, particularly into efforts to form effective alliances. As the case studies in the first two chapters of this book show, enacting feminist commitments to resist the domination of all women and correlatively to respect differences among women has proven to be difficult, a difficulty which frequently makes calls for alliance politics ineffective.

The central argument of this book is that this difficulty persists because of a dis-articulation of diversity from complexity. Learning to work with, rather than contain diversity and its accompanying complexity is the task of alliance building, and yet ethical theory and its assumptions as enacted in politics frequently leads away from this work and toward efforts to contain diversity and flatten complexity. Complexity is under-theorized in both liberal political and economic discourses of pluralism and free markets, and in counter-public discourses and movements constituted around identity politics or a (single-axis) politics of "difference."[9] Even a politics focused on diversity and the elaboration of difference(s) that fails to recognize complexity can run into problems of recuperation. As long as diversity is not articulated in and through complexity, moral commitments to respect diversity and efforts to form alliances will remain ineffective.

A simple commitment to diversity is inadequate because it does not articulate the relations of production which create that diversity. In the contemporary United States, diversity is produced through social processes of differentiation along various interrelated but relatively autonomous axes of differentiation (West 1988). The axes run along lines of gender, race, class, sexuality, religion, ability, age. . . . This list can never be completed as long as capitalist relations of production ensure that we will always produce more units of "difference" (Lorde 1984, 114). These processes of differentiation create social categories which form the matrix of social life into which each individual is born and within which each lives. These units of difference can be produced, however, so as to dis-articulate diversity from complexity. For example, gender difference can be produced as a difference between two, and only two, types of persons—men and women—which does not allow complexity either within or between these two "units" of difference.

Complexity arises, however, because processes of differentiation fail to create coherent units of difference, but instead are implicated in intertwined criss-crossing matrices of conflictual and contradictory relationships. Experiences of living through such social categories never fully fit the boundaries of categorization. An individual is never only or fully a woman. Social sanctions against those who deviate from their ascribed categories, including the fact that one can be accused of not being a "real" woman, imply that slippage between the category "woman" and lives lived by women is a constant possibility. Thus, there are always gaps created by processes of differentiation. Moreover, because the lines of differentiation cross each other, the coherence of categories based on any single "difference" is undermined as any given gender "identity" is differentiated by race, class, and sexuality . . . while racial identity is simultaneously differentiated by gender, class, sexuality. . . . Criss-crossing lines or axes of differentiation create intersections of social relations and open spaces or interstices which cannot be fully represented in a language structured by differentiation. Frequently, the site of intersection is also a gap, an interstice. Hortense Spillers (1992) has argued, for example, that African American women's sexuality is constituted at the intersection of race, gender, and sexuality, which is also an interstice created between "women's sexuality" articulated by white women and African American sexuality articulated by black men.[10] As a result persons and groups act within and, yet, exceed social categories of differentiation. Any particular woman cannot fit the category "woman" or "women" and this mis-fit occurs in more than one direction—she cannot be all of the possibilities of what it might mean to be a woman, and what it means to be a woman cannot articulate all that she is. Given this multi-dimensional mis-fit, diversity will always be accompanied by complexity.

Diversity and its accompanying complexity are central to feminist movements because social processes of differentiation are not simply productive of social differences or the identities through which those differences are lived. They also form the basis of social hierarchies and dominations. Thus, for example, "woman" is not only different from, but also subordinate to "man." This hierarchy is a social domination in the sense described by Michel Foucault (1984b). A hierarchy becomes domination when there are few, if any, avenues for reversal of the relationship or for resistance to the claims of the superordinate party in the hierarchy. Following from this understanding of domination, the central ethical problem is not to establish freedom from power relations, but to resist domination within fields of power (1984b, 18).

By defining domination in this way, Foucault avoids the problematic implication that to be free from domination is also to be free from power relations. Thus, he recognizes that not all power relations, not even all hierarchical power relations, are relations of domination. The asymmetrical institutionalization of power between a teacher and student, for example, is not necessarily a domination. This definition implies that emancipatory projects such as feminist movements always occur within—are never emancipated from—power relations. The purpose of social movement is to resist relations of domination and change the structure of power, not to escape implication in power. This definition also names as domination, however, those rigidly maintained hierarchies, such as gender hierarchy, which have been historically justified as "divinely ordained" or "natural" or "biological" and, therefore, as legitimate. In this sense, Foucault is suspicious of social legitimation for relationships which narrowly circumscribe particular persons and groups from avenues of social power. His example of this type of domination is "the traditional conjugal relationship in the eighteenth and nineteenth centuries."

We cannot say that there was only male power; the woman herself could do a lot of things: be unfaithful to him, extract money from him, refuse him sexually. She was, however, subject to a state of domination in the measure where all that was finally no more than a certain number of tricks which never brought about a reversal of the situation. (Foucault 1984b, 12)

There are several mechanisms for maintaining such domination. Social sanctions can work to restrict the activities of gendered persons to male and female roles and, then, to ascribe powers and privileges to those gendered as "men." Thus, disempowerment can be enacted through mechanisms of exclusion, where the subordinate member of the opposition is excluded from institutions and social relationships which are major sites of power, such as the exclusion of women from political life or voting. Disempowerment can also be enacted through marginalization where a dominant group of persons establishes themselves as the center of activity in relation to which "others" are "included" but peripheral.

Domination is also produced and maintained through discourses—languages and activities in their social and institutional contexts—which work to contain diversity and flatten complexity as persons are induced to try to fit the simple categories of differentiation and complex relationships among axes of differentiation are elided.[11] One of the main discourses to constitute social differentiation as hierarchy and domination is that of binary opposition. Binary oppositions define social differences as oppositional pairs, one of which is defined in terms of the other. Binary oppositions work so effectively by defining a field of opposition so as to make it appear that the entire field of social relations is encompassed. So, for example, gender relations work to produce opposing types of persons where woman is defined in terms of man and where only these two positions are available as "genders." Opposition is created because woman is "not man," implying that woman is "other" than man and that the categories must remain rigidly differentiated. Thus, two possible positions for lived experiences (subject positions) are established: the norm or position of identity, meaning man, and the position of difference, that which is different from or not man, meaning woman. This negative definition further establishes hierarchy between the pair, hierarchy which becomes domination when opportunities for inhabiting the subjectivity of "woman" are so restricted as to make the negative meaning "not man" rigidly determinative of women's possibilities. Such determination denies the possibility of gendered lives which are not "opposed," while simultaneously denying possibilities for multiple gendered positions (for example, hermaphrodites, transgenders, or androgynies). Finally, this opposition denies the multiple meanings of gender as it is itself differentiated by other axes such as "race" or "class" or "sexuality."

Binary oppositions both invoke and contain diversity and complexity, by operating within networks of differentiation. As Catherine Bell (1992) notes, sets of oppositions are hierarchically interrelated so as to generate "a loosely integrated whole in which each element 'defers' to another in an endlessly circular chain of reference" (101).[12] Bell goes on to argue:

> Homologous oppositions (light-dark, good-evil, male-female) can organize taxonomic sets (the set of light, good, and male, or the set of dark, evil, and female) simply by the juxtaposition of activities that use these oppositions. In actual practice only a few elements from a 'set' need be invoked to imply a whole series of relationships and implications. Such homologized spheres are orchestrated (or confused, or collapsed) so as to produce an experience of their basic identity or coherence. This experience of coherence, however, simultaneously facilitates the emergence of some symbolic terms in a dominant relation to others. The sense of general identity of the whole naturalizes such hegemony. (104)

Thus, the oppositions invoke a complex field of interrelated differentiations—the gender opposition male-female also invokes a moral field of good and evil—and, yet, such oppositions also condense the complexity of these interrelations such that male and female appears to be identical to good and evil. Bell's argument demonstrates the need for a theory and practice which addresses the complexity of differentiation, rather than simply focusing on any single binary. Feminist politics cannot be effective if it focuses only on a "gender."

A politics which does not take such complexity into account plays into the "dilemma of difference" in U.S. politics (Minow 1990) and establishes bifurcated choices which sparked the "equality vs. difference" debate within feminism (Scott 1988). When only two positions can be acknowledged—the norm and that which is different from the norm—the norm/difference hierarchy is inscribed as the very definition of "different." In the case of equality versus difference these terms imply that difference must also mean inequality and equality must mean sameness. Thus, within the terms of the "dilemma of difference" only two social moves are allowed, each of which reinforces the normative center: 1) A political focus on difference can trap women in a separate sphere of activity, which because different can never be equal; 2) a focus on equality, when equality is configured as identity or sameness to men, can reestablish "men" as the normative gender to which women must aspire and in relation to which they will always prove inadequate.[13] Minow suggests that this dilemma can only be addressed by shifting the terms of "difference" and challenging the institutions which create difference as a burden to be carried by those identified as different from the norm.

The challenge for feminism is to develop social movements which could effect such change. Scott suggests the need for a double move in order to meet this challenge, "the unmasking of the power relationship constructed by posing equality as the antithesis of difference and the refusal of its consequent dichotomous construction of political choices" (Scott 1988, 44). For Scott this double move opens the door to an alternative strategy which subverts the terms of the dilemma by incorporating the articulation of complexity into a politics of equality in relation to difference. "It is not sameness *or* identity between women and men that we want to claim but a more complicated historically variable diversity than is permitted by the opposition male/female, a diversity that is also differently expressed for different purposes in different contexts" (1988, 46). Thus, it is possible to subvert the dilemma by a politics which articulates both diversity and complexity—a diversity which undercuts the binary nature of gender difference (in Scott's example by recognizing diversity within the categories "women" and "men") and a complexity which can articulate the (historically variable) power relations which constitute "gender." A politics dedicated to subverting binary oppositions is necessary so as to challenge the construction of asymmetrical power relations through the definition of a norm and its "other." Analysis of the "dilemma of difference" also shows, however, why a politics which focuses only on binaries, such as a feminist politics which focuses only on the "opposition" between men and women will ultimately prove inadequate to the complexity of gender(s) (Ong 1988).

A feminist politics addressed only to oppositional gender is part and parcel of a political configuration which isolates binary pairs from each other so that gender, race, class, and sexuality are all constituted as separate areas of analysis and of political action. In this configuration, analyses of race focus on a black/white opposition, class analyses concentrate on the bourgeoisie/proletariat split, the study of sexuality focuses on the hetero/homo binary, while gender analyses become the study of men and women as opposites. This type of knowledge production and its concomitant politics does not ultimately challenge the binary pairs on which it depends, nor can it articulate relationships among marginalized persons and groups. Because alliance politics does not focus on a single axis of social differentiation it shows how relations of domination are produced through shifting, interlocking structures of difference. These complex processes of differentiation work at the margins as well as between center and margin, contributing to the production of hierarchies and dominations within and among marginalized groups.

The singular politics of "difference" produces a version of diversity which is made up of multiple "units" of differences, but which ignores complexity. These coherent "units" of difference are placed in horizontal lists, producing a liberal pluralist version of diversity which assumes coherent separations and clear boundaries. The horizontal placement of various "differences" fails to articulate either power relations or historical conflicts among "different" groups. Chandra Mohanty critiques the production of this version of diversity, arguing that "Difference seen as benign variation (diversity), for instance, rather than as conflict, struggle, or the threat of disruption, bypasses power as well as history to suggest a harmonious empty pluralism" (1994, 146). This version of pluralism cannot articulate complex issues of interaction and inter-relation which produce "differences" and which must be addressed in both alliance formation and political struggle. Instead this practice of pluralism erases these very issues while inscribing lists which will be extended *ad infini-tum* in the attempt to name, ever more accurately, coherent units of diversity which are actually interrelational complexities.

As Mohanty points out, this reductive pluralism facilitates an institutional approach to differences as "diversity management," where historical political struggles are transformed into matters of individual prejudice and misunder-standing to be managed within institutions ranging from the "multi-cultural" university to the "multi-national" corporation. Diversity management em-ploys discourses of authentic "otherness" to discipline those "others" who do not fit the model of authenticity, who do not speak or act like "real women" (Lugones and Spelman 1983, Chow 1993). The units of diversity—for exam-ple, "woman"—control complexity within the categories, while simultane-ously producing a form of diversity which can easily be transformed into ho-mogeneity. The desire within pluralism for difference(s) to speak or show themselves, for example, the desire to hear the "woman's" voice, can further serve as a means of inducing or enforcing "others'" speech within the struc-tures of dominant discourses. Thus, women might speak, but could only be heard in the language already established through their exclusion. In this way, pluralism can once again devolve into singularity as "otherness" comes to mir-ror the center's conception of it*self*.

The problems of a managed diversity dis-articulated from complexity are evident, for example, in the construction of various "studies" programs at con-temporary universities—Women's Studies, American Indian Studies, African American Studies, Mexican American Studies, Latin American Studies, Asian Studies, Judaic Studies, Lesbian/Gay/Bisexual Studies, Cultural Studies.[14] These programs, while in part the outcome of specific political struggles at various sites may have also been institutionalized as (and hence recuperated into) a liberal-pluralist model. This model attempts to recognize, but also con-tain, various pluralisms by separating them into definable, categorized areas of study, which are then induced (frequently through a discourse of "stan-dards") to look more and more like the university "at large."[15] One means of subverting this liberal containment, however, is by the formation of alliances through and across the complex interrelations which are belied by this neat categorization. In such an effort Women's Studies might attempt to recognize the diversity of areas within its program which must be developed to address women's lives; yet, such efforts alone would merely re-enact pluralist contain-ment in which all that women are is supposedly contained within the boundaries of Women's Studies. A more effective subversion would also make connections with and provide support for area studies in which women participate, but which are not defined by gender. To fail to do so is to fail to support women who act within, but are not contained by women's studies (which as I will argue below is any "woman"). Thus, the meaning of "women's studies" itself must be destabilized if it is to be constituted as an alliance among different women rather than as simply representative of the dominative "woman."

As this example shows, dependence on the liberal pluralist version of diversity can create extensive problems for possible alliances within feminist movement(s) and among various social movements. The expectation that feminist politics constructs a movement which makes claims on behalf of "women," while various "other" movements address "other" issues like race and class has been particularly problematic. Not surprisingly the expectation that feminist politics could represent all women as a single category led to foundering on the differences within this particular category. With the liberal model of diversity, differences within women, such as those produced through race, class, and sexuality threaten the very possibility of feminist politics, because there is no way to effectively represent "women" as a coherent unit. Thus, liberal diversity produces tremendous resistance to critiques of dominative feminism as racist, classist, and heterosexist for fear that if these critiques are recognized feminist politics will no longer be possible.

Alliance politics cannot be effected through a simple commitment, even a moral commitment, to diversity. The choice for feminist movements is not whether to value unity or diversity. The valuing of unity alone makes the production of diversity itself problematic and leads to a foundering on differences, yet the choice to value diversity does not necessarily challenge the dominative social relations under which diversity is produced, nor does it effectively materialize alliances. For example, the attempt to materialize an alliance by employing a liberal model of diversity produces the infamously problematic liberal categories "women and minorities."[16] This constitution of alliance cannot account for women who are also "minorities," while it leaves white women's "ethnicity" unmarked. The move of specifying white women and racial/ ethnic minorities is still inadequate, however, in that it fails to articulate a number of complexities. It subsumes women of color under a racial marking, thereby disarticulating their gender; it reduces "minorities" to a racial/ethnic category which dis-articulates other social differentiations, thus, for example, leaving no space to articulate sexual "minorities"; and it completely elides issues of class. Kobena Mercer succinctly states the problems for a politics based on pluralism: " . . . we also need to go beyond the mere concatenation of particularism in the all-too-familiar mantra of 'race, class and gender' . . . if we are to grasp the conflicts and contradictions that exist *within* and *between* each of these various identities at play in contemporary politics (1994, 273–

74, emphasis in original)." Only by re-articulating diversity and complexity can the dangers of liberal pluralism and diversity management be avoided and the problems of alliance politics worked through. The challenge for feminist movement(s), then, is to analyze the complex social relations which produce diversity and rework, rather than simply reproduce, these relationships.

Articulating Diversity through Complexity

The complexity of social relations in and through which diversity is produced imply that there are at least four analytically distinct but interrelated sites of diversity. *Diversity among* persons, groups, and categories refers to the differences that make for specificity, that allow for the articulation of a specific identity. Diversity among persons and groups recognizes that there are multiple positions, for example, multiple racial and ethnic identities, thus, undercutting a focus on binary opposition. The complexity which accompanies diversity, however, indicates that specificity about difference is not in and of itself adequate because the specific locating of "difference" cannot fully account for the intersections and interstices of cross-cutting differentiations. Thus, even as these differentiations produce specific identities by creating boundaries among groups, they also produce *diversity within* individuals and communities. "Diversity within" refers to the differences within persons and groups which are created by the complexity of interrelation. Thus, within any specific identity (relationally defined as specific by differentiation among identities) "other" differences within the identity category (whether individual or group) always remain. Not only are there differences within the category of "women," but each woman is many different things, some of which make her different from other "women" and from the categorical definition of "woman." Diversity within implies that, as Teresa de Lauretis has pointed out, any individual "female subject is a site of differences; differences that are not only sexual or only racial, economic, or (sub)cultural, but all of these together, and often enough at odds with one another. . . . [T]hese differences not only constitute each woman's consciousness and subjective limits, but all together define the *female subject of feminism* in its very specificity, its inherent and at least for now irreconcilable contradiction—these differences, then, cannot be again collapsed into a fixed identity, a sameness of all women as Woman, or a representation of Feminism as a coherent and available image" (1986, 14–15, emphasis in original).

These two sites of diversity—diversity among and diversity within—indicate the ways in which identity and difference, although frequently structured as a binary opposition, are effectively intertwined. The traditional hierarchical binary between identity and difference defines identity in contradistinction to a difference which is outside of and subordinate to identity (as woman is to man). The relationship between diversity among and within demonstrates, however, that difference remains within, even as it is distinguished from, identity. No individual or group consists of parts which are entirely "the same." Yet, an analysis of diversity cannot rest with the identity/difference pairing. The processes which produce this pair are complex and, thus, they also produce excesses. There are two crucial sites for the excesses of differentiation, sites which are most commonly associated with Jacques Derrida's concept of *différance*. *Différance* is the ground of the possibility of differentiation and also its horizon of meaning. This site is a space of radical heterogeneity which is intertwined with the production of specific differences as the ground and limit of their potential meaning. The confounding factor for any claim to difference is that difference(s) are always accompanied by the excesses of *différance*. The boundaries between self and other, for example, are never completely sealed off or secure; rather "the self will be divided from itself, finding within its identity a trace of its other" (Diprose 1994, 77). Thus, *différance* is also the "excessive remainder," that which resists the simple categorization of binary opposition, that which overflows its boundaries (Grosz 1989, xvii).

When diversity is read for complexity beyond binary opposition, this remainder can also be located in the excesses produced by criss-crossing relations of differentiation. This is a site of *diversity between*, referring to those excessive differences which are lived in the interstices and intersections between axes of differentiation. These gaps are also spaces of possibility and limit. Work in these spaces blurs the boundaries of differentiation, making it more difficult for categories to contain diversity and creating new possibilities for connections between and across "differences." These gaps also express the limits of representation (both linguistic and political), of whose interests and needs can be articulated. The limits can be challenged but they can never be fully removed as the "horizon of meaning" recedes before us. Thus, the limits which create gaps in processes of differentiation—both the interstices between differentiations and those between category and lived experiences—can be challenged by new articulations, but they can never be completely "filled." Nor would it be a politically useful project to try to fill completely such gaps. The limits are also spaces of possibility, spaces which have not already been completely written over (overwritten) by domination. The difficult task of alliance politics is to find ways to challenge these limits while keeping open spaces of possibility.

Alliance politics requires work at all of these sites of diversity. Diversity among persons and groups, the difference which also produces identity, is the form of difference which is most frequently recognized in modern public spheres. This "fit" between the public and differences configured as identities makes for both the appeal and the problems of identity politics. If the diversity within identity categories is not recognized, problems are created for alliances as the politics of identity fail to articulate the diverse needs and interests of, for example, "women." Focus only on diversity within, however, fails to recognize how social differentiation always creates gaps, interstices of excessive diversity between categories of "difference." The excesses of *différance* and diversity between remain important as the sites of possibility for change. As spaces whose diversity is not determined by the social processes which fix specific differences (even if only momentarily), these sites point to possibilities for responding to diversity "differently." These spaces simultaneously express the limits of social possibility precisely because its diversity cannot be fixed (even if momentarily). Yet, a politics which celebrates *différance* alone, as if the processes which produce identity and difference could simply be averted, is also inadequate. "Sidestepping" the implications of identity and difference through a singular focus on *différance* avoids interrogating the processes which produce identity and difference in particular forms (Diprose 1994, 81).[17] Thus, persons and societies can never fully live *différance*; rather, they live within and between specific difference(s) in conjunction with the possibilities and limits of *différance*.

This conjunction can be articulated through a focus on the spaces in-between—within and between—processes of differentiation. The complexity which accompanies diversity means that women's moral agency and political action take place within and outside of, in and between, categories and structures of "difference." This project recognizes that if multiplicity is not to flip over into new neutrality, objectivity or universalism it must *in*habit particular positions, while simultaneously moving in the spaces *between* these positions in order to blur the boundaries and divisions.[18] The configuration *in-between* expresses the ways in which action and agency are configured at one and the same time as within and between the boundaries of particular categories and movements: in and between gender and race and class and sexuality, in and between feminist, anti-racist, socialist, anti-homophobic movements, in and between post and modern, in and between gender(s), in and between the category "woman" and women.

The spaces in-between are particularly hard to work with because they are sites of multiple and ambiguous meanings.[19] They lack the clarity of precisely delineated sites of identity and the theoretical purity of the fully open sign. They are also sites of (potential) conflict and contradiction as axes of differentiation intersect and cross each other. Thus, the project of working in and between runs certain risks, the risk of re*in*forcing those positions and the risk of losing a place from which to work and speak as one enters the gaps between such places.[20] The spaces in-between are also sites of great possibility, however. They are excellent sites for "making the connections" (Harrison 1985) across differences as the various ways in which people live in and between differences can be recognized. The spaces in-between contribute to possibilities of living different(ly) by challenging the constraints of particular categories. Thus, complexity not only adds a level of analysis to theories of diversity, it challenges the very meaning of diversity and the meanings ascribed to particular "differences." Commitment to the spaces in-between also points to the possibility of learning how to imagine and work differences differently. Only through imaginative reworkings can we create social spaces where differences need not imply hierarchy and domination.

An alliance politics which works in the spaces in-between, thus, focuses attention and political action on relationships among marginalized, as well as centralized, persons and groups within the context of hierarchical social structures. It allows attention to the ways in which those on the margins challenge and reconfigure the terms of the dominant discourse of difference(s), thus, opening the door to a number of political moves which subvert not only the normative center, but the entire relationship between center and margin, opening the possibility of multiple centers of power, authority, and action. Katie King (1994) provides a useful example of this change in focus by juxtaposing origin stories of second-wave feminism written by white women and that written by Chela Sandoval, which sees white women's organizing as a peripheral concern in relation to historically on-going organizing by women of color.[21] King's juxtaposition graphically presents the possibility of multiple centers of power and action in women's movements whose interrelations are complex by raising the questions: Which center? Which margin?

As King's analysis shows, the margins are themselves centers of complex activity. Complexity comes into play with diversity because these centers are both distinct and interrelated. Perspectives, practices, and traditions shift through movement to various centers of activity (Lugones 1990a, 1990b). Centers also overlap and may conflict and contradict each other, even as they are interlocked in asymmetrical power relations. Thus, relationships among various "differences" do not add up to a single coherent "whole," but rather form a shifting kaleidoscope of complex patterns, not all of which are visible at any single turn. Moreover, differences among marginalized persons and groups have their own margins, the excesses of differentiation found at the intersections and interstices of criss-crossing differentiations. These margins delineate the limits of the possible, but also point to the future which is underdetermined, the possibilities of what might be. The task of both feminist ethics and feminist politics is to ask how we might move into that future.

Why the Ethical?

Why choose the ethical as a site for reworking alliances? Some feminist and lesbian theorists remain concerned that ethics is so deeply implicated in disciplinary practices of control that it can never be useful to feminist or alliance politics. Marilyn Frye, for example, suggests in reviewing *Lesbian Ethics* that lesbians might do better without an "ethics," because ethics plays into disciplinary ideologies about right action.[22] Norms have been a particular site of feminist concern because they are frequently read as constituting prescriptive codes of action. For instance, in the constructive theory of *Lesbian Ethics*, Sarah Hoagland (1988) focuses on the creation of values rather than norms in order to resist a dominant ethics of control. Elizabeth Grosz and Drucilla Cornell make distinctions between ethics and morality in a similar effort to avoid implication in the problematics of a disciplinary discourse. Cornell reverses the order of feminist ethics, naming her project "ethical feminism," as a further distinguishing mark from the discipline of "ethics." In developing a definition of ethics based on the work of Emmanuel Levinas, Elizabeth Grosz states, "Ethics need not imply a moral or normative code, or a series of abstract regulative principles. Rather, it is the working out or negotiation between an other (or others) seen as prior to and pre-given for the subject, or a subject" (1989, xvii).[23] Similarly, for Drucilla Cornell, in contrast to "morality" which is a system of rules or standards by which to justify disapproval of others, the "ethical" indicates, "the aspiration to a non-violent relationship to the Other and to otherness in the widest possible sense" (Benhabib et al. 1995, 78).

These theorists point to important questions about the implication of ethics in discourses of dominating power, but the distinctions which they offer may not be fully effective in resisting this implication. Recent politics has demonstrated, for example, how "values," in conjunction with the term "family," can also be a site of control. Karla F. C. Holloway (1995) points out that a reduction of "values" similar to the reduction of norms to sites of controlling judgment, can occur, where usable values are reduced to marketable "goods" controlled by the logic of exchange in the same way that human beings were marketed under slavery. Moreover, practices of discipline and control can be located in precisely the types of distinctions which these theorists employ, where divisions between ethics and politics or norms and values, can be recuperated into a traditional set of oppositions. In response to Marilyn Frye, Claudia Card (1995) provides a definition of ethics which holds together norms and values, as well as ethics and politics; thus ethics becomes "the study of norms and values, the right and the good, as these enter into or support human well-being, norms that political arrangements can respect (or disregard) and values that politics can promote (or hinder)" (66).

Card's definition recognizes an interdependence between binary pairs—norms/values, right/good, ethics/politics—which delineate fields of debate in both feminist and ethical theory.[24] The divisions which create these pairs—norms/values, right/good, ethics/politics—are often instituted to control diversity. This control is accomplished by recognizing one member of the pair as an appropriate site of diversity, while the other is ascribed a necessary unity which can contain that diversity. So, for example, the division in ethical theory between norms (as the site of a theory of the right) and values (as concerned with the production of the good life) frequently locates values or the concerns of the good life as an appropriate site of moral diversity and even disagreement, while the principles of justice, or the right, form a unitary framework which contains this disagreement. If feminist ethics is to become a site which can articulate both diversity and complexity, however, a methodology which challenges these divisions must be developed.

In order for feminist ethics and politics to subvert this type of containment, norms, values, the relationship between the two, and the power relations within which they operate must be fully investigated and reworked. Analysis of norms in conjunction with values is useful because it allows for analysis of the networks of power relations which both constrain and enable agency. Norms need not be read as prescriptive principles which direct the "correct" action, in order to acknowledge the potential for normative discourse to participate in disciplinary power. I will argue that norms constitute the social matrix which forms the context for action. Norms form the social matrix which structures moral possibilities. Values are social "goods" which are produced by human activity within the context of that matrix. Norms and values are, thus, intertwined (rather than opposed).

If values are goods which are necessary to the possibility of life, as well as goods which make life meaningful, then the "human well-being" alluded to in Card's definition entails various types of "values" or "goods." If values are diverse, then the question of the good life is complicated because there is no single life form which is coherently "good." The good life for one, may not be good for another, and the relationship between "one" and the "other" can structure the question of "good" or "not." Thus, values are not inherent in objects, but are established relationally in and through processes of differentiation. Rosalyn Diprose succinctly illustrates this point through the Foucauldian example of, "[a] managerial space [that] accrues more value (and less surveillance) not because of any inherent value but because of its relation to and difference from the space of manual labor" (1994, 33). Values are not static because as relational positionings shift values may also shift, but these relational positionings and the values available to particular persons and groups in and through these positionings are inscribed by and inscribe power.

Normative matrices create the possibilities and limits for potential shifts in relational positioning and values. Norms give shape to, materialize bodies, including social bodies, thereby materializing relationships in such a way as to differentially value particular bodies. For example, Judith Butler describes the operation of the category of "sex" as a norm which is also, "part of a regulatory practice that produces the bodies it governs, that is, whose regulatory force is made clear as a kind of productive power, the power to produce—demarcate, circulate, differentiate—the bodies it controls" (1993, 1).[25] Thus, the production of bodies takes place through highly regulated practices which are "the forcible reiteration" of ideal constructs or norms. Butler argues that reiteration is a sign that the materialization of norms is never complete—bodies cannot fully comply with norms, and bodies also exceed normative regulation. Just as norms form the social matrices of relational positioning and values, normative enactments also make values. Sarah Hoagland points out how moral agency when enacted makes value. That which is enacted through the iteration of a particular norm is thereby produced as a value. Different re-iterations of norms also make different values.

Given that norms materialize and are materialized by persons and communities, they produce both particular "I"s and particular "we"s. Every person is born into an on-going normative context, the enactment of which literally makes that person. Thus, a given person or community only becomes a person or community through normative enactment. Yet, locating the person in the midst of, rather than prior to, social enactment does not mean that there is no possibility for agency. Just as with processes of social differentiation, there are always gaps, slippages, and excesses produced through the processes of enactment. These gaps open possibilities for resistance to dominating power, possibilities for acting "differently." Normative matrices can be organized in a number of ways, not all of which necessarily further domination and no one of which is necessarily the (singular) path to liberation. Social movements (meaning movements of "different" enactments) create and extend possibilities for changing the shape of a normative matrix.

Because norms are produced out of social activity—are the result of a "material chain of signification," of repeated, but shifting iterations—norms will vary across the locations and communities in which they are produced. Moreover, because these sites of action are both distinct and interrelated, norms also demonstrate the type of complexity demonstrated by social differentiations. The social matrix of norms refers to the interrelated sets of regulatory ideals such as "race" and "class," which, in addition to "sex," materialize bodies and communities (and to which Butler alludes in the footnote to this section). Thus, rather than providing a singular, unitary, or coherent framework to regulate variations in value, norms, along with values, are themselves diverse and complex. These diverse and complex norms and values are interrelated through "moral economies" which intertwine social relations and normative discourse, thus, forming the relations of production for both social differentiations and the normative discourses which materialize those "differences." Each moral economy represents a normative matrix which by defining normative activities also produces normative persons and communities. Moral economies, thus, interrelate moral agency and social differentiations like race, class, sexual identity, and gender. These various economies are overlapping, and therefore, they exert pressure on each other, creating contradictions for moral action. This same interaction among economies, however, also forms possible sites for "freedom," for the construction of agency. By working at sites of intersection of these various economies it is possible to displace normative iterations, to enact norms "differently" and hence to resist or subvert the workings of a particular economy.

The recognition that both norms and values are sites of diversity and complexity, that norms do not form a singular framework which guides interaction among diverse and complex persons and groups, but are rather themselves participants in this diversity and complexity is perhaps the most important contribution which the study of ethics can make to the practice of alliance politics. Learning to work with, rather than contain, diversity and its accompanying complexity is the task of alliances. Reworking how agency is possible in the midst of diversity and complexity, as well as how agency is both empowered and constrained within normative social matrices, is the contribution which ethical theory can make to this task.

The primary criticism of understanding both norms and values as diverse and complex is framed in terms of the problem of moral relativism.[26] Relativism is configured as a problem for ethics because it leaves moral agents without an ultimate decision-making procedure for choosing among diverse ethics. The problem of relativism as it has been constructed in ethical theory has also been constructed as a problem for alliance politics. In the context of alliances relativism raises the question, Can we develop a feminist politics without an ultimate decision-making procedure for deciding among various visions of feminism? I will suggest, however, that the construction of relativism as a "problem" misses an alternative reading of the term. Relativism is not necessarily a situation of criterialess indeterminism, but rather can be seen as a situation in which diverse persons and groups, their norms and values, are *related* to each other in complex ways. The question for ethical theory and alliance politics, then, is not how to decide among these diverse normative visions, but rather how to understand and enact these various and complicated relationships. How, for example, are various universal claims made from different specific perspectives related to each other? How is a particular social matrix structured? How does power operate within and across it? How can we work within this context? Who can we work with?

Agency and Alliance

Placing agency in the context of relationalism challenges modern assumptions that moral agency is located in a self-contained autonomous individual who acts under conditions of freedom. In this traditional understanding agency is located on the side of freedom in an opposition between freedom and determinism. The modern view of self-contained agency has been criticized from a number of perspectives, however. For example, Katie Cannon (1988) in *Black Womanist Ethics* locates womanist agency in a tradition of community struggle, and Sarah Hoagland (1988), contrasting her view with the traditional view of the autonomous self, articulates agency as "autokoenony," as the actions of self in community.[27] Cannon and Hoagland similarly challenge the conception that placing agency within normative matrices of social power relations leaves only a socially *determined* subject.[28] Agency need not be read as completely determined if located within power relations. Katie Cannon demonstrates that the assumption that autonomy in the form of free choice is necessary to moral agency reinforces relations of domination by constructing the dominated as without the freedom of agency and, hence, without morality. Cannon goes on to demonstrate that the assumptions of agency and virtue which focus on free choice and self-control are the values of a capitalist system which reinforces the domination of Black women by constructing them as "either amoral or immoral" (2). For Cannon, alternatively, moral agency is Black women's ability to survive and creatively contribute to the struggle for human wholeness and integrity even in the context of oppression. Similarly, Sarah Hoagland (1988) contends that agency is the creation of value through the choices made in action. In claiming that choice occurs even under oppression, Hoagland emphasizes that agents do not have to control a situation in order to act. Hoagland argues that traditional philosophical assumptions of agency, where autonomy, or control of the self, is understood to be the mark of agency, contribute to a dominative ethics. The assumption that moral agents must be in control serves and structures domination by constructing dominant "selves" as if they are in control, despite dependence on the labor of others and constructing "others" as out of control and, hence, in need of domination "for their own good." Thus, as both Katie Cannon and Sarah Hoagland point out, moral agency is not the exercise of choice under conditions of total "freedom," nor the activity of a subject who is formed prior to the operation of power. Rather, it is in the midst of power relations that agency is undertaken.

If power is part of the context of social activity, a context which both enables and constrains, empowers and determines action, then ethics is no longer faced with an impossible opposition between determinism and agency. Moreover, the self need not be prior to the social context or even activity in order to recognize agency. Rather the self is both empowered through social subjectivity—an individual cannot be a self except through the social—and is at the same time subjected or limited by the possibilities of the social. Agency is built precisely through the actions of subjects working in relationships, actions which in turn produce, maintain, and reproduce subjects and relationships.

This activity is moral labor. In Hoagland's terms, it is the action which produces values (and norms).

Because agency is produced in relationships, rather than found at the moment of individual freedom from relationships, it can only be articulated through complexity. There is never a fully coherent moment of enacting the free and sovereign will, and thus, the moment of agency is always implicated in complicating social relations. This implication in complexity creates an "ethics of ambiguity" (Beauvoir 1972, Hoagland 1988, 204–205), meaning that ethics must be undertaken under ambiguous conditions which challenge the singularity of right action—i.e., which challenge the claim that there is one right action and that any action can be singularly right. Thus, we cannot decide on a given act because it is wholly good and we know it to be so; rather, as Gayatri Spivak suggests, responsibility is "the risk of decision in the face of undecidability." Ethics, then, is faced with the task of contributing to critique and decision, despite this ultimate undecidability and despite the continuing presence of ethical impurity. The question of agency under conditions of domination (or of any type of power relation) is how action can negotiate, resist, subvert, and change these power relations.

An ethics or politics which focuses on complexity reconfigures understandings of bases of social movement, reversing the order of solidarity and identity to make solidarity primary. If even individual persons are constituted through differences within themselves, then any form of moral and/or political agency—whether by an "individual" or a "movement"—is undertaken in and through solidarity across differences. Alliances are not the outcome of connections across pre-determined units of "difference," but are the constitutive subject matter of activity located within diverse and complex social relations. The subject of agency is, thus, a net-work of connections and contestations. The task of alliance politics, then, is how to work with differences so that they are mobilized to challenge dominating power relations. Mobility is important so that differences are not reified, so that persons are not trapped in their differences. This mobilization opens the door to the creation of new movements in which the meanings of both "identities" and "differences" shift. Drucilla Cornell (1993) has suggested that what women hold "in common" occurs through "difference." What is held in common is the set of social relations among women which make them different. Cornell concludes, "this 'in common through difference' is precisely what must be understood through cultural work if there is to be anything like a true solidarity between women" (193).

Moving diversity and complexity to the center of analysis, thus, implies that agency is itself constituted as alliance. Agency is alliance, and alliance produces agency. Working alliances then are moral and political enactments which produce agency and solidarity. We work in and through alliances by undertaking this moral and political labor, and in so doing, we produce ourselves as allies.

Theories at Work

The major theoretical sources for my work are derived from those areas of theory production most closely tied to social movements. In making these theories central, I am interested in crossing and re-crossing the boundary commonly invoked between theory and practice. The theories developed in this text not only keep practice in mind, they develop out of various types of practices, including my own participation in social movements, particularly anti-racist, feminist, and queer movements. My analysis is also obviously influenced by contemporary theories which have been variously labeled postmodern, post-structuralist, and/or deconstruction, theories which are themselves quite diverse and complex. My interest is not to engage the arguments which have emerged around and over these theories *per se*, arguments often constructed through oppositions (between modernism and postmodernism; essentialism and constructionism; agency and determinism). Rather I explore the complexities which these oppositions tend to elide by reworking ethical concepts—particularly agency, norms, values, and tradition—in light of some of these theoretical insights.[29]

I hold the ambiguities among various resources of theory and practice together by using a methodology which works through historical examples. My goal is not to (re)produce history so much as it is to meet the excellent work done by historians of U.S. women's history with questions of ethical analysis.[30] Demonstrating both morality and theory at work, each chapter considers moral speaking and acting in a specific moment of U.S. history and social movement. These examples not only ground the theoretical insights, but they show the process of producing moral knowledge, claims, norms, and values through the work of building relationships and movements, the process of moral labor. This type of boundary-crossing methodology reflects my own (inter)disciplinary location in women's studies and religious studies (each of which is itself an interdisciplinary field of study) and my specific training in an interdisciplinary program called "ethics and society." Feminist ethics frequently encourages a context-based construction of ethical theory, and the study of ethics within the field of religious studies is distinctive in that it focuses on practicing communities. For many of my colleagues these communities are faith communities, whereas for me they are social movements. Thus, my text is not a traditional religious ethics, in that while I do take religious expression and action seriously—I do not, for example, leave aside the faith perspective of self-avowedly religious public actors or ignore the importance of religion in analyzing Katie Cannon's *Black Womanist Ethics*—I do not place my constructive work within a religious or theological context. Rather, I see these constructive efforts as contributions to on-going feminist movement.

Throughout this text, I develop a methodology which holds together ethics and politics, because the division between the two frequently works to provide a problematic containment of diversity and flattening of complexity. In some theories ethics is the site of unity (for example, the unity of *the* moral point of view) which allows for the diversity of political disagreement. Alternatively, ethics is located as the site of private value formation, specifically so as to allow diversity in the private sphere, while politics is the public site of overarching and unified principles of justice and equal treatment (meaning similarity). Ethics in this sense is seen as individual, while politics is social. Thus, individual diversity is supposed to be protected (but is also contained) by relegation to the private sphere of the ethical. This division can contribute to domination as the concerns of particular groups of persons are also contained within and relegated to the privacy of ethics. For example, Ada María Isasi-Díaz argues in En la Lucha, *In the Struggle: Elaborating a* Mujerista *Theology, A Hispanic Women's Liberation Theology* that the individual/social division between ethics and politics is untenable in *mujerista* thought, which always understands ethics as social ethics:

> This follows from the centrality of community in our culture and from the fact that *mujeristas* denounce the split between the personal and the political as a false dichotomy used often to oppress Hispanic Women. (1993, 5)

Joan C. Tronto (1993) (herself a political theorist) argues that it is crucial for feminism to challenge the boundary between ethics and politics. Tronto outlines the ways in which boundary crossings between the ethical and the political are traditionally viewed as problems. Political considerations brought into the context of the moral can be seen as tainting moral considerations with practical concerns that obscure the ideal nature of morality. Conversely, moral concerns in the political realm may be seen as irrelevant distractions from or as idealistic interventions in the pragmatic business of politics. Taking women's public activities seriously, however, necessitates questioning these boundaries, because women's concerns have been traditionally relegated to the realm of the private and the ethical. For the women in the abolition movement whose activities I consider in chapter 1, speaking in public is itself a violation of the boundary between public and private, even as it allowed them to bring moral concerns to bear on political issues. Tronto concludes that "the boundary between morality and politics works not only to protect morality from corruption, but also renders morality relatively powerless to change political events"

(152), and that "the separation of morality and politics keeps us from noticing how profoundly our political conceptions constrain our sense of morality and vice versa" (172).

An analysis which crosses the boundaries between ethics and politics can enrich moral theory. If the normative is the iterative materialization of power relations, then it is always already implicated in the political insofar as the political is concerned with social power. Ethics is intertwined with politics precisely because the conjunction of the two articulates the embodiment of power relations. As both Chandra Mohanty (1994) and Martha Minow (1990) point out, rethinking "difference," or rethinking how norms and values "work," is most effective when placed in the context of histories of social action and institution.[31] Investigation of moral claims which are politically enacted in social movements demonstrates the implications of ethical theories, while it also articulates the moral theories and assumptions which inform social movement and political action. Thus, the intertwining of ethical and political analysis may allow for a re-evaluation of the workings of contemporary democracies.

The book shifts back and forth between ethics and politics while always placing both in the context of social movements. Chapters 1 and 2 provide a reading of interrelations among diverse and complex moral actors through an analysis of shifting moral economies. In the first chapter I investigate the workings of moral economies by analyzing women's claim making from various sites in relation to nineteenth-century abolition movements. The analysis shows how the Grimké sisters, Catharine Beecher, and Sojourner Truth differently articulate women's moral stances toward abolition and toward the meaning of "women's morality." This chapter illustrates complexity in relation to diversity by showing how shifting among the different perspectives also shifts understandings of relationships which make up the whole and, thus, challenges the limits of difference. This chapter also raises the initial questions about the conjunction and disjunction of movements operating under the signs of "race" and "gender." By placing these various claims in relation to each other it is possible to understand not only their difference(s), but how they constitute each other. Through this analysis women's moral activities are shown to produce and simultaneously to subvert the moral economies within which they work.

The second chapter takes up questions of intersection and interstice by investigating social movements of the 1970s. This chapter asks why and how it is that U.S. social movements so frequently cannot sustain alliances, but rather take on the same type of singularity exhibited by the U.S. public sphere. Why, for example, do movements tend to operate under singular signs of "race," "gender," "sexuality," or "class" when this configuration makes alliance politics so difficult? This singularity points to an "economy of the same" which operates in the U.S. public sphere to contain social movements within the public sphere, by positioning diverse movements for change as threatening to the unity of the public; it also works within social movements, so that movements assume that their claims must be based on some unity.[32] As a result, through inducement and enforcement, counter-public social movements too often end up as replicas of the very public sphere which they are trying to change.

Chapters 3 and 4 provide an analysis of how to work with diversity and complexity by recognizing multiple forms of social differentiation and its accompanying complexities in the spaces in-between differences. The third chapter investigates diverse possibilities for ethics by relationally reading texts from the mid–late 1980s, specifically Katie Cannon's *Black Womanist Ethics* and Sarah Lucia Hoagland's *Lesbian Ethics*. Each of these texts provides important new possibilities for moral claim making and response, inventing and extending moral traditions. This relational reading demonstrates the limits as well as the possibilities of working with diversity among and within persons and groups, thus, laying the ground for articulating the spaces in-between differences. The fourth chapter asks how to work with diverse moral possibilities in the context of contemporary publics, reading right-wing claims on and about the "general" public in relation to lesbian, gay, bisexual, and queer claims on and about this same public. This chapter shows how both right-wing and queer publicity can reproduce the public problems of chapter 2—racism, sexism, heterosexism, and class dominance—if the differences of chapter 3 and their correlative complexities are marginalized in action. The chapter also shows how such reproductions can be challenged by making diversity and complexity constitutive of public activities through work in the spaces in-between differences. The conclusion then reworks the relationships between universalism and moral relativism in order to suggest new possibilities for working alliances.

Working Alliances

Alliance politics has proven so difficult for feminist movement because the methodology for forming effective alliances is not self-evident. A commitment to diversity does not, in and of itself, materialize alliance. The case studies in this book show that, historically, feminist movements, working in and among various U.S. economies of differentiation, have worked both to recognize and to consolidate diversity. As chapter 1 shows, insofar as first-wave feminist movement was tied to the struggle for abolition, feminism worked to address issues of race, as well as gender, and to form alliances across racial divisions among women. The complexity of interrelation among economies of differentiation does not allow for women activists to take up coherent positions which simply represent women's diversity, however. Rather, each of the protagonists in chapter 1 must negotiate a set of contradictions. When these negotiations are effective they challenge the liberal pluralist approach to diversity as "units" of difference dis-articulated from complexity. This liberal pluralist model is, however, the dominant structure of articulating diversity in the U.S. Given that it produces a form of diversity that devolves into singularity, economies of differentiation along the lines of "gender," "race," "class," "sexuality," are themselves structured into the dominant "economy of the same," and social movements tend to structure themselves as "the same"—the same as the dominant public, the same as each other, and internally the same (based on commonality or identity). Thus, diversity repeatedly becomes singularity, and movements for social change simply reiterate the public.

The assertion of diversity is also insufficient to alliance formation in that it engages the ambivalence of the term "alliance" itself. Alliances assume the existence of separate, autonomous movements which might come together to form an "alliance"; but, alliances also require the subversion of the autonomy upon which they depend. As the case studies show, attempts to form alliances by first establishing autonomous movement and then forming alliances will tend to fail because the basis of alliance—the complex interrelation among issues and movements—has been undercut by the assertion of autonomy. The case study of 1970s women's movements in chapter 2 shows how a women's liberation movement based on autonomy from left political and civil rights movements desired, but could not effectively form, alliances. In the move to autonomy, the diversity of women's activisms devolved into a predominantly white, heterosexual, and middle-class feminism because implication in interrelation, which is also implication in complexity, was lost. Diversity is once again dis-articulated from complexity, and efforts to form alliances will not work.

If complexity is engaged with diversity, however, the ambivalence between autonomy and alliance can be (re)constructed as ambi-valences, sites of multiple activity and possibility. This reconstruction can take place, in part, by shifting the priority of autonomy and alliance to make alliance primary. To do away with the tension between autonomy and alliance altogether by working only in alliance would suggest the possibility and need for a "super-movement" that could coherently contain all issues, all resistances to domination. Such a move would, however, undermine complexity, just as does the assertion of single-issue movements. Work in the complex space in-between autonomy and alliance would be lost. The likely effect of attempts to create such all-encompassing movement is that autonomy would begin to reassert itself, just as 1970s feminist movement did in relation to a left politics that claimed to cohesively articulate all issues from a single base. Complexity can be engaged through work at the intersections of social movement. The type of articulations at the intersections undertaken by the texts read in chapter 3 work to connect issues across economies of differentiation. As these texts articulate new norms from these sites they also materialize new possibilities for social movements to be constructed out of diversity and complexity. Yet, even articulations at the intersections can produce their own margins, indicating the ongoing need for work. The possibilities for alliances between womanist and lesbian ethics which were created, in part, by the writing of these texts is a space that can be articulated in various ways, including as an interstice. Chapter 4's study of right-wing moves to overwrite the space between "race" and "sexuality" demonstrates that working in alliances also requires reworking the U.S. public sphere, such that it can sustain a complex, rather than a liberal, pluralism. Complex pluralism demands a public sphere which can bring together diverse persons, groups, and movements not in an overarching framework that contains all diversity within its singular frame, but rather through a network of publics held together by the connections between and among them.

Overall, the case studies show that alliance formation is not simply the effect of particular activities in social movement. Rather, to form alliances that work, movements must proceed from diversity and complexity, making alliance primary to movement. Working in alliances, thus, shifts the base of social movement such that movement itself must change. Alliance formation is never a completed project; neither is democratic contestation. The work of producing new norms that can materialize diverse relationships in all of their complexity remains constitutive of on-going moral and political life.

1 | Moral Economies at Work
Diversity, Complexity, and Women's Moral Agency

How do alliances work? When are social movements able to come to-gether to work across differences, and when do they split apart? When do movements successfully bring together issues, actions, and activists? How do conceptions of moral agency enable or constrain the possibilities for working alliances? Which norms, when (re)iterated, materialize alliances? Specifically, what does it mean to make alliances the site of moral agency? How does it change our conception of agency to shift from the individual as the site of agency to alliances as the site of both agency and the constitution of the "in-dividual"? And, how does such a shift (from individual to alliance) alter ethical perspectives and possibilities for action? In order for action or activism to be moral does it not need to articulate a coherent moral perspective? And, does the need for coherence suggest singularity and boundedness, that one particu-lar course of action is the moral course? If alliances presume multiplicity and diversity how can they provide the basis for a specifically moral agency?

This chapter addresses these questions by investigating alliances formed through intersections in social movement, specifically mid-nineteenth-century movements for the abolition of slavery which brought together (albeit imper-fectly) issues of "gender" and "race." Through this example, I will delineate a conception of moral agency which takes moral diversity as its starting point. Reading for moral diversity is not enough, however. These various perspectives articulate each other and so they must also be read in and through the com-plexities of interrelation. Emphasizing the double meaning of articulating mo-rality—articulation through speech and action which is also statement and en-actment of interrelation—opens the door to a model of agency that challenges the boundaries of coherent singularity and yet maintains moral possibilities. Thus, demonstrating how diversity and complexity *work* at the intersections of social movement can also show how alliances *work* as site of moral agency.

Historians have frequently linked the "first wave" of feminist movement in the United States to mid-nineteenth-century movements for the abolition of slavery (Lerner 1971, Kerber et al. 1995). Women activists on behalf of aboli-tion took up new roles, such as public speaking before "mixed" gender audi-ences, while they also extended skills and methods, such as petition drives, which had previously been the purview of women's activities. In the early nineteenth century, two European-born libertarian reformers, Frances Wright and Ernestine Rose, broke the boundary that prevented women from speaking before "mixed audiences" (Yellin 1989, 46–48). Maria Stewart, a free African American woman, was the first American-born woman to leave extant texts of public speeches (Giddings 1984, Stewart 1987). The path established by these women was followed by several women in the abolition movement, including some of the women I consider in this chapter: Angelina and Sarah Grimké, Catharine Beecher, and Sojourner Truth. The Grimké sisters took another step forward when Angelina spoke to the Massachusetts legislature, thus using their (albeit controversial) success as public speakers in the social sphere as a springboard from which to challenge women's exclusion from institutionalized politics (Lerner 1971, 1–12). African American women like Harriet Tubman led movements to free slaves, while both African American and white women formed anti-slavery associations.[33]

These women did not, however, simply move from a private sphere of activity to a public one, bringing with them or formulating along the way, a single woman's moral voice. Each of the activists which I consider in this chapter, intervened in political culture using specifically moral discourses, but they offered a diversity of positions, drawing on various norms and enacting various forms of agency in striving for the goal of abolition.[34] Moreover, even the specific historical voices that I consider do not simply offer a happy plurality or multi-vocality. Rather, women involved in abolition movements were frequently in disagreement with each other about a number of issues, including the best path toward abolition, the appropriate place of women in society and social movements, the nature of women's morality, and, even the question of who or what is a "woman."[35] These different conceptions of women's morality and ethical agency demonstrate moral diversity among women, but an investigation of their interrelations also highlights the complexities that inform possibilities for agency in and through diversity.

This story presents deep contradictions and limitations, and thus, it is a cautionary tale as well as an inspiring one. The contests among women activists were formed in a social field that presented women with a number of problems and limitations in their efforts to enact moralities. Women were particularly faced with the problematics of inclusion and difference, what Martha Minow (1990) has called the "dilemma of difference," a dilemma central to the structure of U.S. law and the public activities which inform the law. In this chapter, I suggest that the contradictions and limitations faced by women working in public alliances are most clearly delineated when we recognize that the claim to speak as women is itself a claim to complexity, one which implicates issues of race, class, and sexuality in women's moralities. This chapter will show how the intersection between issues of "race" and "gender" in the politics of the nineteenth-century U.S. abolition movement, not only informed alliances across both racial and gender division, but also brought these divisions to the center of the social formations they supposedly named—women and men, slave and free. Thus, women's moralities are precisely about contradiction and confrontation, diversity and complexity. The dilemma of difference can never be resolved simply, by either simple inclusion or simple recognition of difference.

Diversity and Complexity

Historian Nancy A. Hewitt (1990) has demonstrated that just as women have always participated in economies of material production, so also they have produced their own norms. Hewitt argues that women have produced moralities within laboring enclaves, enclaves which are race and class specific and which carry specific sexual mores. She identifies, for example, distinctions among slave women, mill girls, and bourgeois wives and mothers. Each specific enclave shared working and living conditions distinct from men of the same race and class, but interrelated with these men and other groups of women and men. Out of lives structured by work within these specific communities, women developed social networks, common rituals, and most importantly for my concern, moral, as well as economic, value(s). These values do not represent a unified women's morality, but rather a set of diverse and sometimes contradictory women's moralities.[36]

The stresses and contradictions of women's positions as laborers within particular economies and the interrelations among various economies make for the complexity which accompanies diversity. For example, historian Paula Giddings (1984, 39–55) has argued that while African American women produced their own set of norms under the extreme conditions of slavery, these norms were still affected by the dominant white society. Giddings argues that, in fact, there were three major and potentially contradictory axes crossing the social field of slave women's norm production—survivals from African society, the moral requirements of the situation of slavery, for example the need to reproduce a sense of self which could ground resistance to slavery, and the norms of the dominant white culture. Giddings makes a similar argument for the multiple and complex axes that influenced free African American women's norm production. So, for example, the nineteenth-century "cult of true womanhood," ideologically invoked as a normative description of white bourgeois women, also had an impact on African American women's norm productive activity. This complexity is an indicator that the contexts within which women act as norm producers are themselves not seamless and coherent, but contain internal contradictions. This complexity also implies that the diversity of women's moral voices cannot be understood as simple parts of a coherent whole. Rather, social conflicts can create contradictory diversity within, as well as among, particular moralities.

Women's moral activity is further complicated by the fact that the enactment of morality involves various forms of moral labor which may or may not be contradictory. Bourgeois wives may produce a moral voice distinctive from dominant public sphere norms, but may reproduce these same norms in their sons by teaching them to be autonomous and competitive, and/or they may use their particular voice to challenge norms of autonomy and competition through moral reform. Mill girls may develop norms of solidarity among themselves, they may work to change the social conditions which determine the structure of their labor, and/or they may internalize bourgeois norms of domesticity and understand their mill work as a temporary step toward achieving those norms. Slave women may produce norms relevant within a community of African Americans, but complex forms of moral labor may be necessary to maintain these norms over against dominant ideologies.

Moral Economies

In order to begin to understand how moral agency works in and through diversity and complexity, I will read particular agencies by locating them in "moral economies." Moral economies are the normative social matrices within which moral agency is constituted and moral action and activism undertaken. Moral economies are sites of normative discourses that work to produce moral persons and their activities. Discourses as defined by Ellen Messer-Davidow (Gardiner 1995) are systematic sets of social relations, referring to a variety of practices and their institutional and social contexts. These normative matrices inscribe "governing power," meaning that moral activity and subjectivity are formed by the (re)iteration of governing norms. Actions or persons that do not admit to the governing power of a particular economy cannot be moral within that economy. For example, the nineteenth-century "cult of true womanhood" (Welter 1966, Cott 1977) established a moral economy along the axis of gender division, interstructured with race and class, such that "true women" (read: white, middle-class wives and mothers) enacted a domestic morality complementary to public sphere norms of individualism and competition among white men. Within such an economy, all those persons whose activity takes place outside of this realm of complementarity, such as women who participated in labor outside their "homes" or men who are excluded from the competitive economy of wage labor, will be excluded from morality, from "womanhood" or "manhood," and, thus, effectively from "personhood." It is in this sense that Katie Cannon (1988) argues that because Black women have labored outside of the bounds of white gender complementarity

Black womanist ethics have been treated as either amoral or immoral by dominant U.S. society. The tie between moral enactment and the recognition of personhood both induces and enforces the production of particular types of persons and their actions through the interactive re-iteration of particular norms.

Various moral economies are overlapping, and therefore, they exert governing force on each other, creating contradictions for moral action. For example, the normative matrix governing "the public," is constructed through claims of universal relevance to all persons, yet this economy interacts with a moral economy of "gender" that normatively distinguishes male and female moral activity. The interaction of the moral economy of the "public" and that of "gender" reinforces "men's activities" as dovetailing with public, thereby, simultaneously reinforcing male dominance and women's exclusion from or marginalization in the public. Thus, moral economies interrelate moral agency and social differentiations like race, class, sexual identity, and gender. This same interaction among economies, however, also forms possible sites for "freedom," for the construction of agency. As the women's activism in this chapter shows, by working at sites where these various economies intersect, it is possible to displace normative iterations, to enact norms "differently" and hence to resist or subvert the workings of a particular economy.

An analytic focus on moral economies highlights the complexity of interrelation, in part by bringing to the fore the dynamic interplay of social relations. Writing about the historical and social context of moral and political action runs the risk of presenting descriptions that over-stabilize context, so that social relations appear not to be constituted by interactions, but rather to be fixed and determined by social structures. Moral economies, while effectively systems of interrelations, are also active and shifting, thus, emphasizing the interplay of dynamic processes. By reading the shifting construction of moral economies across various sites of women's speaking and acting in the nineteenth-century U.S. abolition movement, I am arguing that questions of how a particular ethics is articulated and enacted are not simply internal questions of reasoning, logic, or tradition. Rather, given the ways in which moralities are interrelated in economies particular ethics are also constituted through others around them.

I use the concept of moral economies not simply to establish interrelations and social context for moral speaking and acting, but also to emphasize the ways in which morality requires work and to articulate critically the ways in which this labor is divided.[37] I emphasize the labor necessary to morality because much of the work that women do is moral labor and, like most women's work, that labor is often devalued.[38] Acknowledging moral labor also challenges those views of ethics, such as natural law theories, based on the assumption that morality is given in the structure of nature or reality.[39] Moreover, recognizing that moral labor may be divided challenges social constructivist theories that understand ethics as the "common" product of a particular society as a whole.[40] Finally, reading diverse moral economies as complexly interrelated and, thus, potentially contradictory challenges theories of moral diversity that configure diverse moral perspectives as coherent parts which, when added together, make up a (coherent) whole. While movement across boundaries and among locations may expand moral understandings, contradictions imply that any attempt at complete or comprehensive representation of the moral "universe" will erase some aspects of the context it claims to comprehend.

In order to be effective, moral agents must negotiate these contradictions, and yet, many models of agency do not recognize the complexity of interrelation. This chapter's example illustrates how the various historical protagonists respond to the social conditions in which they worked and, thus, whether their models of agency effectively enabled them to fulfill their stated moral intentions. The chapter investigates how women's social actions work to change society in relation to norms of democracy and equality, while they also challenge and transform long-accepted meanings ascribed to these norms. The analysis shows that historical actors are best able to make ethics work when they can work with and in the complexity which is created by criss-crossing lines of interrelation among diverse moralities. By considering the implication of these historical protagonists in systems/economies of race, class, and sexual relations, relations that have been historically constituted as asymmetrical power relations, I develop a concept of moral agency entangled in complex power relations which frequently imply that with resistance comes complicity as well.[41] The work of moral agents, then, is not to purify oneself or one's position, thus producing an unproblematically "moral" agency, but to negotiate across and even through these complexities. In part, this project works within the discipline of ethics, to move away from the traditional (Kantian) model of the individual, freely acting moral agent for whom intention or "good will" is the central moral question, to a more historically and socially contextualized agency that focuses on both the constraints and the effects of action.[42]

Abolition and Agency

Since my aim is to do moral analysis I have chosen women's activism in nineteenth-century abolition movements as a case study because it is well documented and has been the subject of a great deal of feminist history.[43] This example illustrates a few of the ways in which U.S. women have produced norms and values and constructed themselves as moral agents, thus, providing the opportunity for an analysis of diverse agencies undertaken by women who worked with a stated commitment to remaking both race and gender relations. Because these women worked at the intersections of social relations, placing such an analysis in the context of complex moral economies also allows a (re)-writing of moral possibilities for alliances.

I begin my historical example with Sarah and Angelina Grimké as women who adopted justice language to express their outrage over the evils of slavery and over their own experience of injustice in a sexist society.[44] In adopting a justice perspective, the Grimké sisters worked with a model that emphasized equality among individual persons as the site of agency. Only the "immediate abolition" (Ceplair 1989) of slavery could realize this equality. I then consider Catharine Beecher's response to the Grimkés and her claims that the public activity of the Grimkés undermined the distinctive nature of woman's moral voice and, hence, failed to fulfill the "duty of American females."[45] Catharine Beecher invoked a republican or communitarian perspective which placed the individual moral agent within a community, but which understood that community as coherent and clearly bounded with defined gender roles. Both an end to slavery and a recognition of the "true dignity" (1837, 99) of woman could occur if the community was made the foremost site of agency. The Grimkés and Catharine Beecher engaged in direct conflict over these alternative conceptions of how to accomplish the morally agreed upon goal of ending slavery. While each actor thought that her position provided a necessary critique of the others' moral activity, by reading the positions in relation to one another, I will also demonstrate their interdependence. Sojourner Truth's speeches and activities provided another vision of agency, one that raises important questions about how to understand the equality of individuals, the communal site of agency, and the role of women's moral activity.[46] Truth does not abandon either the language of justice or of women's morality, but she is able to enact them precisely by complicating the question of: Who is a "woman"? And, what kind of work can "she" and should "she" do?

All of these women locate themselves as moral agents in relation to what they understood as an American public. Each finds herself to be working with a series of binary oppositions—between men and women, between slave and free, between public and private. Each places women's morality at the center of activity, but each locates this center differently. As centers of analysis and action shift, hierarchical relations and binary oppositions look different and, thus, each actor works the binaries differently. By asserting a particular agency, activists not only constitute their own position, but work to reconfigure the others. Their mutual critiques constitute an interdependent, and yet, contradictory set of relations within the moral economies that form a shifting context of action for women as moral agents. These mutual critiques also work to challenge and shift the moral economy which the protagonists understand to be the normative matrix governing the U.S. "public." Thus, these various contexts for action must themselves be read as dynamically interactive.

The Grimké Sisters

Sarah and Angelina Grimké, daughters of a wealthy, slave-owning family from Charleston, South Carolina, moved north in order to escape the stifling mores and morals of their birthplace, Sarah in 1821 and Angelina in 1829. While, for each, the reasons for leaving Charleston were complex, including their conversion to the Society of Friends, both women were motivated by a desire to end their participation in the brutal system of slavery (Lerner 1971, 55, 66–86). In the 1830s they became outspoken advocates for the immediate abolition of slavery. The Grimké sisters adopted the justice language of equality and freedom legitimated by a universal creator God. The fundamental equality of souls of all persons was based on a sameness that undercut the type of social and racial hierarchies on which slavery was based. God's creation of each person in equality guaranteed them certain rights and enjoined upon them responsible moral agency. Slavery clearly denied the created equality of humanity by denying to African Americans their freedom, thereby dehumanizing them rather than treating them as responsible moral agents.[47] Thus, locating moral agency in individual human beings, all of whom have equal rights and responsibilities before God, formed the basis of the Grimké sisters' activities to end slavery.

In an analogous argument, the Grimkés claimed that denying women the "right" to participate actively in public sphere debate of moral issues like the abolition of slavery denied them both their freedom and their moral responsibility as enjoined by God. For example the 1837 Anti-Slavery Convention of American Women adopted the following resolution offered by Sarah Grimké:

> RESOLVED, That whereas God has commanded us to "prove all things and hold fast that which is good," therefore, to yield the right, or exercise of free discussion to the demands of avarice, ambition, or worldly policy, would involve us in disobedience to the laws of Jehovah, and that as moral and responsible beings, the women of America are solemnly called upon by the spirit of the age and the signs of the times, fully to discuss the subject of slavery, that they may be prepared to meet that approaching exigency, and be qualified to act as women, and as Christians, on this all-important subject. (Sterling 1987, 12)

Thus, the sisters stressed that because all human beings were equal before God and held by God to the same moral responsibilities, all human beings therefore held the same right to act as moral subjects. On this basis, the sisters both created a public position of agency for themselves and articulated a moral basis for ending slavery.

Through this language of equality the sisters undercut the binary oppositions between men and women, slave and free, and the race-based opposition between Black and white. In so doing, the sisters included themselves and African Americans (slave or free) in the center of both moral agency and public life, a center from which they had been excluded by the sibling evils of slavery, race discrimination, and sex discrimination. They undertook this project in a cross-racial alliance between whites and African Americans in the struggle for abolition, an alliance which for them was based on the connections between the oppression of white women and African American slaves created by the denial of their rights. In fact, this alliance was the grounding for the Grimké sisters' understanding of their own agency. Without the struggle against slavery the Grimkés might never have become public speakers. Moreover, they came to understand the restrictions they faced as women, in relation to the oppressions of slavery, and without this understanding they would not have articulated their own right to act publicly. In this sense, alliance formed the site of their agency, but their model for enacting this alliance also created certain contradictions which served to reinforce dominations: race and class dominations in the abolition movement and U.S. society, as well as domination along the lines of gender and sexuality experienced by the Grimkés. Continuing implication in these dominations undercut their own ability to act, as well as the alliance to which they were committed. Thus, ultimately, the method of simple inclusion of difference, of moving all persons to the center of agency, proved inadequate to either alliance politics or the formation of effective moral agency.

Despite the important moral leverage provided by using the justice language of equality, the most important of the contradictions that the Grimkés had to negotiate developed from the ways in which justice perspective claims of equality at creation erased the complications of existing social relations. The language of equality employed by the Grimkés while based on a fundamental "sameness" at creation was a site at which multiple, various understandings of sameness and difference were negotiated. Thus, claims on behalf of equality allowed for a certain "slippage." Invocations of a fundamentally spiritual equality left open the question of how far to carry equality at creation into the world of social relations.

At times the slippage in equality implied a "sameness" which elided distinctions in relational positioning and led to a form of alliance based on over-identification (Yellin 1989, 24–26). In locating their agency in an alliance of oppression with enslaved African Americans, often based on claims to a metaphorical enchainment which mirrored the enchainment of slavery, white women who conjoined women's rights and abolition might also erase the distinct agencies of those women on whose behalf they struggled. For example, one of Sarah's resolutions adopted at the Anti-Slavery Convention of American Women in 1837, calls for the production of anti-slavery prints so that the "speechless agony of the fettered slave may unceasingly appeal to the heart of the patriot, the philanthropist, and the Christian" (Sterling 1987, 20). The Grimkés worked to gain a public speaking position for white women and yet were able to configure the female slave (depicted in the print) as speechless. Once the enchainment of slaves became the metaphorical basis of white women's agency, then the literal actions of African Americans against slavery tended to be elided. Moreover, the muteness and passivity of the enchained slave, served to reestablish distance between slaves and "the patriot, the philanthropist, and the Christian." As Jennifer Fleischner points out, "narrative reinforcement of the slave woman's *mute* suffering helped to allay cultural anxieties about the propriety of overidentification" (Fleischner 1994, 127–28, emphasis in original). Thus, the claim to equality also allowed for a "slippage" between the equality of souls and the inequality of social relations.

This room for slippage in claims for equality was compounded by a Christian model of moral reform which constructed agency as Christians helping "others" less fortunate than themselves. This model rather than constructing agency within an alliance of equals depended on a certain distance and fundamental difference between the two parties to the relationship. As a result, at the same time that the Grimkés argued that the Christian God had created all persons as equal, the Christian missionary model implicit in the abolition movement carried within it a paternalistic paradigm. Lawrence Friedman (1982), in *Gregarious Saints*, his study of movements for immediate abolition, argues that paternalistic Christianity allowed white abolitionists to claim that African Americans were their fundamental equals, while at the same time treating them as inferiors who needed to be educated and civilized. Contact on an equal basis with African Americans wouldn't just threaten the superiority of whites, but the "difference" which African Americans represented, despite supposed internal equality, might contaminate the purity of moral agency which "gregarious saints" were trying to construct.[48]

The slippage in equality in relation to this paternalism meant that the Grimkés' Christian justice language could still operate within a moral economy which distributed power and action unequally between whites and African Americans. While the Grimkés fought against their own paternalism, they were not completely successful in this project. The sisters understood the problem as a "prejudice" which could be undone through contact between the races, rather than as a problem created by the unequal distribution of power. Friedman quotes Angelina as taking the stance that "You [free Negroes] must be willing to mingle with us whilst we have the prejudice, because it is only by association with you that we shall be able to overcome it. You must not avoid our society whilst we are in this *transition* state. . . . We entreat your aid to help us overcome it" (Friedman 1982, 174). Sarah took an activist position encouraging white abolitionists and African Americans to sit together in places of worship, walk together in the streets, and socialize together. In some respects, particularly in their familial recognition of their African American nephews, the Grimkés were exceptional in their willingness and ability to challenge paternalism and address racial prejudice. Nonetheless, African American abolitionists identified whites' behavior as indicative of a "chord of prejudice," and race relations within the movements became more problematic over time (from the 1830s to the 1850s). African Americans began to lose patience with whites, gradually developing independent organizations and tactics.[49]

In fighting the "chord of prejudice" the Grimké sisters were able, at some points, to challenge the justice perspective's lack of a clear articulation of social relations. The slippages of claims to equality also manifested themselves with regard to the battle for their own rights as women. In a conflict sparked by the publication of a pastoral letter against the sisters' public activity, their colleague, Theodore Weld, whom Angelina eventually married, took the position that the sisters should speak out only on the topic of abolition, not on women's rights.[50] He based his position on the claim that the topic was a needless distraction from the cause of abolition. Weld's commitment to nongendered equality led him to the conclusion that the Grimké sisters could, without a problem, adopt the subject position of non-gendered moral responsibility and speak out against slavery. As the sisters had maintained with regard to racial division, Weld viewed opposition to women's public activity as a matter of prejudice that could be changed through contact with responsible and capable women: "The feeling of opposition to female praying, speaking, etc., which *men* generally have is from a stereotyped notion or persuasion that they are not competent for it. It arises from habitually regarding them as *inferior* beings. . . . But let intelligent woman begin to pray or speak and men begin to be converted to the true doctrine, and when they get familiar with it they like it and lose all their scruples" (Weld to Sarah and Angelina Grimké August 26, 1837, Barnes and Dumond 1934, 433, emphasis in original). The sisters maintained, however, that in order to speak at all they must speak on women's rights, precisely because the subject position of public moral responsibility did not automatically include a position for women, but had to be expanded in order to do so. "The *time* to assert a right is *the* time when *that* right is denied. We *must establish this right* for if we do not, it will be impossible for *us* to go *on with the work of Emancipation*" (Angelina Grimké to Weld and John Greenleaf Whittier August 20, 1837, Barnes and Dumond 1934, 428, emphasis in original).

Part of the argument was over the relationship between issues. For Weld only one issue at a time could be effectively undertaken: "Since the world began, Moral Reform has been successfully advanced only in *one* way, and that has been by uplifting a great *self evident principle* before all eyes. Then after keeping the principle in full blaze till it is *admitted* and *accredited* and the surrounding mass of mind is brought over and *committed* to it, *then* the *de-rivative* principles which radiate in all directions from this main central prin-ciple have been held up in the light of it and the mind having already embraced the central principle, moves *spontaneously outward* over all its *relations*" (Weld to Sarah and Angelina Grimké August 26, 1837, Barnes and Dumond 1934, 432, emphasis in original). For the sisters, the two issues were inextri-cably linked: "And can you not see that women *could* do, and *would* do a hundred times more for the slave if she were not fettered?" (Angelina Grimké to Weld and John Greenleaf Whittier August 20, 1837, Barnes and Dumond 1934, 429, emphasis in original). And, in the same letter, "Anti Slavery men are trying very hard to separate what God hath joined together. I fully believe that so far from keeping different moral reformations entirely distinct that no such attempt can ever be successful" (431). The sisters argue that it is more effective for the cause of abolition to recognize the connection to women's rights. They also argue that it is their moral duty to address women's rights. A woman, like a man, is enjoined to a moral responsibility before God, and if she does not act on this responsibility by fighting against slavery then she "*sur-renders her moral responsibility,* which *no woman has a right* to do" (Angelina Grimké to Weld August 12, 1837, Barnes and Dumond 1934, 416). Yet, in order to fight publicly against slavery she must also fight "for the *rights of woman* as a moral, intelligent, and responsible being" (415).

While this language of equal rights and moral responsibility enabled the sisters to take a stand on women's rights in the battle to articulate a public moral agency for women, it did not enable them to analyze the conditions nec-essary to such an expansion of women's public subjectivity. In particular, dur-ing their speaking tour the Grimkés supported themselves by the inheritance which they had received from their father. This money was more than suf-ficient for their individual needs, and it was only after Angelina's marriage, when there was a family to support, that either of the sisters had any financial concerns. Their economic independence erased a fundamental material differ-ence between themselves and the men with whom they worked. The various roles for public speaking which also offered remuneration, the life of a minis-ter or politician, were open only to men, but the sisters were not dependent on their work as a means of making a living. While men could support themselves by public speaking, the Grimkés could speak publicly and still support them-selves.[51] Thus, a material block to the Grimkés' claims to sameness with men was removed.

In Angelina's case an assumed equality and an agency which focused on the rights and responsibilities of the individual moral agent could not effec-tively articulate the sexual division of labor or the changing economic circum-stances she faced upon marriage, and thus, could not sustain the continuation of her public speaking career. When Angelina Grimké and Theodore Weld married they were determined that their marriage should not have an adverse impact on their work as abolitionists, and as proof of that commitment, Angelina spoke merely two days after the wedding at the inauguration of Abolition Hall in Philadelphia (Lerner 1971, 243). Yet, their personal commitment (as individual, autonomous moral agents) was insufficient to overcome the material conditions of married life for women, particularly the realities of childbirth and child care. Sarah addressed the inequalities between husband and wife in her *Letters on the Inequality of the Sexes*, published in 1838 (Bartlett 1988). She criticized the ways in which a wife upon marriage lost her legal right to act, quoting the eighteenth-century British jurist Sir William Blackstone's description of the doctrine of coverture, that upon marriage "*the very being, or legal existence of the woman* is suspended during the marriage, or at least is incorporated and consolidated into that of the husband under whose wing, protection and cover she performs everything" (Bartlett 1988, 72). Sarah comments, "It would be difficult to frame a law better calculated to destroy the responsibility of women as a moral being, or a free agent" (73). Angelina did not intend to surrender the exercise of her moral responsibilities because of her marriage, yet she never questioned whether her assumption of the role of wife should include traditional motherhood. She was concerned to demonstrate to the world that her public speaking career had not made her an "unnatural" woman, and she questioned herself when the contradictions of her position surfaced (Lerner 1971, 288–93).[52] Eventually the emotional and physical demands of domestic labor, child bearing, and child rearing effectively stopped Angelina's career as a public speaker. Angelina's justice stance provided her with a commitment to equality, one which a moral agency articulated as an individual commitment could not fulfill. Despite her commitments Angelina could not overcome the constraints of "womanhood."

By locating agency in the equality of individuals the Grimké sisters were able to include as moral agents in public discourse those previously excluded, specifically African Americans and white women. This method of approaching "difference" by moving the marginalized to the center of moral activity allowed the Grimkés to challenge slavery with calls for immediate abolition and to challenge restrictions on women's proper sphere for moral action. This model of agency did not, however, allow them to negotiate fully the relational complexities at the intersection of issues of race and gender. Their vision of equality based on sameness in a world of relational differences, particularly differences in power and privilege, allowed for slippages which reinforced, rather than undermining, the hierarchies and binary oppositions which the Grimkés intended to challenge. In particular, the Grimkés' model of agency could not articulate the ways in which bringing together the struggle for racial and sexual justice through claims to mutual or analogous oppression when used as a means of asserting women's agency could elide the agency of African

Americans on whose behalf they struggled, and they could not articulate the complexities of claiming a public position for white women as equal to white men, without articulating the differential burdens and relational positionings of women. Thus, while they worked to maintain an effective alliance with African Americans and to assert the important connections between issues and struggles, justice language alone could not fully articulate this task.

The importance of being able to articulate and work with relational complexities is further highlighted when the slippages and contradictions of the Grimkés' activities are located in relation to the diversity of women's moralities articulated and enacted in movements for abolition and women's rights. Catharine Beecher took a stand against the Grimkés' public action and in support of women's distinctive moral labor. She and Angelina engaged in a direct debate over these issues through Catharine's *An Essay on Slavery and Abolitionism with Reference to the Duty of American Women*, published in 1837, and Angelina's response in *Letters to Catharine E. Beecher, In Reply to an Essay on Slavery and Abolitionism*, published in 1838. While this debate is mutually critical, it is also important to read for the ways in which the dispute represented two sides of an interdependent moral economy. The justice tradition does not articulate a full set of social institutions in America, but is intertwined with a republican tradition, adopted by Beecher, articulating institutions and communities bounded by lines of social differentiation.[53] The justice and republican traditions could be mutually critical, but slippage in the justice language of equality also allowed the two traditions to be mutually reinforcing. Claims of fundamental equality did not necessarily carry over into a critique of the institutions of labor, family, and community, nor did fundamental equality directly imply the social realization of this equality. The Grimkés could subvert some of those conditions by expanding the boundaries of justice with regard to race and gender. They could not, however, undertake this liberationist project without contradiction because the moral economy and its social structures remained intact. Thus, the Grimké sisters faced contradictions they could not articulate and moral commitments they could not fully work out.

Catharine Beecher

Unlike the Grimkés' assurance about the social implications of God's activity, Catharine Beecher, the oldest daughter of evangelical minister Lyman Beecher, was much less convinced of the connection between divine activity and human life. In her well-documented struggle over conversion, which was also a struggle with her father, Catharine never reached a converted position from which to determine a clear relationship between God and her life.[54] Kathryn Kish Sklar (1976) interprets Beecher's struggle as part of an intergenerational movement which transformed Lyman's Calvinistic theology into a pattern for social action. Because of Catharine's particular position as a female heir to the Beecher tradition, however, this transformation to social philosophy was not without its own problems. Throughout the course of her life as a teacher, educational leader, and expert on domestic economy, Catharine attempted to work out the particular role of women in the Calvinist project which Lyman had argued for as a project of U.S. nation-building—the building of a Christian society.[55]

Beecher located women's moral agency relationally, placing it in the context of moral community. Thus, rather than adopting the liberal justice tradition with its erasure of the differences between men and women, Beecher developed her own version of the republican tradition, emphasizing the particular morals of (white, middle-class) women as distinct from men. Beecher did not specifically delineate the boundaries of the community which she understood to be the moral community. In her writings it is clear, however, that she has a specific community in mind, one tied to republican ideals of citizenship and one which incorporates the boundaries and exclusions of citizenship in her time.[56] Beecher's project is to revalue women's moral labor in relation to the white, propertied male citizen of the republic and, thus, to value "woman's" place in the community which she shares with him.

Drawing on the prescriptive ideology of True Womanhood (Welter 1966), Beecher argued that because women did not participate in the competitive activities of public sphere political and economic life, they had a superior moral nature that was the necessary guide to sustaining the republic. Yet, because for Catharine the relationship between God and social action was uncertain, women's special nature as morally superior beings was not guaranteed by God and must be vigilantly protected. Beecher argued that in accepting their restricted social position, American women undertook a self-sacrifice which assured their moral superiority. Beecher claims that women in the United States are equal to men, as is required by the principles of democracy: "In this country it is established, both by opinion and by practice, that women have an equal interest in all social and civil concerns; and that no domestic, civil, or political, institution, is right, that sacrifices her interest to promote that of the other sex." "But," she continues, "in order to secure her the more firmly in all these privileges, it is decided, that, in the domestic relation, she take a subordinate station, and that, in civil and political concerns, her interests be intrusted to the other sex, without her taking any part in voting, or in making and administering laws" (1841, 4). This subordination does not obviate equality, however, because in a democracy the ascription of super- and sub-ordinate roles is a choice. "No woman is forced to obey any husband, but the one she chooses for herself; nor is she obliged to take a husband if she prefers to remain single." And, "Each subject, also, has equal power with every other, to decide who shall be his superior as a ruler" (1841, 3). The tension in these claims, however, is that the parallels that she draws between individual choice and civic and political institutions cannot be sustained. Without the vote, women did not have equal power to choose a ruler, but Beecher maintains that even without the vote women's interests are protected because "in all cases, in which they do feel a concern, their opinions and feelings have a consideration, equal, or even superior to that of the other sex" (1841, 7). Because women voluntarily submit through self-sacrifice, their moral superiority is secured and acknowledged by those to whom their interests are "intrusted." This is not to say that Beecher did not also promote an argument based directly on differences between "man's" and "woman's" nature, but the references to woman's nature are interestingly placed in quotes from Tocqueville's *Democracy in America*.[57] For Beecher, the nature argument is ultimately insufficient because the institutional position of white, middle-class women's labor is critical to her understanding of women's moral agency. In Beecher's schema women's superior morality is earned by the self-sacrifice of restricted activity and could be lost by entry into the public sphere.[58]

In *An Essay on Slavery and Abolitionism with Reference to the Duty of American Women* (1837), Beecher's argument is based on this view of self-sacrifice and the potential threat of losing women's moral superiority. Catharine argues that by entering into public sphere activity, particularly through public speaking, the Grimkés are doing more harm than good in their anti-slavery campaign. Beecher takes the position that slavery is a moral evil and claims to be arguing with the Grimkés over means, not ends (1837, 109–110). The Grimkés' anti-slavery campaign is harmful not just because they have overstepped the bounds of True Womanhood, but because they are enacting the values of the public sphere which women are supposed to buffer. By speaking publicly the Grimkés create dissension which threatens to break up the community. Rather than entering the public sphere, woman's role is to guide man's moral understanding so that moral community can be built and slavery ended through harmony rather than competition: "It is . . . by exhibiting and advocating the principles of charity and peace, that females may exert a wise and appropriate influence, and one which will most certainly tend to bring to an end, not only slavery, but unnumbered other evils and wrongs" (1837, 145–46). For Beecher the potential break up of the union is the great moral evil with regard to the slavery question (1837, 127). Thus, the abolition movement should be directed toward careful transition from the present state of affairs to a resolution acceptable to both sides, "the North" and "the South" (1837, 142–46). It is important to note that the "sides" refer only to division within white society with no reference to the position of slaves. For example, Beecher writes, "Do not Northern men owe a debt of forbearance and sympathy toward their Southern brethren, who have been sorely tried [by the interference of strangers in their domestic affairs]?" (1837, 145). Beecher never directly compares the evil of a split in the union to that of continued suffering by slaves if a resolution to the problem is slow in coming, leaving her in the position of implicitly valuing the connection of predominantly white society over an end to slavery.

In the introduction to her *Treatise on Domestic Economy*, Beecher translates this argument into the claim that women's domestic labor is the basis for moral labor necessary to the maintenance of the republic and should be valued as such. Beecher responds to the hierarchical opposition between the role of men and the role of women in the republic by emphasizing difference rather than emphasizing sameness so as to include women in the center of public sphere activity as did the Grimkés. In this way, Beecher attempts to improve "woman's" condition by increasing the value which society attributes to her labor, particularly her moral labor. She works to move the center of moral activity from the public sphere of citizenship to the private sphere of domestic economy: "Woman is to win every thing by peace and love; by making herself so much respected, esteemed and loved, that to yield to her opinions and to gratify her wishes, will be the free-will offering of the heart. But this is to be all accomplished in the domestic and social circle" (1837, 101).[59] She does not claim a new position for women's agency, as did the Grimkés, but rather moves the center of moral activity toward the margin, revaluing a form of agency already enacted by women. Nonetheless, this strategy of revaluing difference did not prove less contradictory for Beecher.

Beecher faced contradictions with regard to the construction of her own moral agency and in relation to questions of solidarity across race and class lines which she could not effectively negotiate. In the end, Beecher could not directly challenge the hierarchical gender opposition which restricted and devalued women's moral labor, as her position could work to provide the very labor necessary to the maintenance of those discourses that devalued it. Beecher's position presents a clear inability to develop solidarity among women across race and class lines, thus, illustrating the dangers of focusing only on a binary opposition between center and margin without taking into account the complex relationships among marginalized persons and groups. This failure in Beecher's position illustrates the importance of how a community is constructed for communally defined agency or for ethics that focus on the maintenance of connection.[60]

The most obvious contradiction for Beecher's position as a woman was her own violation of the very boundaries and roles which she had established as necessary to the maintenance of women's superior moral nature. She refused dominant roles of gender and sexuality. She never married, never had children, and never practiced the domestic economy which she recommended. Through much of her life she earned her living through fund-raising efforts promoted by public activity, particularly through her publications. Yet, despite the public nature of her activities, Beecher was never able to achieve financial independence. She was always dependent on public good will to support both her projects and herself. Moreover, she was always dependent on men as the board members and trustees of schools or as the figureheads of her project to send teachers to the west. This dependence, in conjunction with Beecher's own middle-class assumptions, marks a primary influence on the formation of her position. Beecher's assumed community is that of middle-class propriety with a clearly defined gendered division of labor. With the publication of the *Domestic Economy*, Beecher became a leader in the movement to define women's labor in the home (what Dolores Hayden [1981] calls "the grand domestic revolution"). The constructions of middle-class propriety were only reinforced by Beecher's financial dependence on prominent men and "the public," a dependence which she recognized as requiring her to act with restraint.[61]

The contradictions of Beecher's position, apparent in her own life, are even more striking with regard to women of different races and classes. The norms that she invokes against the Grimkés—opposing separation and strife in the moral community—draw the boundaries of that community completely without regard to the lives of those persons most directly affected by abolition: slaves. Her concern is about separation and strife between white men and women or among white men. She accepts the status quo definition of community as the white middle-class community which surrounds her, and she also assumes the status quo to be harmonious (non-violent). It is the acrimony aroused by the Grimkés that threatens this harmony. Thus, Beecher's emphasis on connection results in a contradictory disconnection from other women; the violence to which slave women are subjected is beyond the bounds of her communal vision, and so she is separated from their cause. For Beecher, an agency that emphasizes the difference between middle-class white men and women ultimately works to reinforce an exclusionary alliance between them. The connection between middle-class white men and women is maintained by reinforcing relationships based on binary gender roles, while any but the most abstract connection to African American women and men, even in the context of discussing slavery and abolition, is lost.

Why was Catharine Beecher blind to the boundaries of her vision and so to the lives of other women? Why was she willing to argue passionately that women's lives and work should be valued, while failing to challenge the framework of restriction which devalued the lives of even those women who were included in her vision? Historian Jeanne Boydston answers these questions by referring to the limitations established by the conclusion of Catharine's initial struggle with Lyman: Boydston concludes, "Never a rebel by choice, she pursued a more circuitous strategy, seeking to define a public persona congenial to the traditions of her parents, and to work from within to expand women's—

and her own—power" (226). Boydston also points to two central issues for Catharine: her financial dependence upon her family and prominent men and a fear of physical violence perpetrated by men.[62] Whereas, for the Grimkés, solidarity across race, class, and gender boundaries allowed them to face down the threat of violence, Beecher remained hesitant to undertake any action which might "provoke" violence: "And in pointing out the methods of exerting female influence for this object, I am inspired with great confidence, from the conviction that what will be suggested, is that which none will oppose, but all will allow to be not only practicable, but *safe*, suitable, and Christian" (1837, 110, emphasis added). Beecher's position demonstrates some of the dangers of constructing moral agency so as to validate or revalue women's moral agency without challenging the structure of moral economies. Without considering the diversity and complexity of women's moral positioning such a move may fail to challenge an economy which distributes power to white men and restricts the action of white women while denying the importance of the lives and agency of women and men outside the boundaries of white, middle-class families and communities.

An analysis of moral economies also suggests that despite the mutual criticism of the debate between Angelina and Catharine, their two constructions of women's morality are also interdependent.[63] The justice language of equality and public activity was so contradictory for the Grimkés partially because justice represented one aspect of a broader moral economy which included women's special nature as moral beings who fleshed out the world of equal and individual moral agents in families and communities—communities with boundaries drawn along lines of race and class. Nineteenth-century justice language could erase the gender of the speaking moral subject and social relations of equality and inequality because the status quo was ensured elsewhere in American ideology and institution. In this sense liberal and republican discourses worked together to form a moral economy that produced white propertied male citizenship at the center of moral and public activity. While both the Grimké sisters and Catharine Beecher intended to improve the condition of women by emphasizing the importance to society of women's moral labor, neither position ultimately subverted the moral economy within which they worked. The contradictions for women's agency created by this economy made working in alliances difficult for the Grimkés and nearly impossible for Beecher.

Neither the Grimkés nor Catharine Beecher could fully realize alliances because the moral languages with which they worked did not fully articulate the moral economy that formed the conditions for that work. Both the Grimkés' justice claims and Beecher's communitarian ethic hid the social conditions that made possible the illusions of equality and harmony (among white men)—those conditions being women's labor, including the labor of slave women. Sojourner Truth, working for both abolition and women's rights, presents what Jeffrey C. Stewart refers to as "a labor theory of human equality" (Truth 1991, xxxvi). By demanding recognition for her labor as a slave woman and free itinerant preacher, Truth was able to point to the complexities of U.S. moral economies and, in so doing, make "millennialism, abolitionism, and women's rights . . . completely intertwined issues" (1991, xxxvii).

Sojourner Truth

Like the Grimkés and Catharine Beecher, Sojourner Truth drew on her understanding of God's activity in the world in order to develop her own moral agency. She repeatedly refers to an immanent God who is all around her throughout the world and who is directly active in her life—God directs her on the road to freedom, the Spirit calls her to her labors as an itinerant preacher and returns her from life-threatening illness while there remains work for her to do.[64] Thus, Sojourner Truth's understanding of God is more activist than the Grimkés' creator God, and unlike Catharine Beecher's absent God, Sojourner Truth's God directs her moral activity. Truth's religious conversion and her continuing relationship with an immanent God allowed her to undermine her reported internalization of the structures that oppressed her and to begin to develop a critical perspective (Gilbert 1970, 39–41).[65] Gloria I. Joseph (1990) has analyzed Truth's religious perspective as a combination of Christian and African world views. Indeed, it is a combination of religious impulse and her analysis of her position in a dominative political economy as both a slave and free laborer that motivate her to challenge the dominant society as an itinerant lecturer (Gilbert 1970, 97–102).

Sojourner Truth was given the name Isabella when she was born a slave in upstate New York. After escaping from slavery and being legally freed by the state, Isabella eventually was called to the life of an itinerant speaker and took up the name Sojourner, later adding the surname Truth.[66] I do not turn to Sojourner Truth as someone who was able to adopt a non-contradictory position from which to speak women's morality, although she was at times able to turn contradictions into rhetorical challenges. Rather, Truth's work points to the complexities of developing moral agency amid contradictory moral economies. As recorded in *Narrative of Sojourner Truth; A Bondswoman of Olden Time, With a History of Her Labors and Correspondence drawn from Her "Book of Life"*, Truth is able through words and deeds to incorporate certain aspects of prevailing ideologies, both ideals of womanhood and justice claims to rights, into her construction of herself as an itinerant preacher and moral agent within movements for abolition and women's rights.

As Nell Irvin Painter (1996a, 1996b) and Jeffrey Stewart (Truth 1991) have pointed out, this story is itself a complex mediation of Truth's life and actions, a mediation which allowed her to sustain herself materially while it also created her as a symbol disjoined from that material life.

In taking up the life of an itinerant speaker Truth was following a path which was relatively well established at the time. Although there were fewer women than men on the itinerant circuit, she was not alone in this role, nor were audiences unused to hearing women speak at camp meetings and revivals.[67] Truth shared her calling with other African American women preachers like Jarena Lee, Zilpha Elaw, and Old Elizabeth (Williams 1993b).[68] In connecting her speaking to moral reform, Truth was also working in a context of African American women's moral reform activity, including the paradigm for women's political action publicly articulated by Maria Stewart (Giddings 1984, 50). African American women in major urban centers like New York, Philadelphia, and Boston also formed literary and cultural societies which undertook benevolent, mutual assistance, self-help and moral reform activities, thus these societies served African American women as bases for social activism (Boylan 1994, 135, Winch 1994).

Truth was drawing on this context in undertaking her own moral labors, but it was not without contradictions. In developing their moral agency African American women, both slave women and free African American women, faced gender expectations which intersected with racial stereotypes in contradictory ways.[69] African American women were not, like white women, assumed to be virtuous. Rather, racist images regularly pictured them as sexually promiscuous and morally degraded (Boylan 1994, 120). Paula Giddings's analysis of the pressure that dominant gender norms of "True Womanhood" placed on African American self-constitution suggests that while many of antebellum African American women's experiences were denied by norms of True Womanhood, African American women were not simply different or separated from these norms; rather they were affected by these norms even as they pursued their own projects (Giddings 1984, 33–50).[70] There was pressure, for example, on free African American middle-class women to identify with the "cult of domesticity" and demands for moral purity in order to "prove" their "womanhood" and their "morality."[71] Embracing the ideology of domesticity could, however, reinforce dominant standards of both sexual and class "respectability" and work to exacerbate status divisions between middle- and working-class African American women.[72] At the same time, as Evelyn Brooks Higginbotham (1992) argues, African American women could be chided for aspiring to a position not "rightfully" theirs due to their race: "In contrast to the domestic ideal for white women of all classes, the larger society deemed it 'unnatural,' in fact an 'evil,' for black married women 'to play the lady' while their husbands supported them" (260).[73] Anne Boylan concludes that:

Excluded by virtue of their race from white conventions of feminine respectability, African American women were more adventurous in speaking out on
public issues, combining abolitionism with community uplift, and challenging the pronouncements of male leaders. Nevertheless, in their relations with
African American men and in their interactions with white women abolitionists, black women activists encountered barriers of gender, class, and
color that also affected their organizations. African American women never
endorsed standards of feminine respectability as fully as did white women.
But insofar as they adopted these standards in order to establish their claim
to feminine virtue, they found themselves constrained by narrow definitions
of appropriate behavior. (1994, 135; see also 133–34)

This context was particularly contradictory for Sojourner Truth as someone
who had lived and worked as both slave and free. In her public activity, she
could be treated as the authentic symbol of oppression under slavery, as a
marker of the beneficence of white society once she was free, and as someone
who both should and should not aspire to "true womanhood."

As Giddings reports (1984, 52), one major difference between free African
American women and white women was that African Americans did not necessarily see a contradiction between domesticity and political action. For white
women, as the Grimké-Beecher debate shows, the relation between domesticity and political action was a critical and often debilitating problem. In order
for African American women to adopt a paradigm for political action, however, they had to negotiate the complexities of their position. Giddings says of
Maria Stewart, "Her ideas reflected both the fundamentals of the Victorian
ethic and criticism of its inherent biases. Out of that mix emerged a distinctive
ethos which underlined Black women's activism for generations to come. And
as is evident in Stewart's work, it was an ethos that had its contradictions"
(Giddings 1984, 50). Thus, in order to develop a moral agency and undertake moral action, African American women have faced the sometimes contradictory task of "fashion[ing] a set of moral values on their own terms, as well
as mastering, radicalizing, and sometimes destroying the pervasive negative
orientations imposed by the values of the larger society" (Eugene 1988, 29).

Sojourner Truth, as a public speaker working in this context, had to negotiate many of these contradictions. Truth develops a perspective at the intersection of multiple interrelated "axes of sameness/difference" (Christian 1988,
36). Her gender experiences in relation to her race and class (labor) positions
sometimes worked to deny her womanhood, and sometimes worked to pin her
to the identity "woman." At times, her particular position was erased as if
someone in her social location did not exist. At times, her self-positioning was
held up as contradictory to "woman's" position and hence invalid, while at
other times, such as when African American men were given the franchise
while women were not, her activities were restricted as she was pinned to the

identity "woman." And, at times, as Nell Irvin Painter (1996b) points out, she became *the* symbol of either the (naive because illiterate) "truth" of slavery or of strong (because black) "womanhood."[74]

The most famous of these symbolic moments is the "Ar'n't I a Woman?" speech given at the Akron women's rights meeting in 1851, as reported by white abolitionist and feminist Frances Gage in 1863 and reprinted in *The Book of Life* in 1878. In this speech, it is her labor as an African American woman during slavery that challenges the assumptions of True Womanhood— "Look at my arm! I have plowed and planted, and gathered into barns, and no man could head me—and ar'n't I a woman?" Both Jeffrey Stewart and Painter argue that these lines are later interpolations of Gage's. This passage in the 1851 *Anti-Slavery Bugle* report of the speech reads as "I have as much muscle as any man, and can do as much work as any man. I have plowed and reaped and husked and chopped and mowed, and can any man do more than that?" (Truth 1991, xxxiii). The question which Painter raises is how Gage's version of the speech operated so effectively in constructing Sojourner Truth as a "symbol" that remains particularly potent.

The second crucial moment in the construction of Sojourner Truth as symbol was when she was challenged with respect to her gender identity at an abolition meeting in Indiana. Her challenger states, "Your voice is not the voice of a woman, it is the voice of a man, we believe you are a man."[75] At this meeting she responds by direct reference to her embodiment, baring her breast, and using ideals of womanhood against those who confronted her by stating that this unwomanly display of her body is to their shame, not hers. She, thus, also challenges those norms which are too narrow to include her experiences or her physicality. Painter points out that it is her repeated self-positioning as a laborer and mother, in conjunction with her age, dark skin, and apparent naivete which allows her to appeal to her embodied experience in this way. These characteristics contrast her with "the light-skinned, ladylike Negro woman [who] symbolized the enslaved fancy girl, whose sexuality—which could be bought and sold—was her most salient characteristic" (Painter 1994, 155). Thus, Truth's separation of her self positioning from the sexual stereotyping of African American women contributed to her ability to rework dominant paradigms of moral agency. Truth worked at what Evelyn Brooks Higginbotham (1993) has called the "nexus between respectability and protest." Higginbotham argues, "[T]he reigning values in society are sufficiently multivalent to be appropriated and reinterpreted by subordinate groups for their own purposes, even for resistance against the power of the dominant group" (221). Undertaking resistance by playing off of multivalent norms (produced at both dominant and marginalized sites) does not allow for a pure moral agency, free from all constraint, but it does allow for the production of agency within the complexities of power relations. Thus, Truth works to construct an agency which (re)negotiates the contradictions of exclusion, marginalization, and difference.

The circulation of rhetorical moments which make Sojourner Truth a potent symbol for work at the intersection of race and gender is not completely separable from knowledge of her life and work, in part because their circulation through the sale of the *Narrative* was part of materially maintaining herself. As Painter (1994) points out, Truth's life story was implicated in a certain desire for exoticism among the white audiences who took up her cause and who wrote about her. Harriet Beecher Stowe's dramatic description of her as *The Libyan Sibyl* and Frances Dana Gage's report of the "Ar'n't I a Woman?" speech in Southern dialect and in an overdrawn contrast to the white women advocates of women's rights show this exoticism at work. Truth's repeated self-positioning as an ex-slave distinguished her from some of her contemporaries who often chose different routes to agency by, for example, emphasizing literacy and education, as a route to public activity. Painter reports:

> Truth resisted or ignored the temptation, as Frederick Douglass did not, to create an educated persona to display the benefits of freedom. Douglass recalled her poking fun at him as he remade himself: '[Truth] seemed to feel it her duty to trip me up in my speeches and to ridicule my efforts to speak and act like a person of cultivation and refinement.' Douglass, like most other African American abolitionists, made one choice; Truth made another. (Painter 1994, 154–55)

Because Sojourner Truth was to some extent able to remove her body from sexualized images of African American women, she did not have to assert her "respectability" in the ways which were salient for some of her contemporaries. Painter reports (1994, 158) that this strategy was criticized by other African Americans for "reinforcing unfortunate stereotypes of the-black-as-ignorant-primitive." And, yet, adding another layer of complexity, "Though she may have poked fun at young Frederick Douglass, she, like him, absorbed the ideals and practices of people who were more firmly implanted in the metropolitan culture of writing and respectability" (Painter 1996a, 270).[76] As with the Grimkés and Catharine Beecher, Sojourner Truth's strategy was not without contradictions, despite the critical leverage it provided her.

The various projects which Truth undertook in her life and work show how she both resists and plays off of the contradictory demands of "womanhood." She fights for the uplift of her race, but through the particular means open to her as a woman. She acts as a direct care provider to African Americans in and around Washington, D.C., during and directly after the Civil War, protesting the segregation of the City Railway, and working on jobs and resettlement projects.[77] She argues for women's suffrage as a means to improve the living conditions of African Americans. She also argues simultaneously for the vote on the basis of women's nature and knowledge as distinct from men and for an expansion of liberal understandings of rights to include African American women. As a newspaper account of one of her speeches reports, "The Friend [Sojourner Truth] said that woman ought to have her rights for her own benefit, she ought to have them, not only for her own benefit, but for the benefit of the whole creation, not only the women, but all the men on the face of the earth, for they were the mothers of them. Therefore she ought to have her God-given right, and be the equal of men, for she was the resurrection of them" (Gilbert 1970, 218).[78] She worked to claim her rights, going to the polls in Battle Creek, Michigan, where she lived and demanding the right to vote in the 1872 presidential election (Sterling 1984, 412, Gilbert 1970, 231).[79] In her postbellum project of attempting to gain land grants for African Americans, she also challenged the material conditions of racism in the United States and the continuing rights of former slaves to claim a place in the United States in contrast to the project of repatriation to Liberia (Sterling 1984, 399–401, Gilbert 1970, 239). This project was not unproblematic, in that it was conceptualized along the lines of nineteenth-century Indian reservations: "She wants the government instead of feeding them [freedmen] as it does now, to put them on land of their own, as it does the Indians, and teach them to work for themselves" (Gilbert 1970, 221). The complex implications of this project also engaged the intersection of respectability and protest: "She last night gave startling pictures of the degradation and suffering among the colored people at Washington and elsewhere; showed that it would pay the nation to transform those paupers into industrious, moral citizens" (Gilbert 1970, 224). Ultimately, Truth was able to participate near the end of her life in a similar, but differently formulated, project that took place not under the auspices of the federal government, but through the initiative of some African Americans to leave the South after the end of Reconstruction and migrate to Kansas (Painter 1976, 247).[80] These various projects show the multiple levels at which Truth worked and her need for a variety of strategies to negotiate the contradictions she faced. Neither a strategy focused on individual equality and rights, nor a community-based republicanism were sufficient.

The ways in which Truth drew on traditional understandings of women's role, while at the same time undermining them, can be read as contributing to the project of complex subjectivity termed "womanist."[81] Elsa Barkley Brown (1989), for example, describes the womanist consciousness of Maggie Lena Walker in the following terms: "[Walker] drew upon traditional notions of the relationship between men and women at the same time that she countered these very notions. [For example,] Black men could play the role of protector and defender of womanhood by protecting and defending and aiding women's assault on the barriers generally imposed on women" (Brown 1989, 629–30). Sojourner Truth negotiated complexities by using traditions while also fragmenting them in order to reform or rework the pieces into alternative possibilities. She questions notions of unequal labor between women and men without giving up the claim to be a woman herself. She speaks and acts morality as a "woman" without simply reifying the relations of domination which have constructed her womanhood.[82] Working with these complexities allowed Truth to appeal to moral ideals both of justice and of women's "different" moral agency.[83]

Sojourner Truth works to shift the center of morality, refusing a choice that requires *either* simply moving women to the already established and, thus, constraining center of morality *or* moving the center toward women's already established and, thus, equally, if not more, constraining "difference." Sojourner Truth articulated her agency in part through claims to women's morality, although she did so in such a way as to challenge the category "women," constructing it so as to maintain the intersection between gender and race politics and making it a potential site of alliances across race and class lines; yet, her agency was not without its own dangers. Precisely because of the ways in which the category women excluded African Americans, Truth operated in a space of exoticized "otherness," which as Nell Irvin Painter (1994) points out, kept even the symbolism of the challenge "Ar'n't I a Woman?" in interrogative rather than declarative form.

Moral Economies/Moral Diversity

These readings demonstrate some of the diverse ways that women have constructed moral agency and some of the dangers and contradictions which they worked through.[84] Catharine Beecher's interpretation of women's distinctive moral voice placed value on woman's role as provider of the moral labor necessary to the maintenance of moral communities despite a competitive economy and polity. This perspective could not, however, provide the moral resources to challenge directly either the ideology of woman's role or the racist boundaries of the moral community. The Grimkés challenged some of the racism inherent in the white construction of community. They worked to make a place for women to speak in public, by promoting an equality of sameness with the dominant (white and male) public, but this ideology of sameness conflated subject positions, setting up a dynamic of overidentification and simultaneous denial of agency in relation to African American women, particularly slave women. Ultimately the Grimkés had difficulty establishing an alliance that maintained distinctiveness in the midst of connection. Even as they claimed an equality of sameness, once Angelina married, her individual commitment to gender equality could not overcome the simultaneous, social structural demand to maintain the gender-differentiated role of wife and mother, a combination of tasks which proved impossible. Moreover, the ambivalences expressed in the argument between Weld and the Grimkés—over the necessity or effectiveness of moves toward alliance and connection and the argument that gender is not a central political "principle"—appear repeatedly in the work of women's movements. Sojourner Truth subverted the division between a distinctive woman's voice and a strategy of expanding male public discourse by working on each side of the division. Women deserved the vote both because they had a right to it and because they had a moral voice which could improve the public realm. Yet Sojourner Truth also undermined the expectations of "womanhood" which reinforced gender and race restrictions and which deny the realities of women's labor. Sterling (1984) reports the following speech at the Equal Rights Association in 1867: "I would like to go to the polls myself. I own a little house in Battle Creek, Michigan. Well, every year I got a tax to pay. Road tax, school tax, and all these things. Well, there was women there that had a house as well as I. They taxed them to build a road, and they went on the road and worked. It took 'em a good while to get a stump up. Now, that shows that women can work. If they can dig up stumps they can vote. It is easier to vote than dig stumps" (1984, 412). Thus, a woman does not have to be frail to have a distinctive moral voice and a right to vote.

The contradictions faced by these women articulate the "dilemma of difference" (Minow 1990) in U.S. society. More importantly these positions are also *interdependent*. The two sides of the dilemma, either equality or difference, liberal or communitarian, are usually read as conflicting. In this reading of the dilemma, each position works as if it describes a coherent perspective critical of the other and sufficient unto itself. It is the claim to coherence which enables the perspectives to appear as either/or choices, thus hiding their interdependence and inherent contradictions. The examples in this chapter have shown that women's claim to moral action in the U.S. public sphere did not simply engage a binary opposition between public roles for men and private roles for women. Had that been the extent of the problem, the Grimkés' strategy of expanding the liberal paradigm to include a position for women would have been more successful. But the positions of Catharine Beecher and Sojourner Truth show the hidden conditions of liberal ideology. White, propertied men could represent themselves as free and equal because their material and communal needs and values were ensured through the moral and material labor of women—of slave women and African American free laborers and of bourgeois wives and mothers who were to ensure the maintenance and reproduction of liberal ideology through their own distinctive moral purity and their labor as mothers. Refusing the either/or choice when articulating paradigms for agency makes visible the boundaries of the "dilemma" by challenging the coherence of the two sides and demonstrating that they do not articulate the entire field of social relations.

None of these women actors, the Grimkés, Catharine Beecher, or Sojourner

Truth, could occupy without contradiction the position of either sameness with or difference from the dominant "public" which they sought to engage. Thus, these readings challenge the conception of moral agency as a site of either complete coherence or freedom, along with the concept of sameness/ difference as a coherent either/or choice. Letting go of this coherence complicates moral agency, thus leading to accusations, like Weld's, of ineffectiveness. Yet, as the sisters pointed out, the coherence Weld advocated was itself ineffective. Letting go of coherence opens the possibility of an alternative series of choices built by recombining fragments of the various positions into a new set of relationships. While the Grimkés and Catharine Beecher chose positions on either side of the "dilemma"—either sameness or difference—Sojourner Truth adopted a strategy which both appealed to and challenged both sides of the dilemma. While such a strategy did not allow her to form a newly coherent or non-contradictory position, it did allow her to negotiate particular sets of contradictions.

These readings also show the complex set of interrelations which make the context for action. There is not simply a gender economy, which poses the "woman question" at work here. Rather, these women are working in a gendered economy which operates through a binary opposition between "men" and "women," but which intersects with a racialized economy that (re)connects particular groups of men and women and operates through a binary opposition between, in this case, whites and African Americans. This intersection works to place white men's interests and actions at the center of morality, while *separately* marginalizing white women, African American women, and African American men. These economies further intersect with differentiating economies of class and sexuality, producing, for example, sexual respectability as a dominant norm that marks class status, and that works differently for African American women and white women. Thus, it is necessary to cross and break open the boundaries of binary oppositions which segment marginalized groups from public rights and responsibilities and from each other.

Reading for interdependence and contradictions helps to explain how fundamental contradictions within the U.S. polity have been maintained—how, for example, claims to universal equality have historically been accompanied by and possibly even were founded upon hierarchies of race, class, gender, and sexuality. If liberal claims to equality are dependent upon, or at least historically interdependent with, the communal hierarchies, then slippage in abstract justice between, for example, equality of souls and inequality in social relations is not simply the mis-application of justice principles, but is, in fact, inherent in the liberal concept of justice itself. Analogously, communitarian emphasis on the substance of social relations may be unable to articulate these relations in terms other than bounded hierarchies or effectively to challenge abstract liberalism. The communitarian position depends on the very abstraction of liberal equality to produce and maintain communities which claim to be harmonious and to provide freedom and equality, but which are built on violence, constraint, and domination.

Acknowledging moral diversity and abandoning the coherence of dominant paradigms for agency does not necessarily deny women creative possibilities for agency, however. Rather, this move opens alternative possibilities to develop agencies which are counter-coherent, which challenge claims to moral coherence by embracing the complexity of women's agencies. Women can, for their own purposes, play out the contradictions of the multiple discourses which construct their experiences, breaking up and crossing boundaries, rather than allowing these contradictions to present us with unsatisfactory, bifurcated choices. This step can be most effectively undertaken if we undermine the supposed coherence of morality and recognize that moral diversity contributes to the opportunity for subverting contradictions. For women, in all their complexity, to enter public discourse they neither have to be satisfied with expanding existent discourses which can never articulate their lives and work, nor do they have to produce full-blown alternative discourses. In fact, the most effective strategy might be to do both at once—to expand available discourses, while also proliferating alternative accounts of the world which may undermine the available discourse. This strategy, then, implies breaking up power exerted through the illusion of coherence in moral discourses. Diversity and complexity in women's moral voices implies a need to develop solidarity among women across differences. Solidarity does not imply an identity of moral voices, for example between white women and African American women, but a recognition of the relationships among moral voices.

In providing a critique of these various women's agencies I am not suggesting that it is best simply to abandon the models and ethics they enacted, but rather that we work with these models in various ways in order to be able to enact them differently. It is not necessary to abandon languages of justice, equality, or connection and community. I am suggesting, however, that each of these languages does not form a coherent set of norms, nor does any of them ground a coherent moral agency. This view of morality locates agency in the complexities of interrelation. There is no single "right" action which carries no dangers or is immune from critique. Reading diverse agencies relationally creates a space which delineates some of the parameters, some of the possibilities and limits, and some of the dangers of publicly claiming women's "agency." My suggestion is that within that space women work to construct agencies which are themselves "alliances"—recombined parts of the agencies located in different sectors of the moral economy. Precisely through the reconfiguration of these various parts it is possible not only to create agencies which address some of the dangers and expand the parameters of moral agency, but also to reconfigure the moral economies which connect norms to social differentiation, thus expanding the parameters of moral possibility for alliances, for social relations not strictly inscribed by the norms of gender and racial divisions.

Unfortunately, the historical outcome of the alliances created between feminist and anti-racist politics during struggles for the abolition of slavery did not necessarily result in the continuing connection between these issues. In particular, postbellum feminist struggles for women's suffrage frequently worked specifically to dis-articulate feminism from anti-racism, as some white women advocates argued for white women's suffrage on the basis of maintaining racial superiority over immigrants and, once they were enfranchised, African American men (Andolsen 1986). My next chapter investigates the question of how the lessons of alliance are so quickly and often forgotten. Why, if feminist movement is so often born out of the work of diverse movements and alliances, as it was in both the mid-nineteenth and mid-twentieth centuries, are working alliances so difficult to maintain, such that the expression of a desire for alliance seems more consistent than does its enactment?

2 (Re)Producing the Same
Autonomy, Alliance, and Women's Movements

How does intersection become interstice?[85] How do movements formed in the crucible of alliance become representations of singular issues and communities? Why are the lessons of alliances so hard to learn? Or, perhaps more accurately, why are they so quickly and frequently forgotten? Why, for example, did feminist movements constituted in and through action to end slavery, split in the postbellum period with a dominant stream of women's movement adopting racist discourses to promote voting rights for "women," meaning specifically white, American-born women? What were the inducements to leave the intersection at which feminist movement was initiated? And, if it was political efficacy which these feminists sought, why did they believe that abandoning alliances with women of color for a singular vision of white womanhood was more efficacious? Thus, the question for chapter 2 is how does multiplicity become homogeneity? How do internally diverse social movements come to look homogeneous? And, then, how do diverse social movements come to reinforce the homogeneity of the dominant, in this case, of the U.S. public?

In this chapter, I propose to address these questions by investigating the "economy of the same" which structures the U.S. "public" and within which ethical enactments of alliances are played out.[86] Feminist movements are formed not only in relation to economies of differentiation—along lines of race, class, gender, sexuality—but also in relation to an economy which produces "the public." What distinguishes the public economy is its claim not to be related to social differentiation. The public sphere economy makes claims of universal relevance to all persons (at least all persons who are members of the public). The "public" as the undifferentiated location of all persons is, thus, established on the basis of hierarchical oppositions between central positions of non-differentiation (e.g., unity) and marginal positions of differentiated particularity (e.g., diversity).[87] Diversity then is the marginalized term in a series of binaries—singularity-diversity, unity-diversity, coherence-diversity—none of which is necessarily a direct opposition, but each of which can establish diversity as a threat to appropriate order. Thus, the economy of the same interacts with economies of differentiation, creating the contradictions faced by the protagonists in chapter 1.

This economy works not only to contain social movements within the public sphere by positioning diverse movements for change as threatening to the unity of the public; it also works within social movements, so that movements assume that their claims must be based on some unity. As a result, through inducement and enforcement, counter-public social movements too often end up as replicas of the very public sphere which they are trying to change. Clear examples of this economy at work surface at those points when women have challenged dominant feminist movements for failing to recognize diversity, points which have occurred throughout the histories of feminist movement. The responses to such challenges when framed as critiques of fragmentation and distraction have invoked a sense of opposition between the unity of "women" and the diversity asserted by those who felt they were marginalized by this very unity.

The strength and persistence of the desire for singularity and unity and the repeated assertion of its necessity to morality and politics is, thus, the product of an economy of the same which operates in the U.S. public sphere to recuperate claims for change based on different perspectives. The pressures faced by alliances within a public sphere dominated by an economy of the same, are the inducements to abandon alliances and to reproduce a politics of singularity. The reason that the inducement to participate in the economy of the same is so effective is not just the dilemma of difference, the way in which claims to either equality or difference always fail, but also the ways in which social movements produce themselves as "the same." Thus, the inducements of this moral economy work repeatedly to produce "the same" type of person and "the same" type of movement. To be "the same" is not to be allied, however. The assumption that similarity makes commonality makes alliance makes effective movement is mistaken. Rather, the economy of the same continually reasserts interstice in place of intersection and, thus, produces the repetitive insistence of the need for, but the failure to, work in alliances.

The economy of the same plays off not only the dilemma of difference, but also the ways in which alliance is itself an ambivalent term, dependent upon, but also subversive of, autonomous movements which might come together to form an "alliance." The ambivalent dynamic between alliance and autonomy is frequently replayed in the case study for this chapter—1970s women's movements—as the need to establish a distinctly "women's" movement asserts an autonomy from the alliances which made such movement possible or as the intersection of gay and women's liberation becomes the autonomous movement "lesbian-feminism." Yet, distinctiveness was not always asserted as autonomy, nor did intersections always become new, separate movements. Women's struggles around multiple issues, including race and class, could and sometimes did maintain themselves as sites of alliance formation among multiple movements. These approaches to the complexity of women's movement open the possibility for reworking the relationship between autonomy and alliance, making it the site of multiple, ambi-valent possibility, rather than ambivalent singularity.

Second-Wave Feminist Movement

The 1960s and 1970s in the United States were, like the mid-nineteenth century, a time of extensive social movement, including a resurgence in feminist activity. Yet, like the mid-nineteenth century, this "second wave" of feminist movement developed in relation to multiple movements and issues, but sometimes became predominantly white and middle class. Why were the lessons of first-wave feminism and the loss of early alliances not heeded, but instead repeated, nearly a century later? How could a feminist movement initiated through a number of other social movements including civil rights movements for racial and economic justice, left political movements, and post-Stonewall lesbian and gay rights movements develop into a predominantly white, middle-class, and heterosexual movement? The simplest answer is that racism, classism, and heterosexism were at work. This answer is incomplete, however, in that it doesn't tell us much about the operation of racism and/or classism and/or heterosexism. Nor does it tell us much about the specific dominative practices at work. It is not clear, for example, that early second-wave white feminists were racist in the same ways that their nineteenth-century counterparts were. The specific type of white supremacy displayed by Elizabeth Cady Stanton, where she argued that white women should get the vote in order to maintain the dominance of respectable white society over immigrants and freed African Americans, is not necessarily in evidence in the 1970s. Thus, second-wave feminism is a distinct case, one which raises important questions about the ability of contemporary movements to address the problems of either first- or second-wave movement. In 1994 Nell Irvin Painter raised the issue of why more than a century later Sojourner Truth's question, "Aren't I a woman?," still carries such rhetorical power. Does it not imply a failure to form any kind of effective alliance which could serve as the basis for a category "women" which is articulated across race and class lines? By focusing on how dominative practices operate in and through a discursive context in this particular case, it is possible to interrogate why dominative practices constantly reappear within and between movements, why alliance politics is repeatedly so difficult, and how to resist or intervene more effectively in the operation of such dynamics.

The importance of issues of diversity and alliance across a range of issues—race, class, and sexuality—is clear in early second-wave feminist texts from the late 1960s and early 1970s. The question of alliances is raised centrally in the introductions to both *The Black Woman* (Cade 1970) and *Sister-*

hood is Powerful (Morgan 1970), while texts aimed at addressing issues of differences among women appear in the early 1970s, including *Class and Feminism* (Bunch and Myron 1974), a collection of essays from the Furies written in 1972 and published in 1974,[88] and Jill Johnston's *Lesbian Nation*, published in 1973, and based on articles by Johnston appearing in *The Village Voice* from 1970 to 1972.[89] Moreover, the role of women of color, working-class women, and movements for racial justice and class revolution in the formation of second-wave feminist movements is clear in many histories of the time period like Evans (1980), Giddings (1984), Sacks (1989), Garcia (1990), and Crawford et al. (1990).[90]

In feminist theory texts of the 1980s and 1990s, however, it sometimes appears as if early 1970s discussions and debates over differences and alliances never took place. In these stories, "different" women—women of color, working-class women, lesbians (the never-ending list)—and issues of "difference" (perhaps better termed issues of "dominance")—racism, classism, heterosexism—disappear from the 1970s, which is cast as the decade of white, middle-class, heterosexual "feminism." "Differences" then reappear in the 1980s to contest this narrowly defined feminist movement. These stories tend to disarticulate the connections between second-wave feminism and movements like the civil rights movements of the 1950s and 1960s, and they belie the on-going work of women of color, working-class women, and lesbians as feminist work. Rethinking these stories in light of a rereading of early feminist movement texts raises a number of important issues, because the ways in which they construct the "problem" of diversity for feminist movement also delineate how they construct a solution to the "problem." The story seems to imply that, if the 1970s was the decade of monolithic feminism, and the 1980s brought differences to the fore, then perhaps the 1990s will be a decade of alliances.

There are a number of variations on the story which indicate how the "problem" of difference, or the lack thereof, is projected onto the 1970s. Sometimes "diversity" is an academic distinction which later becomes important politically, while sometimes issues of difference—race, class, sex—are political matters which only later become sites of theoretical concern. One major variation of the story is a narrative of historical progression in which feminism moves from being narrowly defined, lacking diversity and incapable of alliance, to a contemporary period in which these issues are beginning to be addressed, ultimately pointing to a positive future. Hester Eisenstein and Alice Jardine (1985) in the introduction to *The Future of Difference*, for example, take the view that Women's Studies, like the women's movement, started out with a view of the unity of women's experiences, a view which then shifted: "As the women's movement grew more diverse, it was being forced to confront and to debate issues of difference—most notably those of race and class—as, for example, in discussions and organizing efforts around the issues of abortion and forced sterilization. Thus, the discussion and the acknowledgment of differences among women was increasingly a political as well as an academic necessity" (xix). This narrative not only removes women of color and working-class women, along with discussion of issues of diversity, from early feminism, it also completely elides issues of sexuality other than heterosexuality, despite the fact that such issues were frequently at the center of early feminist debates.

Nancy K. Miller and Jane Gallop (Hirsch and Keller 1990) similarly locate the beginning of the importance of "race" to white feminists as the mid-1980s, although they emphasize the shift as of theoretical import. They state that in the early 1980s they were not particularly concerned with "race," in contrast to their concern and "anxiety" in the late 1980s. Miller states, "It's as though race had to become a problem for *theory* before it could be taken seriously by white feminists" (Hirsch and Keller 1990, 353, emphasis in original). What happened between 1970 when race was an issue of theoretical importance for both the contributors to *The Black Woman* and *Sisterhood is Powerful* and 1985 when Miller and Gallop locate a major change in consciousness about race for white feminists?[91] Note my concern here is not so much to question the particular tellers of the story as to inquire into the social forces that constructed the history portrayed by Miller and Gallop. What is the politics which led to the forgetting of race as an issue of feminist theory that made it seem newly "serious" in 1985? They attribute, in part, white feminists' attention being drawn to the issue of race to Adrienne Rich's "Notes Toward a Politics of Location," published in 1984. Why is it an essay by a white woman on race that signaled this change? Why is it an essay from the early–mid 1980s, rather than the early–mid 1970s that made "race" something to be taken seriously by "white feminists"?

It could be argued that part of the issue from the 1970s to the 1980s is a shift in the center of feminist theorizing from movement sites to academic sites. The texts from the 1970s which I read in this chapter were primarily produced as movement texts. While some of the authors or contributors, Toni Cade for example, did have connections to universities, most did not. Moreover, the texts were published by mainstream or feminist publishing houses, not academic presses. Was it perhaps that the issue of diversity had to be "relearned" by academic feminists/feminisms? A more recent movement-related text, Carol Anne Douglas's (1990) *Love and Politics*, published by Ism Press, demonstrates versions of the same story, however. Douglas uses two historical narratives about feminism in relation to issues of race, class, and imperialism. In the first chapter called "Defining Ourselves" she subscribes to the narrative that 1970s feminist movement did not live up to its promise to identify with "all women": "By the late 1970s, many Black feminists and other feminists of Color were saying that white feminists had not sufficiently lived up to this ideal of dealing with racism and creating a feminism by and for all women" (17). In the next chapter she adds the narrative of historical progress: "The problem of universalism is not so much a flaw in generalization *per se*, as in who is creating the theory. This is changing as Women of Color living in northern countries and women in Third World countries develop theories. Sharing access to ideas and research resources is the responsibility of northern feminists" (39). While the "this" that is changing is not clearly specified, it is apparently a claim that white women have been the ones producing theories, because "this" is now changing as women of color "develop theories." Yet, white women remain the center of feminism to which diversity is added as it is "the responsibility of northern feminists" to share feminist resources.

In her introduction to *White Women, Race Matters: The Social Construction of Whiteness*, Ruth Frankenberg (1993) similarly appeals to "false universalism." Although she narrates the story in a more careful and complex manner, she still begins her narrative with the 1980s and maintains the past tense:

> Through the 1980s and into the present, work predominantly by women of color has been transforming feminist analysis, drawing attention to the white-centeredness, and more generally the false universalizing claims, of much feminist discourse. Ethnocentrism based on the racial specificity of white women's lives, it was pointed out, limits feminist analysis and strategy in areas such as the family and reproductive rights. In the realm of theory women of color were the first to advance frameworks for understanding the intersection in women's lives of gender, sexuality, race, and class as well as visions and concepts of multiracial coalition work. (8)[92]

I do not disagree that false universalism is a problem. Robin Morgan's assertion in the introduction to *Sisterhood is Powerful* of a universal social location for "women" is very much part of the problem, but there is also a more complicated story, belied by the appeal to false universalism and Frankenberg's use of the past tense in telling this story.

These complications to the story are crucial to understanding the continuing failure of alliance building. It is not that texts in the 1970s were not concerned with alliances. Alliance (or coalition) is a central question, raised, for example, in the introductions to both *Sisterhood is Powerful* and *The Black Woman*. It is not that white feminists simply forgot about or did not take diversity into account. Rather, it is the means of responding to diversity and understanding alliance that is at issue. Morgan touts universal sisterhood in *Sisterhood is Powerful* precisely because of diversity among women, a diversity demonstrated (somewhat) in the contributions to the anthology.

This distinction is so crucial because it shifts the locus of the problem of, in this case, racism in feminist theory and movement from false universalism—the assumption that all women are the same—to the politics of difference itself. Frankenberg makes this move in the next paragraph: "The issue here was [is?] not only that white women's daily experiences *differed* from those of our sisters of color. If that had been the case, simply adding more accounts by women from a variety of racial locations would have resolved the problem. Instead it became clear that white feminist women accounting for our experience were missing its 'racialness' and that we were not seeing what was going on around us: In other words, we lacked an awareness of how our positions in society were constructed in relation to those of women—and men—of color" (9). Here Frankenberg focuses on a problem of relation. The problem is not a lack of diversity but the specific relationships, in this case racial domination, through which differences are constructed. Similarly, my concern is the relational implications of diversity, implications that I argue can be articulated only through complexity. Thus, I am also concerned to follow the mechanisms by which diversity, for example the diversity touted and even celebrated in *Sisterhood is Powerful*, devolves into sameness over and over again.

Similarly, complexity is necessary to the story of the relations between lesbian and feminist movement. In 1995, as part of a project of "separating lesbian theory from feminist theory," Cheshire Calhoun writes, "Although historically the first demand was that '[r]ace and class oppression . . . be recognized as feminist issues with as much relevance as sexism,' recognizing the oppression of lesbians (and gay men) seems a natural next step" (1995, 14). Calhoun is here citing bell hooks's 1984 book *Feminist Theory: From Margin to Center*. Why in 1995 does bell hooks's 1984 argument look like "historically the first demand" when *The Black Woman* was published in 1970?[93] Why in 1995 does it seem that recognizing the oppression of lesbians as a feminist issue is a "logical next step," apparently yet to be taken, when Becki Ross (1995) reports that it was precisely the project of mid–late 1970s lesbian-feminist organizations like the Lesbian Organization of Toronto (LOOT) (1976–1980) to do this work and to distinguish lesbian politics from mainstream "feminism"? The traditional story is that lesbian-feminism conflated lesbians and feminism, thus, in Calhoun's terms "closeting" lesbians within feminism rather than distinguishing the two. While this reading articulates part of the history, it leaves out much of the on-going complexity in the relationship between lesbian and feminist theory and politics. If both Ross and Calhoun are correct, if the work of separating lesbian from feminist movement was undertaken in the 1970s and if it needs to be undertaken (again) in the 1990s, how did the loss of a lesbian theory and politics which could be articulated with, but not "closeted" within, feminist politics occur?[94]

The repeated reference to the 1980s as the beginning of diversity produces a number of narrative implications.[95] It places the "problem" of a monolithic "feminism" and resultant dominations within feminism safely in the past.

Also, even as it locates the problem in the 1970s, in another sense this narrative protects the image of (1970s) feminism by allowing for the assumption that any movement, in order to first establish itself, must make (the mistake of) a monolithic assertion of its subject. It naturalizes the progression from singularity to diversity. Yes, feminism was once monolithic, but now that is changing and it will only get better from here. If however, diversity is an issue in the 1970s, if women's movements were diverse *before* the production of a predominantly white, middle-class, heterosexual movement, then this natural progression may not happen. Telling the story in this alternate manner implies that singularity is repeatedly constituted *out of* diversity. Singularity is not the natural state of any movement in its beginning stages, it is the product of movement itself. Moreover, if singularity is *repeatedly* constituted out of diversity, then the move of asserting diversity is at some level ineffective. It is not the "logical next step" in a linear progression toward non-dominative feminist movement, but is instead part of a cyclical process that repetitively (re)produces dominations.

Perhaps most chillingly, the narrative of progression appealed to in the 1990s is used in virtually the same manner by Robin Morgan in 1970. In the Introduction to *Sisterhood is Powerful* she writes, "Until recently, the [women's liberation] movement seemed to be composed mostly of young white women from middle-class backgrounds. . . . But this is beginning to change" (1970, xxix),[96] or, "Only recently people have begun to discover that the women's movement *is* diverse in class origins" (xxxi, emphasis in original).[97] Bringing together these questions and claims made over a twenty-five-year period indicates that the "problem" of racism, classism, and heterosexism within feminist movement is not one that can be either located or corrected in the simple passage of time. What is the function for Morgan in positing that the movement was biased "until recently"? Does not this story and its assumption of progress elide precisely the historical process which constituted the women's movement as mostly "young, white and middle-class"? Does this story not also elide the historical role of the African American and Mexican American women whose writings are available in *The Black Woman* and *Sisterhood is Powerful* and who have been organizing in and with "women's movements"? Does it not thereby create a narrative in which the diversity and complexity of women's movements are denied in the past and present, and yet connection and alliances are constantly sought after in the future?

Rather than describing a movement which somehow "started out" or "became" predominantly white and middle class and only now is becoming diverse, these stories indicate tensions between identity and difference, autonomy and alliance in movement, tensions which persist into the current historical moment. These tensions tend continually to (re)produce movements as the "same," continually reproducing feminist movement as white, middle-class, and heterosexual, and thereby continually reproducing the same problems for alliance formation. Thus, we see the need for reiteration of claims for diversity in 1970, in 1985, and in 1995. How do these tensions work themselves out in the texts of feminist movement from the 1970s, and what do these workings tell us about the problems feminists face in alliance building in the 1990s? The repetition of these stories about 1970s feminism indicates that they are written out of a consensus that carries the force of "common sense" (Belsey 1980) within feminist theory. Thus, a rereading of 1970s texts is useful precisely to question the status of this consensus. One of the questions that these stories do not address, for example, is: How did the diversity of the early 1980s get (re)produced? Was it not dependent upon early diversity of feminist movements, not just within the cover of Morgan's book, but also among women's movements?

Reading these texts from the 1970s helps to clarify why the frequent calls for alliance formation as part of feminist politics have not been particularly successful in materializing alliances. The configuration of autonomy and alliance varies in these texts from the 1970s, and these variations can contribute to an explanation of how diversity in feminist movements is asserted and then often lost or forgotten, sometimes undermined in the same text(s) which make the assertion. These texts also illuminate the production of a feminist movement that (in its autonomy) is not an alliance. The predominantly white, middle-class, and heterosexual women's movement often described in the 1990s in the passive voice or as factual data about the 1970s, the movement which has existed "until recently" or which will soon change, is not a necessary fact of women's movement or even an unfortunate, but unavoidable, necessity of saying "women." It is instead produced in particular historical moments, often out of a diversity of women activists and of their activisms and movements.

The Black Woman: An Anthology

The importance of the anthology *The Black Woman* (Cade 1970) in the formation of 1970s women's movements cannot be underestimated. As Cheryl Clarke (1993) says, "Toni Cade Bambara's *The Black Woman: An Anthology* (1970) was the first autonomous collection of writings with feminist leanings published by Black women or any women of color in response to the resurgence of feminism in the late 1960s" (215). The anthology includes poetry and prose, fiction and non-fiction. The original publication dates of those essays in the collection which had been published previously range from 1962 to 1969.

In the first paragraph of *The Black Woman*, Toni Cade states that "we are involved in a struggle for liberation: liberation from the exploitative and dehumanizing system of racism, from the manipulative control of a corporate society; liberation from the constrictive norms of 'mainstream' culture, from the synthetic myths that encourage us to fashion ourselves rashly from without (reaction) rather than from within (creation)" (7). From the beginning Black women's struggles are about multiple issues, and Cade goes on to describe how it is that Black women are so frequently erased in the production of knowledge which might ground such a struggle. Experts are generally white and male, but even when they are Black and male their knowledge is "derived from their needs, their fantasies, their second-hand knowledge, their agreement with other experts" (9).[98] Similarly, with the production of knowledge by white women,

> But of course there have been women who have been able to think better than they've been trained and have produced the canon of literature fondly referred to as "feminist literature": Anais Nin, Simone de Beauvoir, Doris Lessing, Betty Friedan, etc. And the question for us arises: how relevant are the truths, the experiences, the findings of white women to Black women? Are women after all simply women? I don't know that our priorities are the same, that our concerns and methods are the same, or even similar enough so that we can afford to depend on this new field of experts (white, female).
>
> It is rather obvious that we do not. It is obvious that we are turning to each other. (9)

In the center of this passage is the crucial question for the conceptualization of women's movement: "Are women after all simply women?" Is it the work of women's movement to articulate the issues of women simply as women, or is something more required? Does thinking of women's movement as simply about women produce knowledge that marginalizes Black women from "women's" movement? This question is so crucial because it points to one mechanism in the production of a women's movement that is not relevant to Black women. Women's movement is not necessarily, nor did it start out as, "white" women's movement. Rather it is produced as such through particular actions, in this case through political analysis that thinks of women "simply as women." My question is, of course, What type of complexity is needed to produce a different kind of women's movement?

Cade makes the first move toward complexity in configuring Black women as both the center of knowledge and activity and active in multiple struggles. Cade argues that the move of turning toward each other is the particular characteristic of 1960s struggle: "What characterizes the current movement of the 60's is a turning away from the larger society and a turning toward each other. Our art, protest, dialogue no longer spring from the impulse to entertain, or to indulge or enlighten the conscience of the enemy; white people, whiteness, or racism; men, maleness, or chauvinism; America or imperialism . . . depending on your viewpoint and your terror" (7, ellipsis in original). She goes on to describe the activities that come out of "turning toward each other":

> Throughout the country in recent years, Black women have been forming work-study groups, discussion clubs, cooperative nurseries, cooperative businesses, consumer education groups, women's workshops on the campuses, women's caucuses within existing organizations, Afro-American women's magazines. From time to time they have organized seminars on the Role of the Black Woman, conferences on the Crisis Facing the Black Woman, have provided tapes on the Attitude of European Men Toward Black Women, working papers on the Position of the Black Women in America; they have begun correspondence with sisters in Vietnam, Guatemala, Algeria, Ghana on the Liberation Struggle and the Woman, formed alliances on a Third World Women plank. (9–10)

Thus, this move toward autonomy for Black women's movement does not extract women's issues from other sets of issues and struggles, but rather works to articulate Black women within these struggles. Cade provides no common position of women which marks women's movement. Rather, the production of knowledge about women is an open question. Cade does provide a list of tasks for the movement, including knowledge production about "ourselves" through projects that would, for example, "present the working papers of the various groups around the country" and "provide a forum of opinion from the YWCA to the Black Women Enraged" (11). There is no expectation that, in order to turn to each other, Black women will necessarily separate themselves from the other issues and struggles in which they are involved. Cade's list is marked by a number of issues: public school education, stereotypes of "the matriarch and the evil Black bitch," migrant workers, consumer education, cooperative economics, Black studies and a Black university, and "the whole area of sensuality, sex" (11). The question is not necessarily whether Black women should form their own organizations or stay in other movement organizations. Whichever organizational move is made, the question is how to remain active in multiple struggles. In the list of contributors to *The Black Woman*, each entry begins by naming such activities, "Active in SNCC's Black Women's Liberation Committee, the National Council of Negro Women, and several Black women's study groups" (Frances Beale)[99]; "Active in Women's League of Voters and discussion groups" (Helen Cade Brehon); "Active in Movement since first march on Washington. Has chaired numerous community-teachers conferences in Michigan" (Grace Lee Boggs); "Frequent traveler to Africa with architect husband Max Bond" (Jean Carey Bond); "Active in anti-poverty projects in California" (Carole Brown). Thus, locating the Black woman in the center of movement requires multiple centers of activity.[100]

Like Cade's introduction, the first prose piece of the collection, Paule

Marshall's 1962 story "Reena," raises this multitude of issues in telling the story of the title character's efforts to form a life committed to "doing something about social issues" (25). Reena engages the major struggles of the time. She participates in Left and student movements and is suspended from college as part of McCarthy-era purges of radicals. She also experiences racism within these movements and doubts whether they effectively address the issues of workers. She eventually withdraws her participation (28–29). She is reinstated at college and graduates, but then faces race- and gender-segregated labor markets, making it nearly impossible for her to find a job in journalism, the field for which she was educated. The only job that she can find is as an investigator for the welfare service. This job allows her to develop an understanding of the intersections of class, race, and gender issues for poor Black women and demonstrates how the welfare system exploits both welfare workers and "clients." The story also addresses class differences within Black communities, challenging the political commitments of the Black middle class to maintain connections to the issues of poor and working-class communities (32). The story articulates the intertwining of sexuality and racism and sexism. Reena's relationships with men confound and are confounded by the interrelation of these issues. She is interrupted in her initial attempts at organizing by a relationship (25), she realizes that in a subsequent interracial relationship both she and her lover use the relationship to work out racial issues (28), and after some years of happy marriage, it too founders on frustrations induced by racism (35).[101]

The complexities of sexuality in relation to gender roles highlight what Cheryl Clarke emphasizes as the watershed importance of Toni Cade Bambara's essay "On the Issue of Roles." Clarke states, "Though I was not a lesbian in 1970, I was nonetheless struck by Bambara's stunning proposal for the resolution of antagonisms between Black women and Black men in her essay, 'On the Issue of Roles':

> Perhaps we [black people] need to let go of manhood and femininity and concentrate on blackhood. . . . It perhaps takes less heart to pick up the gun than to face the task of creating a new identity, a new self, perhaps an *androgynous* self, via commitment to struggle. (Cade Bambara 1970, 103; emphasis added)

Though Bambara was not a lesbian either and none of the articles in her anthology dealt with lesbianism, she and the other contributors—among them Alice Walker, Sherley Anne Williams (Shirley Williams), Audre Lorde, Frances Beale, Nikki Giovanni—were clearly preoccupied, as was I, with gender role expectations and male domination in the Black community/movement" (Clarke 1993, 215).

The various contributors also describe different aspects of Black struggles.

Joanne Grant describes Ella J. Baker's participation in the organization of the Mississippi Freedom Democratic Party and the struggle of rural Black Mississippians to participate in democratic processes, while other contributors focus on issues in urban settings including the need for radical education, change in the welfare system, reproductive freedom, and the need to develop unity across class divisions (Pat Robinson and Group "Poor Black Women's Study Papers by Poor Black Women of Mount Vernon, New York").[102] Many of the contributors debunk the Moynihan report (U.S. Department of Labor 1965) and the "myth of Black matriarchy."

These contributors are often skeptical of white feminists' appeal to a mythic matriarchal past, given the ways in which the term is used against Black women. For example, Toni Cade in "On the Issue of Roles" is interested in investigating the possibilities for alternative conceptions of society in a pre-colonial and pre-capitalist history, but argues that pre-capitalist societies were not necessarily woman-dominated, but rather were societies without rigid sex roles (102). Contributors are also critical of a predominantly white and middle-class feminist movement, although they are clear that Black women's issues are feminist issues:

> As the movement toward the liberation of women grows, the Black woman will find herself, if she is at all sensitive to the issues of feminism, in a serious dilemma. For the Black movement is primarily concerned with the liberation of Blacks as a class and does not promote women's liberation as a priority. Indeed, the movement is for the most part spearheaded by males. The feminist movement, on the other hand, is concerned with the oppression of women as a class, but is almost totally composed of white females. Thus the Black woman finds herself on the outside of both political entities, in spite of the fact that she is the object of both forms of oppression. (Lindsey in Cade, 85)[103]

The "but" in the penultimate sentence in this passage is crucial in that it shows the expectation that Black women's issues should be included in the movement addressed to ending the oppression of "women as a class." There is no sense here that the issues of women as a class include only those that are separable from race and/or economic class. The argument is rather that "the feminist movement" has not lived up to the breadth invoked by "women as a class."

Like other 1960s struggles Cade's move toward autonomy is made in conjunction with a desire for alliance, in this case an alliance with Third World women in anti-imperialist struggles. Cade's blueprint of movement work includes, "set up a comparative study of the woman's role as she saw it in all the Third World Nations," and "chart the steps necessary for forming a working alliance with all non-white women of the world for the formation of, among other things, a clearing house for the exchange of information" (11). This particular expression of desire for alliance is clearly produced in relation to the growing awareness of connections between struggles against racial domination within the U.S. and struggles against imperialism, particularly U.S. imperialism, in the Third World. Many of the contributors to the anthology see Black American struggles as contiguous with "Third World" struggles. Frances Beale's discussion of "bedroom politics" includes critique of U.S.-sponsored sterilization clinics in "non-white countries, especially India" (96) and Puerto Rico. Ann Cook uses the term "Africans" to refer to "all people of Africa whether in Africa or the Western Hemisphere" (149), connecting issues of Black consciousness in the United States to those throughout North and South America and Africa (154).

This desire for and move toward connections also enacts certain ambivalences. Several contributors are critical of a certain "romanticism" in the picture of revolutionary struggle modeled on African revolution. Frances Covington's essay "Are the Revolutionary Techniques Employed in *The Battle of Algiers* Applicable in Harlem?" is concerned to show "that the idea of importing techniques of revolution that were successful in one place may prove disastrous in another place" (251). Cade argues that a romanticized view of revolution tends to forgo "hard organizing" and the long-term work of developing a mass-based political movement (110). The appeal to connection to Africa was not necessarily simply about "Africa," but could also work as a means of constructing African American identity. Kobena Mercer (1994) has analyzed, for example, how 1960s appeals to Africa in the form of hairstyles like the "Afro" or "natural," were not necessarily appeals to Africa "as it is" (112), but to a construction of "a collective sense of black American identity" (113). Similarly, in *The Black Woman*, Paule Marshall's character Reena uses a desire for connection to Africa as a means of articulating a stance more radical than a politics of integration into U.S. society: "It is important that [my children] see Black people who have truly a place and history of their own and who are building for a new and, hopefully, more sensible world" (36); and "I question whether I want to be integrated into America as it stands now, with its complacency and materialism, its soullessness" (37).

The ways in which the contributors to *The Black Woman* describe relationships among oppressions and struggles vary. Several contributors use a materialist analysis. Francis Beale's (90–100) essay (which is reprinted in *Sisterhood is Powerful*) connects racism and sexism to capitalist super-exploitation and the development of a reserve labor force. Kay Lindsey (85–89) ties the sexual division of labor and the institution of the family to support of the state, arguing that the system is set up to control Black women's bodies, ultimately placing their labor and their sexuality in service of the state. Toni Cade argues, however, that there may not be an existing framework that can effectively bring together the various issues that constitute Black women's movement(s):

> Perhaps we need to face the terrifying and overwhelming possibility that there are no models, that we shall have to create from scratch. Doctrinaire Marxism is basically incompatible with Black nationalism; New Left politics is incompatible with Black nationalism; doctrinaire socialism is incompatible with Black revolution; capitalism, lord knows is out. (109)

Cade argues that revolution begins with a reworking of the self (109). Only in and through such struggle can truly new and revolutionary possibilities begin to emerge.

Cade's insight that no single oppression can be located as the base oppression and hence the central site of revolution marks a crucial shift in the conceptualization of radical politics in the United States. The shift in analysis from a single base to multiple simultaneous and interlocking oppressions opens the door to rethinking diversity among women in and through complexity. This shift was carried further by the Combahee River Collective, which initially formed in 1974. They present a clear statement of the *simultaneity* of oppression in the "Combahee River Collective Statement" (written in 1977, initially published in Eisenstein 1978, and reprinted in Moraga and Anzaldúa 1981 and Smith 1983):

> The most general statement of our politics at the present time would be that we are actively committed to struggling against racial, sexual, heterosexual, and class oppression, and see as our particular task the development of integrated analysis and practice based upon the fact that the major systems of oppression are interlocking. The synthesis of these oppressions creates the conditions of our lives. As Black women we see Black feminism as the logical political movement to combat the manifold and simultaneous oppressions that all women of color face. (Combahee 1983, 272)

The Combahee Statement argues that this analysis of simultaneous, interlocking oppressions comes out of valuing Black women's lives and activisms at the intersections of oppressions and issues. "Above all else, our politics initially sprang from the shared belief that Black women are inherently valuable, that our liberation is a necessity not as an adjunct to somebody else's but because of our need as human persons for autonomy" (274). This claim is based on the need to assert the importance of Black women's liberation and to criticize the inability of other movements to adequately address Black women: "This may seem so obvious as to sound simplistic, but it is apparent that no other ostensibly progressive movement has ever considered our specific oppression as a priority or worked seriously for the ending of that oppression. . . . This focusing on our own oppression is embodied in the concept of identity politics. We believe that the most profound and potentially most radical politics come directly out of our own identity, as opposed to working to end someone else's oppression" (274–75). Thus, as do many other women's movements of the

1970s, the Combahee River Collective establishes its strength by beginning from the point of women's lives and work and building a critique of one's "own oppression."

The promise, possibilities, and problematics of "identity politics" became central to subsequent debates in feminist theory. And, yet, in the Combahee Statement this endorsement of identity politics is followed by several paragraphs explaining the complexity of identity for the members of the collective, the need for solidarity (with Black men, with other oppressed peoples, against capitalism), and the multiple issues which must be addressed in order to combat "our own oppression." This complexity is articulated through the analysis of simultaneous, interlocking oppressions, an analysis which is often severed from "identity politics" in subsequent theorizing. Thus, part of what marks the Combahee River Collective statement as a breakthrough is not necessarily a shift to identity, but the move to the simultaneity and interrelation of oppressions and issues, thereby tying identity to complexity. There is no sense that the desired identity politics is about establishing an "autonomous" movement separate from "other" issues. Rather, the statement articulates simultaneous and intersecting axes of oppression, precisely because "identity" is placed in the context of these intersections. The pursuit of "identity politics" in the 1980s, however, often separated the two aspects of Combahee's claims, making "identity" rather than complexity the primary site of analysis and action, and, thus, reasserting an autonomy which desires, but cannot enact, alliance.

Sisterhood is Powerful: An Anthology of Writings from the Women's Liberation Movement

Sisterhood is Powerful: An Anthology of Writings from the Women's Liberation Movement (Morgan 1970) is a "somewhat diverse" (Roof 1995) anthology that works not only to collect documents "from" the women's liberation movement, but also to establish women's liberation as an autonomous movement. The tensions between autonomy and alliance are particularly evident in the disjunction between Morgan's description of the women's liberation movement and the diversity of the contributions to the volume. The problems in the introduction cannot be simply attributed to Morgan, however. Rather, the problem is an issue in the construction of movement. Specifically, Morgan is impelled to make certain moves because she understands herself to be acting as spokeswoman for, to be introducing, not only the anthology, but the "women's liberation movement."

Like the Combahee River Collective, Robin Morgan is interested in addressing her own oppression and creating solidarity, yet, the way she envisions both the autonomy of the women's movement and the basis for solidarity leads away from rather than toward complexity. These tensions are evident through-out Morgan's Introduction as she works both to establish women's liberation as an autonomous movement distinct from other "left" politics and to claim possibilities for alliance. Morgan begins the Introduction with a description of her own political trajectory from a self-described "politico," a woman who saw women's liberation as a wing of or a tool in and for the larger Left "Move-ment," to spokeswoman for the specifically "women's" liberation movement. She criticizes her dedication to addressing "other people's oppression" (xvi) as "Lady Bountiful" actions that reinscribed her own privileges, "because it isn't until you begin to fight in your own cause that you a) become really com-mitted to winning, and b) become a genuine ally of other people struggling for their freedom" (xvii). Thus, establishing an autonomous women's liberation movement, one that is not simply a wing of a larger "Left," is seen as a step toward establishing new, more genuine alliances with "other people struggling for their freedom." These "genuine" alliances are supposed to shift women's movement away from the liberal white, middle-class endeavor of doing good for under-privileged people. And, yet, this move also contains the confounded question of who makes up the women's liberation movement. What does women's liberation mean, if it is for Morgan, her "own cause"? Does it address primarily white, middle-class women "like her" who have been acting on be-half of others but are now acting on behalf of themselves?[104] Are any women part of "other *people* struggling for their freedom"? How does "women's" lib-eration relate to women in these other struggles? Or is Morgan already caught in a conundrum? Does making "women's movement" autonomous from, even if then to be allied with, other movements narrow the meaning of women's liberation to those (white, middle-class, heterosexual) women for whom other movements are not "their own" struggles for freedom?

Morgan seeks to address these questions and negotiate her way through the conundrum by using a methodology that is common to progressive move-ments—the claiming of equivalence among oppressions and liberation move-ments.[105] Morgan initially establishes the claim to equivalence by arguing that women's liberation "is also the first movement that has the potential of cutting across all class, race, age, economic, and geographical barriers—since women in every group must play essentially the same role, albeit with different sets and costumes: the multiple role of wife, mother, sexual object, baby-producer, 'sup-plementary-income statistic,' helpmate, nurturer, hostess, etc. To reflect this potential, contributors from those different groups speak in this book—and frequently disagree with each other" (xx). While this claim works to show that women's liberation does address women in other movements, it moves from a position established by white, middle-class women, established in the Introduction by Morgan's own life, across barriers of social differentiation to the position of other women who are equivalent to (white, middle-class) women. Even the phrasing "from these different groups," indicates a white, middle-class center of the movement to which other women—those across barriers—are made equivalent. Because the "different groups" are named as axes of social differentiation—"class, race," etc.—rather than as specific class or racial groups or communities, white women are situated as not "class[ed]" or "race[d]." And, significantly, sexuality is not an axis of differentiation, a "barrier," which Morgan includes in her list. It cannot be included because the position that the list establishes as the site of equivalence among women is specifically that of heterosexuality.[106] Notably, Morgan acknowledges in an attempt to avoid tokenism that the women from these "different groups" disagree with each other.[107] What they apparently do not disagree with is the list that makes them equivalent as women. Morgan cannot acknowledge this type of disagreement, because to do so would undercut women's liberation as an autonomous movement that simultaneously cuts across social barriers. It would specify the "women" who women's liberation addresses and problematize relations among "women" who did not coincide with this specificity. Thus, moving from a center (assumed to be white, middle-class, and heterosexual) across "barriers" toward the margins in order to establish equivalence does not establish the alliance that Morgan desires.

On the other hand, Morgan also makes a claim for equivalence that moves in the other direction—from "other" movements to "the women's liberation movement"—through an argument from analogy. Morgan claims an equivalence between "other" movements and women's liberation while also pointing to the failure of other movements to take women's concerns seriously. It is this failure that necessitates an autonomous women's movement: "women more and more came to see the necessity of an independent women's movement, creating its own theory, politics, tactics, and directing itself toward goals of its own self-interest (which was also the self-interest of more than half the world's population)" (xxiv), or:

> The current women's movement was begun largely, although not completely, by women who had been active in the civil-rights movement, in the anti-war movement, in student movements, and in the Left generally. There's something contagious about demanding freedom, especially where women, who comprise the oldest oppressed group on the face of the planet, are concerned. (xxiii)

Here women's movement is based on and made equivalent to the claims of other movements—"there's something contagious about demanding freedom"—and simultaneously, made fundamental—"women, who comprise the oldest oppressed group on the face of the planet." Later in the Introduction, these dual claims are made again specifically to answer the charge that women's liberation is not based on concerns equal to those of other movements:

> *How*, we are asked, *can you talk about the comparatively insignificant oppression of women, when set beside the issues of racism and imperialism?*
> This is a male-supremacist question. Not only because of its arrogance, but because of its ignorance. First, it dares to weigh and compute human suffering, and it places oppressed groups in competition with each other (an old, and very capitalistic, trick: divide and conquer). Second, the question fails to even minimally grasp the profoundly radical analysis beginning to emerge from revolutionary feminism: that capitalism, imperialism, and racism are *symptoms* of male supremacy—sexism. (xxxix, emphasis in original)

Oppressions should not be ranked, all movements should be considered as equal, and by inference, if so considered they will also become connected rather than divided. Yet, even as they are considered equal, sexism forms the fundamental base of oppression.

Why the need for both claims together, particularly when on the surface they appear contradictory? Obviously, Morgan makes this move because she needs to emphasize the importance of women's liberation, its standing as "real" politics, when put in relation to "[t]he blood of Vietnam, Laos, and Cambodia, [that] is mixing with the blood of Jackson, Watts, and Detroit" (xxxvii–xxxix). But she also needs a method of making the connections between movements which equivalence posits but cannot materialize. Equivalent movements might be equally valid, but they are not necessarily connected. They have not challenged the capitalist move of divide and conquer, but have simply aligned themselves horizontally. The methodology which Morgan adopts to make these connections is a displacement of the logic of a base contradiction. Thus, she continues:

> Racism as a major contradiction, for example, is surely based on the first "alienizing" act: the basic primary contradiction that occurred with the enslavement of half the human species by the other half. (xxxix)

Sexism is equivalent to (the U.S. history of) racism. Sexism is also enslavement. If racism is simultaneously based on sexism, then women's liberation is not only equivalent, it is *connected*, to anti-racist movement. There is a basis for alliance.[108] Thus, these two claims together establish both the autonomy of women's liberation and the basis to posit an alliance. In their contradictory relation, these claims mark the fundamental ambivalence of a feminist movement that strives to articulate the position and movement of women while recognizing that women and movements are diverse.

The ambivalence between autonomy and alliance leads Morgan directly

into the problematic that posits feminist movement as "until recently . . . composed of young white women from middle-class backgrounds," thus defining
"other" women's movements as outside the bounds of feminism. For example,
in talking about welfare rights organizing, Morgan states,

> Women's liberation cells have, separately and together, been working toward
> what would be a perfectly organic alliance with welfare rights organizations,
> which are made up of women, most of whom are black and brown. We share
> a common root as *women* much more natural to both groups than the very
> *machismo* style of male-dominated organizations, black, brown *and white*.
> (xxix–xxx, emphasis in original)

Although welfare rights organizations are made up of women, they are not by
themselves "women's liberation cells." Rather, an alliance, albeit a "perfectly
organic" one, between women's liberation and welfare organizing is necessary to institute welfare rights as a women's liberation issue. This alliance is
grounded in the shared "natural root" between white women and Black and
brown women "as women," and yet by stating the desire for alliance in this
way Morgan has already separated that which she hopes to bring together in
alliance.[109]

Claims to equivalence allow for the circulation of a political logic, and this
circulation enables particular types of social movement which would otherwise be foreclosed.[110] Claims to equivalence allow women's liberation to establish a position as a specifically political movement, rather than a private set of
complaints, worthy of the same revolutionary fervor invested in other Left
movements. They allow Morgan and others to challenge dominative practices
directed at women within "other" movements. These moves—claiming the
political importance of gender oppression and moving in resistance to gender-
based dominative practices in Left movements—are crucially important, but
the methodology on which they are based ultimately betrays Morgan's desires
for women's liberation. Instead, this methodology establishes a feminist movement which is itself implicated in the type of dominative practices it would
challenge. Thus, Morgan ends up (re)producing the same type of narrow
movement that she criticizes, a reproduction that clearly runs against her
stated intentions of naming (and thus bringing into being) a women's movement that cuts across social barriers.

Here, we see the economy of the same at work. As a spokeswoman introducing "the women's liberation movement" to the public, Morgan articulates
a feminism that runs counter to, but also must make sense within, the public
to which she speaks. Feminism becomes a social movement which can make
sense in the U.S. public, in part because it participates in some of the very same
assumptions that ground the public. As Judith Roof (1995) argues, "It is precisely the presence of this narrative ideology [of emancipatory knowledge pro-

duction] that makes Morgan's anthology both cogent and persuasive—already familiar and functioning with the larger meta-narrative that the collection serves" (61).[111] The story which Morgan tells in the Introduction of coherent oppression and liberation is one which is consistently (re)told as both a modern meta-narrative and the founding narrative of the United States. Thus, feminism is ultimately (re)produced as "the same": the same as itself (diversity is elided through the assertion of common oppression in the Introduction) and the same as the U.S. public—re-enacting the American revolution of oppression and liberation.

What Morgan's claims do not allow is a negotiation of the complexities that they invoke. How can women's liberation both challenge the treatment of women in left movements and remain connected to those movements and causes? Is an autonomous movement the only or best choice of strategy for making this challenge? Is there a complex means of conceptualizing and enacting relations among movements that does not establish the conundrum of autonomy that undercuts alliance? The implication of my analysis is not that women should have shunned the move toward autonomous movement, or that they should have stayed subsumed within "other movements." This type of "inclusion" is itself a dominative practice. Rather, I am arguing that the relationship between autonomy and alliance must be reworked by complicating it. Part of what makes the Introduction to *The Black Woman* different from *Sisterhood is Powerful* is that there is no assumption that an "autonomous" Black women's movement must be separate and unique (the traditional hallmarks of modern "autonomy") in relation to other movements. Rather, Black women's activism(s) are both autonomous and constructed in and through various political movements. There is still a space of absence and desire for alliance— "other third world women." Cade does not fully accomplish the connections which she desires, but there are spaces of connection (that Morgan does not accomplish) between Cade's articulation of a politics of "ourselves" and various issues and locations.

Some diversity and complexity is evident in the contributions to *Sisterhood is Powerful*. The contributions demonstrate various understandings of relationships among oppressions and among movements. They do not necessarily argue for a "collective women's consciousness" or for the need to develop one out of diversity. Frances Beal, in her essay "Double Jeopardy: To Be Black and Female" (which appears in both *The Black Woman* and *Sisterhood is Powerful*), argues that "the System of capitalism (and its afterbirth—racism) under which we all live, has attempted by many devious ways and means to destroy the humanity of all people, and particularly the humanity of black people" (382). Eleanor Homes Norton sees racial, class, and sexual oppression as different, but intertwined. Thus, she argues that racism is distinct from capitalism, the difference in oppression between exploitation and slavery

(399). She argues that one of the crucial roles that Black women's struggle for liberation can play is in forging a different pattern of family relationship than that of the "white, middle-class" nuclear family. Marge Piercy uses a Marxist analysis of labor structures within the movement to demonstrate the need for an autonomous women's liberation movement. Karen Sacks argues that women's oppression is based on their super-exploitation as a reserve labor force within capitalism, an argument which Beal also makes and extends in order to describe the role of Black men and women as super-exploited. Judith Ann connects analysis of her own experiences as a clerical worker with a Marxist analysis of the Secretarial Proletariat and a critique of the racism and sexism of the U.S. labor movement (109). Thus, unlike the Introduction, the contributors offer various articulations of women's movement which open the door to alliances in a number of directions.

The contributors also variously configure the relationships or potential relationships between "women's liberation" and (other) women's movements. Carol Glassman provides an analysis of the welfare system as perpetuating both class and sex oppression. Thus, she argues for "an analysis of the welfare system that sees it as part of the larger problem of women's oppression" (126), but she also notes that "[the welfare rights movement] does not see itself as a women's movement, rather, it is a movement that happens to have as its constituency mostly women" (126). Enriqueta Longauex y Vasquez in the essay "The Mexican-American Woman" raises concerns similar to those raised by contributors to *The Black Woman* (including Beale). For example, Longauex y Vasquez argues that the prospect of alliances among women's movements is unlikely precisely because of the ways in which "women's liberation alone" can operate as autonomous from other movements, including "the Mexican-American movement" (432).[112] With respect to sexuality, while many contributors share Morgan's view that (hetero)sexuality is the center of women's oppression, Gene Damon, writing as a representative of the Daughters of Bilitis (formed in 1955), argues that workers for lesbian civil rights are not necessarily more welcome in feminist organizations than in any other political organization, including other homophile organizations, or society at large (341). Alternatively, Martha Shelly argues in "Notes of a Radical Lesbian," that "Lesbianism is one road to freedom—freedom from oppression by men"; thus, lesbianism can be a specifically feminist undertaking (343). Again, the contributors engage the complexities of alliance formation that are elided by Morgan's claims to equivalence in the Introduction.

Sisterhood is Powerful articulates a politics of diversity: Women are a diverse (but equivalently situated) group, and diverse movements are necessary to a truly revolutionary politics. From its opening gesture on, *Sisterhood is Powerful* also articulates the need for alliances. Why, then, is this diversity contained in the Introduction within a model of equivalence and collective consciousness? I would suggest that Morgan takes on the conundrum of autonomy and alliance in order to speak the language of movement. Iris Marion Young describes this dilemma in 1994: "On the one hand, without some sense in which 'woman' is the name of a social collective there is nothing specific about feminist politics. On the other hand, any effort to identify the attributes of this collective appears to undermine feminist politics by leaving out some women whom feminists ought to include" (714). Are these the only two choices however? In order to make sense of feminist politics is it necessary to name something "specific" (autonomous?) about feminism? And is the issue betrayed by this need for "some sense," one of inclusion? After all, Morgan betrays the diversity of the collection, specifically by trying to name a feminism that "includes" all women across social "barriers."

The problems in *Sisterhood is Powerful* are precisely problems in the politics of diversity. In the Introduction, the problems develop out of Morgan's methods of inclusion and connection. The first is the construction in the Introduction of a women's movement which assumes through the construction of women as a coherent group opposed to men that women's liberation is a white, middle-class heterosexual women's movement. Aihwa Ong (1988) has pointed out the ways in which feminist politics, in articulating itself specifically in opposition to patriarchy, must create a coherent oppressed group, "women," that simultaneously dis-articulates connections to and among diverse "women."[113] The other problem is the way in which the diversity of the contributions is lined up as variations on a single theme in the anthology as a whole. The differences of the contributions do not complicate the meaning of "woman." Thus, diversity is constructed as a series of autonomies within feminist movement, rather than as complicated interrelations which are articulated both within feminist movement and which challenge its boundaries. "Women," although diverse, remains a "simple" category, in Cade's terms, or a transparent concept which grounds various diverse experiences, but which is itself uncomplicated. Neither the appeal to the fundamental commonality of women, nor the line-up of variations on the theme "woman" effectively forms an alliance or even expresses the complexity of interrelation which is the context of alliance formation. Individual contributions may express complexity and move toward alliances, but their placement in the line-up of the anthology as a whole contains these moves. Thus, the problem of diversity is not simply a problem of "lack" enacted by a monolithic movement without enough diversity; nor can the problem be solved by calls for alliances.

Lesbian Nation: The Feminist Solution

Like feminism, lesbian movements did not necessarily begin as white, middle-class movements only later to be joined by lesbians of color or as middle-class movements only later to be joined by working-class lesbians. While some early homophile organizations may have been predominantly white and middle-class, the Stonewall uprising was itself composed of a racially diverse group of mostly working-class gay men and drag queens, and lesbians of color participated in the movements which grew out of the uprising (Duberman 1993).[114] As Cheryl Clarke reports:

> I was studying at Rutgers University right after Stonewall and saw the beginning of the gay liberation movement there, led by Black gay activist Lionel Cuffie. Cuffie's anti-sexist and anti-heterosexist politics helped me see the connections among oppressions of Black people, women, and gay men and lesbians. In 1973, at one of the early gay conferences at Rutgers University—trying to resolve the confusion of a Black identity and lesbian desire—I witnessed a contingent of *out* Black lesbians from New York City. When I heard those women—one of whom had been a classmate of mine at Howard University—talk boldly about the intersections of race, class, gender and their impact on Black women who were lesbians and our accountability to be struggling against and organizing around our oppression as well as celebrating our liberation from traditional and boring gender role expectations, I was transformed and asked myself the question: *With these women out here, why am I in the closet?* (Clarke 1993, 216, emphasis in original)

Nonetheless, the anxieties and conflicts over autonomy and alliance within an overarching economy of the same replayed themselves (albeit differently) in the workings of lesbian movement. As with the instantiation of feminist movement in *Sisterhood is Powerful*, the lesbian movement that is perhaps most identified with the 1970s, lesbian-feminism, developed as predominantly young, white, and middle-class (Ross 1995, 54). Moreover, the push toward singularity is so insistent that even the alliance named by the conjunction of lesbian and feminist often came to represent a reduction of lesbian and feminist movement to the operation of a single "magical sign" (King 1986).[115] Thus, the eventual autonomy of lesbian-feminism operated in two senses: in a movement defined as "separate" from both (hetero)feminism and (male)gay liberation, and/or in moves to conflate lesbianism and feminism in both theory and practice so as to make lesbian-feminism the one (singular) true feminism. *Lesbian Nation* is also unlike *Sisterhood is Powerful* because Jill Johnston did not set out to establish an autonomous movement which *then* desired alliance. Rather Johnston worked specifically to create an alliance among the two movements with which she identified. But, if what came out of *Lesbian Nation* was an autonomy that Johnston did not initially seek, then the interesting question is, Why, even when alliance is made primary to autonomy, is autonomy produced?

Jill Johnston's (1973) *Lesbian Nation: The Feminist Solution* is an attempt to articulate an intersection between two movements, the resurgent feminist movement of the 1970s, a movement that was for Johnston organizationally fluid, and the post-Stonewall gay liberation movement, primarily embodied for Johnston in the Gay Liberation Front and Daughters of Bilitis.[116] While both of these movements—"gay" and "women's" liberation—inform her consciousness and actions, she also finds both inadequate to the politics she is working to articulate. Johnston refers to the intersection of movement as "Gay/Feminist" (153). By working at this political site, Johnston is attempting to shift the center and meaning of the two movements whose intersection it names. In the book, Johnston does enact the transposition described by Katie King (1994, 125) from Ti-Grace Atkinson's formulation "that lesbianism was *a* practice and feminism was *a* theory" (Johnston 1973, 117, emphasis added) to feminism as *the* theory and lesbianism as *the* practice (166). In so doing, Johnston makes lesbianism "the feminist solution": "When theory and practice come together we'll have the revolution. Until all women are lesbians there will be no true political revolution. No feminist per se has advanced a solution outside of accommodation to the man" (166).[117] Johnston also advocates "[G]etting it together with women. Or separatism" (181) as the "solution."[118] In short, *"Until all women are lesbians there will be no true political revolution"* (271, emphasis in original). These moves, however, do not define the text as a whole, nor are they the only possible basis for a politics which "comes out" of this text.

Lesbian Nation narrates the intertwined processes of constituting an identity termed "lesbian" and of establishing a consciousness enacted in movement which made this identity the intersection of the personal and the political. Johnston is clear throughout the book that identity is constituted by movement. For example, in describing the pre-Stonewall 1950s and 1960s in the essay "There wasn't a Dyke in the Land," she states, "There was only lesbian activity, no lesbian identity. . . . Identity is what you can say you are according to what they say you can be. And not least of the categories of identity is that of sexual status under the law which allowed no other orientation than that of heterosexuality" (68).[119] She is also clear about the need to change norms in order to change social possibilities: "I never said I was a dyke even to a dyke because there wasn't a dyke in the land who thought she should be a dyke or even that she was a dyke so how could we talk about it. Helen Marie Parks was my best friend in north carolina that one whole year and we never talked about it as I said there was nothing to talk about. . . . We knew certain things were wrong and certain things were right and we were probably wrong since we never questioned the right and wrong code if we had we might have been talking about something" (48). Thus, Johnston makes the point, later articulated by academic theorists, that the understanding of sexuality as identity is constructed in particular historical moments (D'Emilio 1983).

Johnston similarly argues that before the women's movement "We were not women and we were not lesbians. We were people. We were people with a difference. But all people from a liberal point of view were individuals or exceptions or special cases" (77). Johnston is here arguing against a liberalism that privatizes "differences." The major "consciousness raising" which movement provides is the politicizing of differences, the constitution of differences as a matter of political importance and not just personal preference. With the liberal approach to differences "people" always devolves to "men."

This entire essay is framed by the possibilities of what could come "to be" through movement. It begins with an analogical reference to the 1950s and 1960s civil rights movements and the possibility of using a "lesbian nation bus" to collect old (pre-movement) friends and "bring them up to date" (47) and ends with Johnston's own initial involvement in cultural and social movement: "The feminist revolution was still a few years away, and gay liberation was even more remote. There *was* something however, and that was the cultural revolution of hip and beat and black jazz and the twist and the drugs: all incipient makings of drop-out and the later radical left and a woman's movement" (72). This cultural site brought together various "outsiders," including "the children of new york's great population of disenchanted immigrants . . . [who] were getting it on culturally with another group of outsiders the amerikan blacks, and as a misplaced person with a forgotten history of rebellion of my own, the halcyon years of boarding school delinquency, I could relate to all this chaos and craziness" (72–73). How, out of this mix did gay/feminism come to be what it became?

The answer to this question is complex in that Johnston's ambivalent movement between alliance and autonomy in relation to gay and women's liberation also carried implications for the construction of lesbian-feminism in relation to issues of race and class as predominantly white and middle-class. The political necessity of *Lesbian Nation*, of forming an alliance called gay/feminism, comes out of failures in both gay and feminist movements.[120] Johnston articulates these failures in terms of her own political history: "The angry lesbian naturally at first joined forces with gay men in the camaraderie of the shared interest of loving one's own sex and the illusion of an 'outside' oppressor common to both. . . . In the fast realization of the sexism of her gay brothers, who, after all, partake in the general male privilege, the lesbians made the correct and inevitable withdrawal from organizational and personal alliance with gay men to align themselves with the feminists, who were ill prepared to accept their most rebellious element" (184). Johnston here articulates how a political identity can be constituted through an us/them construction which places the agent of oppression outside of the movement. Such a construction can meld a coalitional identity, for example gay men and lesbians, but it does not create the conditions for dealing with domination within movements and, thus, that initial coalition can easily be lost.

Feminism was, however, equally unprepared to respond to diversity within movement. Johnston points out that the same form of liberalism that necessitates feminist politics could also be enacted with respect to lesbianism as a difference *within* feminism (178). In this version of feminism, lesbians are acceptable within the women's movement as long as they enact a personal rather than politicized difference, if, for example, they "fall in love with a *person*. A special person. Who just *happens* to be a woman" (178, emphasis in original). Here, lesbians are simply "women with a difference" in the same way that women are "people with a difference." It is at this point that Johnston establishes "lesbian" as a (separate) identity that cannot be contained within feminism, but can only be articulated at the intersection of gay/feminism. Johnston is also critical of a pluralist or interest-group approach to gay politics: "to be gayer without developing a concomitant feminist consciousness was to merely consider yourself part of a special oppressed minority group without reference to the large political questions, the big picture, the overview of repressed female sexuality in relation to which your special oppression as a gay person was inextricably entwined, especially as a lesbian" (111). Perhaps most interestingly, she is frequently called upon or takes it upon herself to represent the lesbian "difference" to feminism. Some of the actions for which she was most (in)famous—swimming topless at a feminist fund-raiser or providing a lesbian demo at a panel discussion focused on Germaine Greer and Norman Mailer—were precisely challenges to a consolidation of "women's movement" that excluded the (politicized) lesbian. Yet, feminist movement seemed inured to such challenges, as gestures toward feminist "inclusion" of lesbians, when, for example, Johnston was invited to participate in a "gay-straight" consciousness-raising group, simply proved to re-enact "woman" (the center of the movement) as heterosexual and "lesbian" as different from and therefore marginalized in relation to that center.

In order to form the gay/feminist alliance that she sees as necessary, Johnston asserts a new basis for alliance that makes sexual liberation the basis for women's liberation. Ironically, Johnston uses the base of oppression model to displace women's liberation onto sexuality for analogous reasons to those which led Morgan to assert gender in place of class at the base. Johnston is working to assert the importance of the lesbian issue as a specifically political issue in relation to a feminist movement that refuses this recognition. For example, Johnston describes the following conversation with Betty Friedan in her usual style (described as "irreverent" by commentators):

> What went wrong between Betty Friedan and me was a lapse of sexual interest. I liked her below the chin and was ready to talk at that level but she got super huffy when I asked if there shouldn't be a pub(l)ic conjunction between Women's Liberation and the Gay Liberation Front. Her eyes went big 'n' bulgy and her lipstick leered crimson and she said crisply enunciating

each word that "it" is not an issue. What? She repeated. *And*, there's no relationship between the movements. Well, and she softened a moment. I *am* against all oppression. (120)

Yet, Johnston doesn't simply displace feminist movement in favor of lesbian movement. She uses the feminist critique of heterosexuality as the obvious basis for alliance. Organizing heterosexuality as the main problem makes lesbianism specifically feminist and ties gay liberation and women's liberation together through the figure of "the lesbian."[121] This assertion of sexuality as the base of oppression and revolution includes a critique of the ways in which feminist movement had made sexual issues central because "All the feminist issues—abortion, child care, prostitution, political representation, equal pay—are in relation to the man. In other words in relation to reproductive sexuality" (152). Yet, the assertion of the critique of heterosexuality as the singular base also makes lesbians the only true feminists and can, thereby, work to distinguish rather than ally lesbians and feminists. Thus, the conflation of lesbian + feminist as *the* "feminist solution" both reflected and constituted one among various splits between "gay" and "straight" women that moved lesbian-feminism toward autonomy (King 1990).

This split was also reflective and constitutive of splits over "other" issues as well. Even as it asserted distinction from heterosexual feminist movement, lesbian-feminism was, in part, informed by and intertwined with the dominant feminist analysis of gender oppression as first and foremost oppression through (hetero)sexuality. In this way lesbian-feminism could reiterate the narrow version of feminist movement that Johnston critiques. Yet, lesbian-feminism also simultaneously replicates some of feminist movement's dominative practice, including class domination and racism. For example, much has now been written about the ways in which lesbian-feminist movement dislocated some lesbians, such as working-class lesbians and lesbians of color, who did not identify with the dominant feminist movement (in even the alienated fashion of Johnston) and who worked and lived at other sites of cultural formation and movement (Lorde 1982, 1984, Nestle 1987, Nestle ed. 1992, Kennedy and Davis 1993, Feinberg 1993).

Johnston enacts several of the practices which have been identified as contributing to the formation of a dominative lesbian-feminism, including the critique of butch-femme role-playing that is often tied to lesbian-feminist exclusions of working-class lesbians. Interestingly, Johnston's text is resistant to the "desexualized" or "non-aggressive" sexual practice which is frequently attributed as the link between lesbianism and feminism or the site which allowed for the conflation of the two. Johnston was, in fact, denounced as a "lesbian chauvinist" or "male-identified woman" (185) for her assertions of active lesbian sexuality. Johnston describes an encounter at a lecture given by Ti-Grace

Atkinson where "she told us that the female dynamic is love and the male dynamic is sex. translated: Man-Sex-Evil. versus Woman-Love-Good" (117–18). At this event, Johnston is confused about her own position in relation to this feminist theory,[122] but she later writes the essay "The Making of a Lesbian Chauvinist" (148–64), which is a defense of "the aggressive assertion of your sexual and sensual needs and interests" (154). Johnston identifies passivity as "*the* accommodation of a woman to her oppression" and, thus, argues that aggressive assertions of sexuality, not erasures of sexuality in favor of (romantic) love, are fundamentally feminist. For Johnston, love may be a female dynamic, but it is so only insofar as it articulates female oppression. Johnston identifies the feminist critique of an assertive lesbian sexuality as a refusal to recognize the implications of the gay liberation movement (149) and as an attempt to "discredit the lesbian as the upsetting gadfly of the feminist movement" (148). Here it is the external challenge of gay liberation as "the axis for revolutionary change" that challenges feminist movement not just to include lesbians within the movement, but to shift its very basis. Feminists must recognize that lesbians are central to feminist movement in part because they simultaneously stake a claim in a gay liberation movement beyond the boundaries of feminism. It is precisely because lesbians both are within and exceed feminist movement (and will continue to do so) that they are so important to feminism.

Adding another layer of complexity, however, Johnston also uses this critique of passivity against butch-femme role-playing, the site at which the exclusion of many lesbians from lesbian-feminism occurred. Johnston configures butch-femme as "playing the aggressive or passive roles at their extremes" (155). The new sexuality in which all women express their sexual desires aggressively will produce "the elimination of butch and femme as we realize our true androgynous nature must inevitably mean the collapse of the heterosexual institution with its role playing dualities which are defined as the domination of one sex over another and with it all enclaves of sexuality such as love between women which have aped the normative institution" (155). Both butch-femme and lesbian-feminist-love are here positioned as replicating dominant heterosexual norms. This positioning contrasts with the configuration in which they are solidified as opposites by leveling the charge that butch-femme replicates heterosexuality while lesbian-feminist-love does not. Nonetheless, Johnston's argument does enact the displacement of butch-femme role-playing, defining it as outside lesbian-feminism. Johnston could not tie these practices and lesbian-feminism's antagonistic relationship to these practices to class issues. Johnston reports that for a long time she was simply unaware of the lesbian bar culture of this time period, which as many commentators have noted was a location for the development of predominantly working-class lesbian cultures (Kennedy and Davis 1993, Lorde 1982). When she does come into contact with bar culture—notably in London, not New York where she lives—

she takes a primary piece of her political consciousness from this encounter, a critique of monogamy as tied to heterosexist narratives of the family (206). Yet, this encounter leads her to extend, rather than to challenge, her critique of butch-femme role-playing, a critique which is the basis for lesbian-feminism's supersession of these practices. Thus, while Johnston's position does indicate the complicated relationship between lesbianism and feminism, which is open to various possible articulations, it does not successfully initiate a version of lesbian-feminism that can sustain alliances across class divisions among lesbians. The equation of lesbian and feminist and nonaggressive sexuality is not a necessary outcome of allying feminist and lesbian movements.[123]

A similar enactment, but not exact duplication, of this mechanism occurs with respect to race, one of the deepest ambivalences that Johnston expresses. Here, gestures toward alliance also inscribe a distance and lack of intersection between "the black cause" and "gay/feminism":

> I am, by the way, more in sympathy with the black cause than ever before, and in fact with all causes, for it has recently occurred to me that all causes are the same cause (as my critic said, we are all in the same boat) and that what we're doing here then is educating the members of ourselves to certain needs which have gone unheeded or unrecognized or worse damned and vilified and thrust underground so that we can all coexist more happily together. (136–37)

What does it mean to say all causes are the same cause? Does this type of claim ground, necessitate, or even facilitate an alliance among "causes"? This passage seems to suggest that it does, that to recognize all of our needs is to go through a process of mutual education which would facilitate such an alliance. But, no where else in the text does Johnston indicate a desire for such a process or even much recognition of Black lesbians. Rather, the rest of the references to the Black cause are arguments from analogy that serve to establish the basis for gay/feminism as a political "cause" just like the Black cause. Analogy to the Black cause seems particularly to provide a mechanism for the expression of social rage. Here, African Americans and anti-racist movement do the emotional work in providing the site for the expression of otherwise inappropriate emotions.[124] As I have suggested, the argument from analogy is a means of distancing movements from each other even as claims to likeness or similarity are the basis of argument.

The question of mutual education is not one which should be passed over too quickly, however. As described in the passage above, it sounds like a relatively easy (straightforward?) process that could lead to harmony. Yet, when such practices are undertaken, they are often the site of foundering in attempts to form alliance. The difficulties of this process, particularly her participation in a "gay-straight consciousness raising group" are what most frustrate Johnston in relation to feminist movement and make her even question whether feminism is a movement worthy of the name ("movement schmoovement," 232–37): "My encounter with the uptown feminists was on its last lap. I couldn't tolerate their straightness and they couldn't tolerate my challenges. These so-called consciousness raising meetings about finished me off" (224–25). Thus, here we see the (often painful) ambivalences of alliance and autonomy once again. Johnston abandons race and class analysis through the replacement of the base with sexism, and yet, the alliance gay/feminism which this replacement is intended to effect does not materialize. Instead, the result is a lesbian-feminist movement, relatively autonomous from both gay liberation and women's liberation. Gestures toward alliance can also articulate gaps in movement which become the space for the institution of new autonomous movements. Johnston's gay-straight encounter within feminism and her own articulation of connection to the "black cause" while gesturing toward alliance, effectively create the space for a lesbian-feminist movement that is separate.

While the specific gestures of Johnston's text were not always replicated in lesbian-feminist movement activity, the overall trajectory toward autonomy was often repeated.[125] "Lesbian + feminist" came to name not so much an alliance as an autonomous movement defined over against both gay and feminist movements, a painful autonomy which is the result of continuing encounters with sexism and heterosexism in the two movements.[126] Ross (1995) argues that some members of the LOOT collective see the accomplishment of lesbian-feminism as precisely the constitution of a lesbian political identity that allowed lesbians to participate in multiple movements later specifically as lesbians (229). And, yet, the form which this constitution takes, the terms in and through which a new movement and/or identity is constituted have implications for later possibilities of alliance. If, for example, lesbian is constituted as a political identity in ways which exclude working-class lesbians from this identity, locating them as excess to the identity, just as lesbians are located as the excess to "women" as a political identity, then (as I shall argue in the following chapters) both institutions and movements will tend to replicate this exclusion despite intentions and work directed toward alliances. Nonetheless, it is not the case that lesbian-feminist movement always reiterated dominations. As the essays in *Class and Feminism*, produced by the lesbian-feminist collective The Furies, show, lesbian-feminist movement often developed complex analyses of multiple oppressions.

Class and Feminism

The back of the book *Class and Feminism* (Bunch and Myron 1974) claims that:

Class and Feminism examines how class differences affect women in the women's movement. Written by members of The Furies, each article synthesizes both a political and personal view of how class has functioned in the author's own experience. This book, therefore, brings the personal dynamics of class conflict together with an overall political analysis that is unique in discussions of class in the women's movement.

The focus of these essays (written in 1972, but published in 1974), then, is the operation of class within the women's movement and within the Furies collective. The essays connect analysis of experiences of living and working in the collective with an understanding of "class as a political mechanism for maintaining no[t] only capitalism but also patriarchy and white supremacy. More simply class, sexism, and racism" (7). Unlike contributors to *Sisterhood is Powerful* who depend more directly on Marxist analysis, the authors in *Class and Feminism* argue that Marxist analysis tends toward an abstraction about class relations that supports the continuation of Left movements which do not address either class behavior and conflict within movement or the connections among class, sexism, and racism.[127] As Rita Mae Brown says, "Class is much more than Marx's definition of relationship to the means of production. Class involves your behavior, your basic assumptions about life, your experiences (determined by your class) validate those assumptions, how you are taught to behave, what you expect from yourself and from others, your concept of a future, how you understand problems and solve them, how you think, feel, act" (15). They are here critical of precisely the type of abstraction that Johnston enacts, where class functions as the base of analysis, but is abstracted from the particular practices and struggles of working-class communities.

The Furies also argue that attention to class conflict among women is necessary to the development of a women's movement which is not predominantly middle-class in both values and politics. In particular, they agree with Morgan that there is a perception that women's liberation is middle-class despite the fact that many women in the movement are working-class or "lower class."[128] Yet, the presence of lower or working-class women in the movement does not in and of itself challenge the class structure and particularly the class values of the movement as Morgan seems to imply. The Furies argue that middle-class values tend to dominate both in setting the political agenda of the movement and in setting standards of behavior among women working in the movement. Thus, it is not enough for women's liberation to include "women from working-class origins." Rather, beyond simple inclusion, the terms of inclusion, the mechanisms of power relations, particularly class-based behaviors, attitudes, and values, and the political agenda are all at issue.

The inability of women's liberation to address these issues contributes to a movement which is unable to form effective alliances, either across class divisions within the movement, or among issues of classism, racism, and sexism. Once again, the Introduction presents a less complex view of the inter-relations among oppressions than do the contributions, using the familiar feminist analysis that class relations are based on patriarchy as the fundamental oppression.[129] Most of the essays do not focus on a conception of base oppression, but like the Combahee River Collective statement, are more concerned with the intertwining of various oppressions. This shift in analysis from gender as the base oppression to an intertwining of oppressions is undoubtedly the expression of the continuation of class conflict in a Lesbian/Feminist collective which was supposed to have separated itself from patriarchal oppression.

In addition to shifting the analysis of oppression, this collection of essays establishes an alternative understanding of the basis of alliances across social differentiations. Alliance is not necessarily based on the development of a collective consciousness or on the natural/organic connections flowing from a common womanhood or an equivalent positioning as women. Rather, alliance is based on "taking effective action to eliminate or at least work against class, race, and heterosexual oppression" (10).[130] This shift implies that simply being from a working-class background is not enough to make one an ally in movement against either sexism or class oppression. In fact, the essays are often concerned with the ways in which working-class women, as well as middle-class women, can fail to be allies in class struggle and with the complex relations among lower, working, and middle-class women.[131] According to Rita Mae Brown, "The fact is that there are class/race differences between lesbians and those differences have to be wiped out because they keep us apart and keep us at each others' throats. . . . the more privileged you were in that old world, the more you must work to free yourself from that destructiveness so that you can build the new world. But we have all lived in America and in some ways we all have to change" (22).

Thus, neither organic position, nor social location, but action is the crucial factor in constituting alliances across divisions: "Finally we must all work to break down the barriers of class as well as race and sexism. Barriers that are symbols of the destructive hierarchy that male culture has created to make itself feel superior" (11). The shift from organic position to action as the basis of alliance is crucial because it recognizes that the sites of intersection between movements can be constructed as either alliances or interstices, gaps between movements. The practice of articulation, of making, rather than simply claiming, connection is what makes alliances work.

Tasha Petersen is specifically critical of the type of gesture toward alliance made by Morgan: "But they included me in the 'we' when they would talk about how 'we' in the women's liberation movement are white middle class women and 'we' have to begin to relate to lower class and Black women" (31). Petersen is critical not only of her invisibility as a lower-class woman in this formulation of "we," but also of its constitution of a particular form of divide between "we" middle-class women in women's liberation and (they?) lower-class or Black women with whom "we" must ally, but who are not part of "us." Petersen continues, "Middle class women like to group lower class people together in one big unified group. . . . Lower class people are not all the same. They come from different backgrounds with different circumstances to their lives" (31). Thus, this move to constitute a "we" in conjunction with a gesture to alliance with "them" not included in the "we," elides diversity within both "we" and "them" categories and creates an interstice or gap out of the intersection between the two.

In *Class and Feminism* the question of values is central to creating new political possibilities. The question of middle-class dominance is not simply one of perception or even consciousness as described by Morgan. A value system that makes a particular type of discipline and control central simultaneously inscribes the dominance of a particular set of issues and the control of particular groups of persons within feminism. These values materialize both the individual bodies of women and the structure of a movement which is "feminist," such that Nancy Myron can say that feminists "carry around a minuscule version of a larger oppressive power system" (40). The authors are especially concerned with the ways in which "the protestant ethic" (37) induces class practices which constitute the social barriers among women of different classes. As Nancy Myron writes,

> One of the reasons that poverty continues in the richest country in the world is because people are brainwashed with the protestant ethic. If you're successful, it's because you work hard and are a good, clean, ambitious American. If you are poor you haven't tried hard enough, therefore you are lazy and useless and poverty is your punishment. (37)

In this way, the "protestant ethic" materializes class division, and new sets of values are necessary to the possibility of materializing non-dominative feminist movement.

A number of the essays (Brown, Myron, Reid) focus on the narrative of class values and mobility as a primary site at which various oppressions become intertwined. Myron reports on the intertwining of class values and sexism through a narrative of sexuality that accuses poor women of being sexually "easy," the opposite of disciplined embodiment valued by the protestant ethic (38). Coletta Reid tells a similar story: "During my freshman year I had a crush on a farm boy—dirty fingernails, workboots and all. I never got up enough courage to do more than ride around in his old car after school, but soon I heard around school that I was 'easy.' I spent the next three years living down a reputation for looseness. All of us poor farm girls had to prove we were moral, while it was assumed of the businessmen's daughters" (65). The narrative of class mobility and moral worth also contributes to racism in at least two ways. Rita Mae Brown points out that in conjunction with a system of tokenization, the narrative of class mobility allows Americans to believe that racism is not really a social problem as tokenized people of color who have "made it" show that any "disadvantaged person" can make it (14). Myron argues that the narrative of class mobility also induces white women to believe that they can be class mobile because they are white and are therefore superior:

> I grew up in poverty but I had white skin privilege. Despite all my feelings of inferiority I could still "improve" my lot and even make it in the middle class. . . . And as poor as we were, we still weren't as poor as the Blacks in Roxbury. I latched on to this one confirmation of my superiority with much enthusiasm. It was only when I started to put my racism in a broader political context that I was really able to deal with it (39).

Making the connections analytically among the class system, sexism, dominance articulated through sexuality, and racism offers Myron a form of politics by which she can both affirm the importance of class struggle and challenge her own implication in the various oppressions that she names. Again, the ultimate basis of alliance is action, changes in behavior which contribute to a feminist revolution (41).[132] These changes in behavior are interdependent with challenges to dominant value systems (like the "protestant ethic"). Thus, for alliance formation three things are necessary: a political analysis that connects various forms of oppression, changes in the value system that induces particular forms of oppressive practice, and changes in behavior to enable alliances within political movement:

> Working class women want us to stop supporting the class system by accepting its middle class values, stop resting on our privileges and start confronting and challenging class oppressive behavior in ourselves and other middle class women. They do not want to be the only ones who fight against classist behavior. If they are, they might as well separate into their own movement. (Bunch and Reid 80)

Here we see the tension between autonomy and alliance configured in a different way, focused on alliance within movements as the only means to stop an unending splintering. *Class and Feminism* is written in a context where lesbian-feminists have already formed "their own movement," and yet differences within that context are not resolved by the move to autonomy. If working-class women form "their own movement" what would it look like?

The formation of separate movements around a given axis of oppression does not resolve the problems of difference(s), it only shifts the center of activity. For example, to make class the center of activity, rather than sexuality/gender as in lesbian feminism, shifts activity, but reasserts questions of difference in an alternate form as gender/sexuality differences within class struggle.

Class and Feminism is an attempt to address this diversity within the collective structure of The Furies. A politics that addresses differences within a movement invokes a number of complexities, including the complexity of inter-relation among various axes of oppression. This complexity implies that autonomous movement will never fulfill its own claims, but is always already implicated in alliance. Moreover, the attempt to establish autonomy as prior to alliance will lead to a reassertion of the type of dominative power relations social movements like feminism or lesbian-feminism claim to resist. Thus, the boundary between "my own" as opposed to "others'" oppression that Morgan articulates as clear, is itself complicated. The Furies argue alternatively that:

> For many middle class women the women's movement has meant a reprieve from working on somebody else's revolution. Having gotten in touch with their own oppression, they are unwilling to see themselves as oppressors again, especially as oppressors of other women. It is crucial that we stop this before our movement gets torn apart by middle class women's refusal to deal with their class privilege. (62)

Claims to autonomy, equivalence, and difference remain important tools in struggles to challenge complex dominations. A claim to autonomy allowed both *The Black Woman* and *Sisterhood is Powerful* to assert the importance of gender politics in relation to late 1960s progressive movements, the logic of equivalence allowed Jill Johnston to point out that feminist movement could depoliticize lesbianism in the same way that left movement had depoliticized gender. Assertion of differences allowed The Furies to articulate class issues within their collective and to begin to articulate an alliance across these differences. But these claims and the politics that they engender also have limits which feminist movements have repeatedly encountered and rarely transformed.

Ambi-valences and Women's Movement

The examples from this chapter show that the production of dominative feminism, of a predominantly white, middle-class, or heterosexual women's movement, takes place out of a much more complicated diversity of practices and movements. Autonomy is not the simple or necessary precedent for alliance. Rather, it is in working through the tensions between autonomy and alliance that dominative practices are often (re)produced. Each text read in this chapter couples the assertion of an autonomous site of movement with the expression of desire for alliance. The texts do not, however, establish the relationship between the two terms in the same manner. In *The Black Woman* the diversity of issues addressed by the contributors is seen as constitutive of black women's movement, rather than as a contrast to a needed unity. The complexity of interrelations among issues is seen as part of movement possibility, not as the effects of a single locus. This configuration of diversity, complexity, and movement allowed for an (eventual) articulation of simultaneous and interlocking oppressions which were not reducible to a single base. It also allowed for the articulation of identity politics in relation to complexity. Yet, these moves did not necessarily articulate alliances to other marginalized groups. Cade places a desire for alliance with "other" Third World women's groups in her introduction which is not necessarily realized in the contributions. The contributions show a tension in movement, between, for example, romanticized notions of African American connections to Africa and the work of constituting alliance. In *Sisterhood is Powerful*, Morgan uses a number of techniques to establish the diversity within the anthology as an autonomous "women's liberation movement" and to express the desire for alliance with other movements, including (paradoxically) movements like welfare rights which are predominantly women's movements. Morgan tries to find a single site, a center of women's oppression, which is the site of unity in the diversity among women, and in so doing she enacts an assumption that women's oppression and women's liberation is predominantly white, middle-class, and heterosexual. In *Lesbian Nation* Jill Johnston starts from a position constituted by two contemporaneous movements, gay and women's liberation. And yet, she ends up articulating the space between these two apparently autonomous movements, the space which she wants to construct as the alliance Gay/Feminism, as a separate autonomous movement, lesbian nation. This failure in alliance is indicative of the circulation of the logic of autonomy and the possibilities this circulation opens for the constitution of new political identities— feminist or lesbian—but it also demonstrates the limits of this same logic. If *Lesbian Nation* reasserts the political import or substance of this gap between (autonomous) movements, *Class and Feminism* reasserts the existence of politically important diversity within (autonomous) movements. Assuming an autonomous and collective lesbian-feminism, the Furies collective must still work with and form alliances across the class differences of its members in order to effect movement. The work which they incite is necessary because the relations of class which they name are marked not only by difference, but by domination.

The problems in movement indicated by these texts are not based on a simple failure to recognize diversity or even on the desire to consolidate somehow this diversity. Each text moves both to recognize and to consolidate diversity. The interesting question involves the effects of the various methodologies employed to work through the complex interrelations of diversity and collectivity. Sisterhood has, for example, served as one of the most powerful and as one of the most criticized metaphors of connection among women and

women's movements.[133] If movements which start from diverse and complex
social positions constantly reiterate themselves as singular and autonomous
movements, what are the social forces which induce this reiteration?

The on-going ambivalences between autonomy and alliance in all of these
texts and the force by which autonomy is continually reproduced, even in cases
like Jill Johnston's "gay/feminism" which sets out with the express purpose of
forming an alliance, indicate the workings of an "economy of the same" in the
U.S. public sphere. In the case of "gay/feminism" becoming "lesbian nation,"
the need of each movement (gay and women's liberation) to constitute itself as
a social movement made of persons who are the "same" (as each other) and
the resultant inability to deal with diversity within each movement is an insti-
gating factor. Yet, this imperative toward the same sets up the failure of each
movement to recognize fully all of those who might be named by "gay" or
"women." Johnston argues that each movement fails to recognize lesbians.
The logic of response to this failure, the institution of a new social location or
identity from which to act with others who are "the same" — who are, for example, also lesbian — solidifies this move. Significantly, this logic of similarity
within movement also furthers the constitution of counter-cultural social
movement as replication of the dominant culture.

The reproduction of this economy in social movement structures the repeated dis-articulation of movements that might otherwise be allied. Thus,
women's movement in the 1970s developed in relation to movements for racial
and economic justice, and yet, a logic of autonomy, always in tension with
a desire for alliance, repeatedly dis-articulated these issues and movements.
Sometimes women's movement was pushed to the side (or rear) of the "real"
issues of, for example, socialist politics, and sometimes women moved to demonstrate their unique and common claims to oppression and liberation. Sometimes the diversity of women and of women's issues was recognized but recuperated as complexity was denied. Sometimes the gaps between movements
were filled by new autonomous movements rather than by connections between existing movements, and sometimes (albeit infrequently) women were
able to maintain both the diversity and complexity of women's issues and
movements. This last possibility was rare in part because it does not articulate
well with and in the dominant U.S. economy of the same and, hence, from one
perspective looks least effective. Yet the move for effectiveness, when effectiveness is construed only in terms of making "sense" in the U.S. public, also undercuts possibilities for alliances that could form the basis of broad (or in the
language of the 1970s "revolutionary") social change. It is, after all, as Toni
Cade points out in the Introduction to *The Black Woman*, in part a refusal to
focus their claims on the dominant U.S. public that allows Black women to be
for themselves so as to maintain the complexity of their activisms.

As the 1980s and 1990s stories about 1970s feminism reveal, contemporary feminist movement frequently defines itself over against the 1970s. Given the texts presented in this chapter, the vision of the 1970s used in these definitions is inaccurate. For example, 1990s texts often assert that 1970s lesbian-feminism was puritanical or desexualized whereas 1990s lesbians and feminists are pro-sex.[134] Jill Johnston, however, railed against a puritanical conflation of lesbianism and feminism and attempted to find a workable foundation for the gay/feminism alliance, even as she criticized butch-femme role-playing. *Sisterhood is Powerful* is "somewhat diverse" along lines of race, class, and sexuality, as are most 1990s anthologies edited by white women. More than doing a dis-service to the 1970s these stories of contemporary self-definition also erase the contests, conflicts, contradictions, and complexities that 1970s feminist movements addressed and, hence, they lose sight of the moments at which a narrowly based movement is built.

Thus, the problem is not simply that diversity was not recognized in the 1970s while the 1980s was the decade of differences.[135] Movement-inspired texts show that there was recognition of diversity both within and among women's movements. As the texts read in this chapter show, major issues of "difference" identified in the 1980s—gender, race, class, and sexuality—were all central parts of 1970s discussion and movement formation. In fact, it was precisely this diversity and how to appropriately respond to it with which the authors struggled. The conundrum of 1970s movement, of responding to the diversity of women and yet articulating an autonomous women's movement, one which could possibly be in alliance with other movements, has not yet been solved in feminist theory or practice. Nineteen seventies movements struggled to establish and maintain differences—among and within movements—while simultaneously remaining open to alliances. The reiteration of these same struggles throughout the 1980s and into the 1990s points out that a politics which is simply dedicated to diversity and differences will not successfully address issues of domination—sexism, racism, classism, heterosexism—within and among movements, nor will it provide an adequate basis for alliance formation. As long as feminist movements continue to act based on the assumption that in order to be feminist, women's movement must be primarily autonomous, unique and separate from other forms of social movement, then autonomy will always be accompanied by the failure of desire for alliance, precisely because those who are the object of desire have already been defined as outside the movement.

What would it look like to undertake alliance building that did not begin from this point? What would it look like to reverse the order of primacy in the relationship between autonomy and alliance, to make alliance the first step? Could the ambivalences expressed in the 1970s be produced not as points where movement is narrowed, but as ambi-valences, as sites of multiple possibility where various intersections could be constructed? Is it possible to articulate feminist movement in a way that does not reinscribe "white, middle-class, heterosexual" women as the center of activity? The next two chapters consider these questions, but they suggest that in order to produce a feminist politics that can sustain alliance, it is necessary to change some of the basic assumptions about feminism. Feminism, in its autonomous form, has made gender primary to women's movement. The focus on gender is what Morgan uses to distinguish women's liberation from other left movements, but this focus also narrows the possible meaning of feminism in relation to women's movement. The next two chapters undertake the exploration of diversity and complexity in feminist ethics, beginning not with the autonomy of gender issues, but from the point of view some of those "differences" defined out of feminism by the focus on gender. This shift away from gender as the defining characteristic of feminist concern makes alliance primary to feminism. Feminist movement, then, begins not with an autonomous center which can then be diversified and complicated, but with diversity and complexity.

3 | Articulating Norms
Reworking Difference and Relationality

How is it possible to subvert the dominant economy of the same which effectively recuperated much of 1970s feminist movement(s)? If the assertion of "difference" is not in and of itself enough; if the politics of difference(s) can simply devolve into the reiteration of the same (specifically into a reiteration of the dominant), how can movements effectively form alliances? In the past two chapters, I have investigated how economies of social differentiation work within a broader economy of the same, so that units of "difference" are constantly produced and, ultimately, produced as the same type of difference. Within this economy, women's movement tends to reiterate, to re-produce, the public sphere that it works to change.

Social movements have been unable to form alliances effectively not just because they face such economies of social differentiation in relation to an economy of the same, but also because these economies are moral economies. Social differentiation is accomplished not simply by producing persons, groups, and communities as different from one another, but by doing so through the power of "regulatory ideals." This chapter explores the ability to iterate norms so as to produce complex differences at the intersections of economies of differentiation in order to investigate how contemporary norms might challenge the dominant economy of the same, producing new possibilities for moral agencies and working in alliances.

Norms are crucial to the materialization of complex differences—differences not contained by any single economy of differentiation—because norms materialize human subjectivity. As Judith Butler points out, a norm works through "regulatory practice that produces the bodies it governs, that is whose regulatory force is made clear as a kind of productive power, the power to produce—demarcate, circulate, differentiate—the bodies it controls" (1993, 1). The focus on productive power is crucial because it indicates the on-going implication of empowerment in regulation. Particular materializations—realizations of human being—are made possible, but also regulated, through norms. Thus, practices make human subjectivity (including particular forms of embodiment).[136] The repetition or reiteration of normatively required practices makes one into a "person" which is why those who refuse such practices can also be denied "personhood."[137] For example, the constant repetition of gendered practices—from the proclamation at (or before) birth of "it's a girl" or "it's a boy" through everyday modes of dress and activity—produces gendered human beings. The shift from an "it" to a gendered being ("girl" or "boy") who is a person signifies the way in which gender norms materialize person-hood. In this sense, "gender is not something we have, but something we do that ultimately determines who we are" (Franke, forthcoming). These prac-tices are not freely chosen, they are socially enforced, and this enforcement is the regulatory power of norms. Reiteration of norms is thus a means of re-inforcing of "sedimenting" (Butler 1988, 523) particular forms of social prac-tice.[138]

Repetition or "reiteration" can also be a site for change, however. As Butler states, "That this reiteration is necessary is a sign that materialization is never quite complete, that bodies never quite comply with the norms by which their materialization is impelled. Indeed, it is the instabilities, the possibilities for rematerialization, opened up by this process that mark one domain in which the force of the regulatory law can be turned against itself to spawn rearticu-lations that call into question the hegemonic force of that very regulatory law" (2). Thus, one site of social change is in the surpluses and slippages in the prac-tice of reiterating norms. Margaret Drewal (1992) argues that repetitive prac-tices gain both their power *and* their openness to innovation from a "play" on the original. Each performance or iteration of, for example, a ritual tradition is both the original (the original words, actions, etc.) and new—original—in the moment. Tradition is in this second sense made up of (re)new(ed) practices. This play on the original allows innovation in that it draws on the power of the past while simultaneously inventing past, present, future, and the relation-ship among them.[139]

In this chapter I focus on the struggle to (re)articulate different norms and values as a challenge to and reworking of "the very terms of symbolic legiti-macy and intelligibility," specifically a challenge to and reworking of the dominant economy of the same and the economies of differentiation on which it depends. Rearticulation is necessary because of the ways in which domi-nance continually re-iterates or re-asserts itself. The connection between anti-racist and feminist movement, although established at the beginning of both first- and second-wave U.S. feminism, was never complete; white supremacist divisions among women reasserted themselves in both the nineteenth and twentieth centuries. Yet, conversely, the iteration of racism and white suprem-acy is also never complete, and its articulation can be continually interrupted. The work of social change is both to intervene in such dominative (re)itera-tions and to (re)work traditions in Drewal's sense, thus, creating change not as the wholly new, but as the (re)invention of the past, present, and future.

I employ "articulate" in both senses of the word: to express in words and to join together. (Re)articulation means not only a reinvention of certain traditional meanings, but also new connections among social actors or movements. In short, rearticulation produces both new meanings and new relationships. Because surplus and slippage in the meanings of (re)iterations are not necessarily under the control of the performer, these relationships are what stabilize the meaning of any political action.[140] Whether, for example, the effects of a particular action are progressive or conservative depends not simply on the act itself, but on its relational placement, on the articulations that connect it to other actions (Laclau and Mouffe 1985).[141] This second meaning of articulation, thus, defines another important site for social change and activity.[142] The regulatory power of normative reiterations was described in chapter 2. The practices of the women's liberation movement described by Morgan reiterated the dominant economy of the same because they were not their own origin, but were instead innovative iterations of both preceding social movements and of dominant public norms. The possibilities of feminist subjectivity, the meanings of feminist movement, were formed by both feminist enactment of specifically normative claims for "liberation" and by the need to make sense normatively to the U.S. public. Thus, feminist movements did not fully control the meaning of their normative iterations, and the intent to form alliances was undercut by the regulatory power of the norms to which they appealed. In order to make *sense* to both left-wing political movements and the U.S. public as a social movement, Robin Morgan delineated an autonomous women's liberation that could not sustain even the diversity of the anthology she introduced. The double meaning of articulation suggests, however, that connections among progressive activities and movements could work to partially "fix" the meanings of norms as counter-posed to dominant economies. The connections among issues articulated in *The Black Woman* and *Class and Feminism* shifted the meanings of both "women" and "liberation." Differences alone, different norms that operate without alliances, remain open to recuperation. Alliances, connections among movements, are necessary to the possibility of radical social change.[143] This chapter explores some of the possibilities for rearticulation at the intersections of social movement, specifically the chapter investigates how the articulation, in the sense of the naming, of new norms creates possibilities for the articulation, in the sense of connecting, of intersecting issues.

Relational Reading

How can such connections among movements be produced? In calls for alliance, the basis of alliance remains a question. Morgan speaks of an organic or natural connection between feminist and welfare rights movement, organic because based on the bodies of those women who participate in welfare rights. If, however, we reject both the dominative and essentialist aspects of this move, the question of basis remains an open one. Thus far, I have suggested that no singular basis for alliance, whether in terms of organic similarity, fundamental oppression, or the equivalence of all struggles against domination, can be assumed. Rather the bases of alliances must be created within the context of the relations of production of those "differences" that necessitate alliance—both the economies of differentiation that produce particular differences and the economy of the same within which these economies operate.

Working with norms is crucial to the process by which alliances are built (and new values created) because norms materialize both the empowering and constraining or regulating operation of these economies. The power relations established by these economies are both contradictory and complex, meaning that the norms that materialize a particular difference are related to other norms outside that particular economy in complicated ways. Moreover, within these complicated social fields, norms are themselves produced through contestation, through the conflicts and struggles by which contradictions are worked out.

This theory places norms in the context of histories of struggle and complicates understandings of moral communities. Chandra Mohanty, for example, raises the question of how differences are actively constructed in history and suggests a reading of "traditions, cultures, and beliefs" as constituted in historical struggles: "Culture itself is thus redefined as incorporating individual and collective memories, dreams, and history that are contested and transformed through the political praxis of day-to-day living" (1994, 162). This alternative reading then opens the possibility of working in and with "different" traditional and cultural norms as part of the work of producing "cultures of dissent." No "community" is wholly unto itself with its "own" set of norms and values. The contradictions of multiple intersecting traditions and communities are further sites of excess and slippage and, thus, are sites where change is possible. Once again, the task of radical social change is to see this slippage not as a perpetual failure, a failure to create a coherent tradition or community pure and complete unto itself, but as a site of potential power, creativity, and connection. Kobena Mercer (1994, 27), for example, has suggested that it is better to think of traditions as "translations" in order to describe how traditions are translated under conditions of geographical and cultural mobility. Traditions are enacted through translations into new contexts, translations which not only shift the meaning of a particular tradition, but also rework the relationship among various traditions in a multi-cultural context. If norms and their relations of production must be historically contextualized in this way, then the work of building alliances is dependent upon how the specifics of particular relations must be worked through.[144]

In order to contribute to that work, I undertake a relational reading among three sites of ethical possibility, the norms and values articulated by Katie Can-

non's *Black Womanist Ethics*, Sarah Hoagland's *Lesbian Ethics,* and the possibilities for a complex feminist ethics which these texts engage. I suggest that
feminist ethics can recognize the boundaries that have been staked by these
texts (in a particular historical moment and in a particular way) and still recognize the claims which these women who position themselves outside of feminism may make on feminist ethics/movements/politics.[145] *Black Womanist
Ethics* and *Lesbian Ethics* make claims on feminism, both directly and indirectly. The texts provide a critique of dominant ethics, a critique which is applicable to some aspects of feminist ethics as well. At certain points *Black
Womanist Ethics* also presents an invitation to friendship for those feminists
who would join in resisting the domination of multiple groups of women.

Most importantly, reading feminism in relation to these texts offers an alternative basis for an understanding of feminist movement as constituted by
alliances. If feminism is a "women's liberation movement" it will need to address the multiple issues of social differentiation and domination that affect
"women." Yet, because complexity accompanies diversity, feminist movement
cannot adopt a simple method of inclusion that would place all of these concerns within a single movement. Neither can feminist politics claim effectively
that it deals with gender "separately" from womanist or lesbian movements.
Feminist movement must be able to both include the concerns of womanist and
lesbian politics, because these concerns are "women's" concerns *and* recognize the ways in which womanist and lesbian organizing exceeds feminism.
This model differs from autonomous assertion of gender politics as the (singular) basis for feminism in that it makes gender relative to multiple issues of
women's movement. Because diversity *within* movement is always related to
"external" diversities, gender politics is then relatively autonomous—not conflated with, but in relation to—various forms of social movement.[146] Most importantly, feminist movement is not co-extensive with gender politics. From
this perspective feminist movement is a network of various movements, related
to each other in complicated ways.

Reading *Black Womanist Ethics* and *Lesbian Ethics* is a way to begin to
think feminist movement as not founded in autonomy, but in alliance. If feminist movement is a complex network constructed in and between differences,
then reading these texts for differences is one step in articulating that network.
The work of these texts is also crucial because both of them work at the intersections of normative matrices or moral economies, and thus, also at the intersections of movements based on autonomy. Cannon locates her text at the intersection of "race, sex, and class" (1995, 24), an intersection which in the
terms of autonomous social movement had been made an interstice (Spillers
1992), a space between movements that is not fully articulated. Cannon argues that the space in which Black womanists work to constitute their ethics

has been defined as "outside" of ethics, as either "immoral or amoral" (2). To rearticulate the space outside dominant normative matrices as a space of life, is also to change the structure of dominant ethics that depends for its definition and boundaries on naming Black women "amoral or immoral." Thus, Cannon argues, "My overall goal in this project is to recast the very terms and terrain of religious scholarship" (1995, 23). Cannon's goal is not simply to articulate the unarticulated, to fill in and occupy an interstice by asserting it as a space of moral subjectivity. She is also challenging the dominant ethics which denies that subjectivity to Black women. She is (re)articulating not just Black womanist ethics, but ethics itself. Nonetheless, this project cannot be (re)subsumed under "broader" categories. Cannon argues against what she terms "pseudo-inclusivity," that would "[subsume] African American women's scholarship under categories of White women and Black men," (1995, 24). Thus, she maintains both the specificity of the womanist project and its broader implications.

Hoagland is similarly working at an intersection of normative matrices, the intersection between "gender" and "sexuality," but her task is different in that this intersection has been constructed differently. Her project is similar to the "uncloseting" of lesbianism in relation to feminism suggested by Cheshire Calhoun (1995). Hoagland sets out to challenge a conflation between gender and sexuality that she argues has developed out of the articulation of the intersection as the conflated term "lesbian-feminist." Hoagland's (1988, 7) text assumes that the conversion of Ti-Grace Atkinson's claim "feminism is a theory, lesbianism is a practice" to "feminism is the theory, lesbianism is the practice" has been accomplished, and through this conversion lesbianism has been reduced to a practice which can only be articulated through feminist theory.[147] Thus, lesbianism has been subsumed under feminism as a sexual practice which (mutely) enacts a gender theory (and politics). Hoagland challenges this conflation by producing lesbian theory, specifically lesbian ethics. Thus, Hoagland works to challenge the moral economy of (hetero)sexuality, and in so doing, works to rearticulate the intersection between gender and sexuality.

Writing about these texts, themselves written in the 1980s, in the 1990s, it would be easy simply to filter them through the (now) all too familiar critiques of essentialism and identity politics. The power of these critiques is that they challenge the ways in which identity politics can discipline those who are the subject of identity, setting off the demand that any woman produce herself as a "real" woman or womanist or lesbian; yet the critique of identity can operate in a disciplinary fashion just as does that which it criticizes.[148] Thus, at the end of the 1980s and into the 1990s we have seen attempts to undo, destabilize, or otherwise complicate the assumptions and oppositions through which these critiques were made (Fuss 1989, Spivak 1990, Weed and Schor

1989). In the current context, to read these texts simply as assertions of "identity" is to miss the complexity of the normative work that they take on and the possibilities for alliance formation that work produces. Moreover, the simple critique of essentialism itself "essentializes" identities. All "identities" operate in the same manner. One purpose for reading these texts in the 1990s is precisely to read for the ways in which they work "differently." Although alike in some facets, particularly in their critique of dominant and dominative ethics, these texts are in many ways not like each other and not like other, specifically feminist, texts. They negotiate major issues that have been the topic of feminist debate, issues like the relationship between separation and alliance or the terrain of modernism and postmodernism, or the issue of universalism and relativism quite differently, and in so doing they reconfigure and open new possibilities within these debates.

Reading these texts for complex differences as well as for the ways in which they express the historical moment of identity politics in which they were written also raises important issues for alliance politics. Alliances are necessary because of diversity and complexity. If all identities did operate in basically the same way, then the mode of movement which is conflation or unification, where we are all simply fighting the same struggle would be effective, as would the interest-group pluralism that articulates the politics of diversity. Alliances are necessitated by the failures of these modes of interaction. The crucial question and difficulty that is raised, however, is how alike and how different can allies be. One needs and becomes an ally only out of "differences," and yet it is often assumed that alliance must at some level be based on similarity; that "different" women can become allies because they are all women (witness Morgan's appeal to the organic similarity of feminists and women who participate in welfare rights movement). If we abandon the organic base of similarity, the question can become one of how different or in what ways different allies can or should be. The "differences" that these texts present are sometimes difficult for feminists to assimilate. Cannon's text is, for example, expressly theological, certainly different than most mainstream "feminist theory."[149] Hoagland's text comes from a very different location in terms of the "traditions" upon which it draws. Her term "autokoenony," for example, obviously draws upon Greek philosophy. Hoagland also takes a separatist stance that challenges not only feminist theory, but my own focus on alliance politics. Nonetheless, there is much that might ally my work with hers. I would suggest that this type of challenge is part of the work that is building relationships among allies who disagree, and who can work together even without resolving all such disagreement.

A similar challenge for alliance building is raised by the split between modernism and postmodernism that often follows the lines of the identity politics/anti-essentialist split. To simply refuse to work with those on one side or the other of this divide is both to dismiss potentially productive alliances and to disregard the complexity of the social formations named by "post" and "modern." Inderpal Grewal and Caren Kaplan (1994) sum up the issue as follows: "If Western theorists of postmodernism cannot allow for unequal, uneven, and non-synchronous expressions of modernity in reading and interpreting the cultural productions of the so-called Third World, for example, any possibility for solidarity between feminists and others who work with differences is obstructed" (5). The question with which I approach these texts is not "Do we agree?"—a question that carries its own disciplining apparatus; if we don't agree, then we are split, and so if we want to stay together we must police disagreement. The question which motivates the readings of this chapter is "Can we work together?"

Black Womanist Ethics

Katie Cannon's book *Black Womanist Ethics* begins with a claim to specificity—to the historically specific nature of Black or African American women's ethical agency.[150] Cannon is interested in articulating an ethic that has been produced by Black women under specific historical conditions, an ethic that both the academic discipline of ethics and mainstream culture have often failed to recognize as an expression of moral agency. Cannon spends a good part of the text specifying the social location and historical conditions, particularly the conditions of labor, under which Black women have produced a particular set of norms. Cannon emphasizes the conditions of labor because of the structure of labor that connects relations of gender, race, and class such that in Cannon's terms "Blackworkingwoman" is a single concept.[151] Moreover, U.S. society has historically defined Black women as their labor: "Of all Western slaveholding areas, it was in the United States that slaves were defined most completely as sources of capital accumulation and commodities" (1995, 29). Yet, the labor by which Black women were defined was not capitalist wage labor, but "was coerced without wages, extorted by brute force" (1995, 31). Thus, slaves were excluded from agency within the capitalist market:

> Classified as pieces of movable property, devoid of the minimum human rights society conferred on others, my great-grandparents could neither own property nor make contracts. As slaves, they were not permitted to buy or sell anything at all except as their masters' agents. (1995, 30)

After reconstruction, the exploitation of African American labor continued in new forms. Drawing on the work of social theorist Oliver C. Cox, Cannon points out that through the various means of lynching, intimidation, economic force, and control of the political system, "Southern Whites gradually regained monopoly power over the constitutionally freed labor supply and relegated Black people to non-citizenship" (Cannon 1995, 159). Cannon summarizes, "Cox's unshakable conclusion is that Blacks have always occupied and will continue to occupy the lowest rungs of the labor hierarchy. Racism cannot be eliminated *unless* this division of labor is broken" (Cannon 1995, 157, emphasis in original). While some tokenistic economic mobility may be available to African Americans, it only works to promote the illusion of widely available mobility: "Racism, race antagonism, and the illusion of mobility are not only compatible with but also contribute to the successful functioning of capitalist society" (Cannon 1995, 158). Nonetheless, from the time of slavery African Americans created a specific culture and a set of norms and values: "In spite of every institutional constraint, Afro-American slaves were able to create another world, a counterculture within the White-defined world, complete with their own folklore, spirituals, and religious practices. . . . Against all odds, Afro-American slaves created a culture saturated with their own values and heavily laden with their dreams" (1995, 33). Given the history of labor that Cannon recounts, these values were necessarily distinct from dominant values tied to capitalist production.

Through the process of specification, Cannon makes a strong claim on behalf of ethical differences. Cannon places the claim to difference at the beginning of the text on page 2:

> When I turned specifically to reading in theological ethics I discovered that the assumptions of the dominant ethical systems implied that the doing of Christian ethics in the Black community was either immoral or amoral. The cherished ethical ideas predicated upon the existence of freedom and a wide range of choices proved null and void in situations of oppression. The real-lived texture of Black life requires moral agency that may run contrary to the ethical boundaries of mainline Protestantism. Blacks may use action guides which have never been considered within the scope of traditional codes of faithful living. Racism, gender discrimination and economic exploitation, as inherited, age-long complexes require the Black community to create and cultivate values and virtues in their own terms so that they can prevail against the odds with moral integrity. (1988, 2)

Thus, because their relationship to capitalism is fundamentally different from that of Protestants who can embrace the "spirit of capitalism" in their ethics, Black women will produce different norms.

Cannon's claim to difference also includes a critique of white, particularly middle-class, ethics and of white standards of femininity.[152] Perhaps Cannon's most important indictment of white ethics is that it has served to further systems of domination in the name of ethics:

For example, dominant ethics makes a virtue of qualities that lead to economic success—self-reliance, frugality, and industry. . . . But, when the oligarchic economic powers and the consequent political power they generate, own and control capital and distribute credit as part of a legitimating system to justify the supposed inherent inferiority of Blacks, these same values prove to be ineffectual. (1988, 2)

Thus, Cannon's claim of specificity on behalf of Black womanist ethics does not imply the need merely to create a space within white dominant ethics (and culture) to recognize the "difference" of Black women. Rather, the co-construction of whiteness with racism implies that recognition of or respect for Black womanist ethics requires a questioning of, and change in, white ethics.[153] Neither, however, does the criticism of white ethics imply that all ethics should become womanist—such a move would dissolve Cannon's claim to difference in the other direction, this time appropriating instead of refusing Black women's agency.

Cannon contrasts dominant ethical virtues such as frugality and industry, which are geared toward economic success, and those virtues necessary to resist the very economic system legitimated by dominant ethics. Rather than placing free choice at the center of ethical responsibility, Cannon focuses on virtues that enable Black women in their struggle for survival.[154] She argues that Black women carry a particular responsibility for both their own survival and enrichment of communities as based on a vision of community relatedness.[155] Responsibility in and for community leads to responsibility to act on behalf of social reform (1988, 20–21).[156] Thus, responsibility for survival and enrichment of community delineates the particular moral labor taken on by Black women, which includes production of norms relevant to their situation, the maintenance and reproduction of those norms through oral, literary, and ritual traditions, and response to the imperative for social change.[157] Perhaps the most strenuous aspect of this moral labor is Black women's enactment of their norms in the face of social forces which would deny them their agency.

By allowing Black women to appeal to their own conditions of life rather than to fixed rules or absolute principles and by de-centering a range of choices as the meaning of freedom, womanist ethics enables womanist accomplishments "allow[ing] them to prevail against the odds with moral integrity" (75):

Throughout the various periods of their history in the United States, Black women have used their creativity to carve out 'living space' within the intricate web of multilayered oppression. From the beginning, they had to contend with the ethical ambiguity of racism, sexism and other sources of fragmentation in this acclaimed land of freedom, justice and equality. The Black woman's literary tradition delineates the many ways that ordinary Black women have fashioned value patterns and ethical procedures in their own terms, as well as mastering, transcending, radicalizing and sometimes destroying pervasive, negative orientations imposed by the mores of the larger society. (1988, 76)

Cannon is working to enrich understandings of Black women's moral agency, demonstrating the meaningfulness of morality and agency even under conditions of domination. She also wishes to recognize the breadth of Black women's agency by establishing her text as simply one text which can contribute to this project:[158]

> My goal is not to arrive at my own prescriptive or normative ethic. Rather, what I am pursuing is an investigation (a) that will help Black women, and others who care, to understand and to appreciate the richness of their own moral struggle through the life of the common people and the oral tradition; (b) to further understandings of some of the differences between ethics of life under oppression and established moral approaches which take for granted freedom and a wide range of choices. I am being suggestive of one possible ethical approach, not exhaustive. (1988, 5–6)

Thus, Cannon's text remains open to alternative understandings by other Black women.[159] For example, Cannon's text is expressly theological and, while she expresses the hope that "Black feminists who have given up on the community of faith will gain new insights concerning the reasonableness of theological ethics in deepening the Black woman's character," theological ethics does not delineate the entire field of womanist ethics (1988, 6). Cannon's claim to specificity also does not dissolve the possibility of moral relationships with persons who don't work within womanist ethics. "Others who care" can learn about and from the richness of Black women's moral struggle without reading womanist ethics as prescriptive for all of moral life. This move allows for the integrity of her womanist position, on-going relationships with "others who care," including feminists who care, and diversity and complexity in moral life.

The full range of Cannon's text, however, is not summed up by the claim for specificity. In the last chapter of the book Cannon connects Black women's moral agency to communal traditions grounded in Black Church theology, particularly drawing upon the work of Black church theologians Howard Thurman and Martin Luther King, Jr.[160] Cannon argues that the Black Church in the United States represents a unique religion created by slaves who were able to combine West African religious survivals with colonial Christianity to make a "Christianity truly their own" (1988, 17). Part of this Black Church tradition includes universal claims to the inherent worth of every human being, the enduring connection between love and justice, and the grounding of moral agency in a struggle for wholeness and inclusive community.[161]

By connecting individual to communal/social agency via claims to human integrity and wholeness, Cannon argues that Black women's struggles to enact their vision of agency can contribute to a universal struggle for human dignity and wholeness. Yet, in developing an understanding of Black women's contribution to this universal struggle, it is important not to vitiate the strong claim to specificity which Cannon makes at the beginning of the book.[162] In particular, the universal claims upon which Cannon draws cannot be read as part of the dominant liberal tradition in the U.S.—the tradition which Cannon specifically criticizes. Theologians like Thurman and King may have drawn on the liberal tradition, but in placing claims in the Black Church context, they are no longer simply liberal.

By claiming both specificity and universalism, Cannon is doing something very complex which challenges the reading of universalism and particularism as a binary opposition.[163] Her claims also challenge the related binaries of modernism/postmodernism and universalism/relativism insofar as universalism is associated with modernism and particularity with postmodernism and then both particularity and postmodernism are then linked to the threat of relativism. In claiming both particularity and universalism, Cannon is making claims that exceed the narrow purview of binary oppositions that simply reinscribe the center-margin, sameness-difference relation of dominance. K. Anthony Appiah (1991) has undertaken a similar critique of such binaries by describing contemporary African texts as "misleadingly postmodern." Appiah argues that post-colonial African morality rejects Euro-American postmodern relativism through an appeal to non-modernist universals, non-modernist because of a refusal of modern rationalism as the ground for such a claim.[164] Following Appiah, I would argue that Cannon's ethic in its specific universalism is resistant to the dominant ethical configurations of both modernism and postmodernism.

Cannon grounds her universal claims in the Black church tradition—a tradition distinct from both enlightenment universals based on a universal notion of rationality that supersedes other forms of truth and from a Euro-American Christianity that understands its revelation as a unique and dominant form of truth. James Evans (1990) argues that the Black Church tradition has been different from and "strangely ill at ease in the modern world" (207) and "within yet outside of the discursive arena of European-American Christianity" (217). This tradition provides a narrative understanding of truth(s) that distinguishes African American Christian universal claims from either enlightenment rationalist universals or the revealed universals of Euro-American Christianity:

> African-American Christians have never shared classical Protestantism's reluctance to grant revelatory potential to other world religions. Through the sharing of stories, histories and herstories, the search for what is authentically human is advanced and it is then possible to have difference without domination. (219)

Thus, it is by grounding her claims in this particular structure of truth that Cannon is able to articulate the simultaneity of and the complex relationship between specificity and universalism in womanist ethics.

What does Cannon's text suggest about the production of feminist movement starting from the moment of diversity among women? In responding to Cannon's ethics, feminists who are drawing on traditions different from the particularities of African American Christianity cannot simply appropriate Cannon's methodology of avoiding the modernist/postmodernist binary. Cannon's text does, however, demonstrate the possibility of configuring moral agency outside of the conundrum of that binary, as well as the universalist/relativist binary. Feminists can respond to Cannon's text as a challenge to develop their own methods of negotiating across the terrain delineated by such binaries. Cannon's text also calls on feminists, as "others who care" to learn to respond to the particular claims of womanists and to recognize their location in a complex world of moral claims, a world that cannot be delineated by simple binary oppositions. While such a stance indicates some of the limits of feminism, it also opens spaces for creativity. Cannon has shown that it is possible to allow for diversity in forms of truth and structures of responsibility and still make moral claims on each other in our differences. Thus, her text opens the door to possibilities even for those women who don't adopt her particular method (whether, for example, white feminists, Black feminists, or nontheological womanists) to develop methodologies that contribute to moral relationships in diversity.

Black Womanist Ethics employs a complex analysis of womanist ethics that constitutes both boundaries and connections in articulating Black women's moral agency. As such, the book makes a contribution to the project of developing Black women's agency in its diversity and complexity. My reading of the text and placement of it within the structure of a feminist text is a way of responding to Cannon's text in the hope of contributing to feminist agency which can respond to rather than elide the presence of women of color. It is a contribution to the possibility of feminist movement which is respectful of and responsive to the specificity of differences without simply reifying social categories. In particular, the specificity of womanist ethics calls on feminists to respond to the moral agenda established by womanists and contribute to the struggle for survival and human integrity without taking over or appropriating this struggle.[165]

Sarah Lucia Hoagland's *Lesbian Ethics*

Like Katie Cannon's text, Sarah Lucia Hoagland's *Lesbian Ethics* (1988) both describes and constitutes an ethics articulated in relation to a specific community. Hoagland's text contains certain structural similarities to Cannon's. Hoagland criticizes a dominant moral economy, an economy which she terms "heterosexualist." This economy structures the domination of lesbians (and women) and tends to label lesbian agency as immoral or amoral, or sometimes as apolitical. Despite these structural similarities, Hoagland adopts a very different ethical stance than does Cannon. Rather than emphasizing the specificity of lesbian claims in conjunction with a strong set of universalist claims, Hoagland takes up a separatist stance so as to refuse to contribute in any way to the moral economy that structures lesbian oppression. It is important for feminists to respond to Hoagland's ethic, not because she makes specific claims on feminism, but because she establishes her separatist stance as entailing specific moral and political implications that are important to feminists. Her stance entails a critique of the ways in which feminist ethics might participate in heterosexualist structures and assumptions and in so doing (re)enact dominative practices in relation to lesbians. Thus, the hallmark of Hoagland's lesbian ethics is its position as separate from the moral economy of heterosexualism.

Heterosexualism is the structure of social control based on the existence of two, and only two, genders. This system defines women in relation to men and thus inscribes women's location as always connected, but subordinate, to men. This system erases lesbian existence as incomprehensible given that lesbians refuse this relationship to men, thus refusing the demands of womanhood and of gender itself (1988, 7).[166] Here Hoagland is drawing on the work of Monique Wittig, who distinguishes lesbian(s) from woman/women who are always defined in relation to men. Wittig argues that only by refusing womanhood can gender subordination be resisted. Lesbian ethics, then, is both separate from and critical of feminism insofar as feminism makes use of, and therefore reinforces, the category "women." Nonetheless, lesbian ethics also articulates with the feminist project of resisting gender subordination.

Hoagland enacts the project of separating from heterosexualism through the production of an ethics because ethics is a site for the construction and legitimation of social relations. Just as Cannon points out the ways in which dominant culture ethics in the United States legitimates capitalist economics and that the virtues inculcated are the virtues of capitalist success (frugality, delayed gratification, etc.), so Hoagland argues that the ethics of heterosexualism, a system that normalizes domination and subordination, is bound to inculcate virtues that will reinforce the system. In the chapters following her claim on behalf of separation from heterosexualism, Hoagland delineates how traditionally "feminine" virtues such as altruism and self-sacrifice, in conjunction with sanctions against women's selfishness and the expression of women's anger, undermine women's agency and legitimate subordination to men. Complementary "masculine" virtues, emphasizing autonomy and control, foster male power in moral situations, this power often devolving into paternalism.

Autonomy participates in an ideology of control by producing moral agents whose central moral task is to control themselves (despite the fact that such control is illusory). The traditional emphasis on free choice as the condition of the possibility of ethics makes it difficult to claim agency under conditions of oppression. If a person can be moral only when "he" can autonomously control "his" actions (and in order to do so, he must control the situation around him), then oppressive social relations that deny such control to persons can also deny the possibility of agency. If, however, morality implies making choices as a person who faces limits and is interdependent with other persons, then the possibility of claiming agency despite oppression is opened up.

Within a heterosexualist moral economy, reason and emotion are generally separated, often so that labor can be divided, men doing reasoning work such as norm production, women doing emotional labor such as the inculcation of altruism on behalf of norm maintenance and reproduction. In this moral economy, emotion is to be in the service of reason, always under rational control. Thus, the norms of a heterosexualist moral economy incite women to take on relational labor to develop and maintain relationships whose terms are established by male control and to which men striving for autonomy contribute little of their own labor. For Hoagland, any ethics structured by the moral economy of heterosexualism will not enable lesbians' (or women's) moral agency.

By separating from heterosexualism, however, possibilities for lesbian agency, including the possibility to develop an alternative ethics, open up. In separating from heterosexualism, lesbians refuse to contribute their labor to heterosexualist relationships and instead direct their labor toward projects of their own. Through such a separation and reinvestment, lesbians are valuing themselves and the projects they consider important, and hence they are, as Hoagland states, creating new meaning and value. As Hoagland points out, production of values and the relations of their production is at issue for social movements. Values are goods which are produced through action, through movement. They are fundamentally relational goods that establish or reinforce a particular set of social relations. Insofar as lesbians' labor is separate from heterosexualism, the norms produced and the virtues enacted will be alternative to the norms and virtues of the heterosexualist moral economy.

In articulating the alternative ethics produced by lesbians as they labor on behalf of their own lives, Hoagland contrasts a morality that enables agency with the controlling emphasis of heterosexualist morality: "I have always regarded morality, ideally, as a system whose aim is, not to control individuals, but to *make possible*, to encourage and enable, individual development" (1988, 285). The moral act of "attending" is distinguished from invocations of morality which are used to control a situation. Attending implies responding to a situation within the limits of one's agency without attempting thereby to control the situation or other persons. Similarly, a morality that emphasizes "engaging" a moral situation is contrasted with a binding morality that attempts to enforce moral imperatives through the invocation of duty and obligation.[167] "Autokoenony," the view of the self as both distinct from and embedded in sets of relationships is contrasted with autonomy as the hallmark of the moral self.[168] Autokoenony allows for a recognition of the interdependence of moral agents without a complete loss of a sense of bounded selves. From the position of possibility created by separating from heterosexualism, Hoagland incites a "moral revolution" that can enable lesbian agency and might also lead to the end of heterosexuality, gender domination, and the (moral) existence of women and men.

As with Katie Cannon's text, I read *Lesbian Ethics* as refusing the limitations of the modern/postmodern dualism. The moral economy of heterosexualism, particularly the modern emphasis on autonomy, from lesbian ethics is understood by Hoagland to be separate, is (in the modern period) based on the establishment of two (and only two) distinct genders. Hoagland resists this modern social organization, and hence a modern ethics, by separating from heterosexualism and developing an ethics grounded in a community located as immoral or amoral within modernity. Hoagland's text also resists certain marks of postmodernism, however. Postmodernism is generally understood to eschew revolutionary claims and to be willing to draw on the past rather than claim the importance of wholly new beginnings. Hoagland fashions her claims in terms of a moral revolution, rather than reform, and in her separatist ethic, refuses to draw on modern ethics as providing even the fragments of a new moral position.

The question of how to respond to Hoagland's text from a feminist position is complex and depends upon how the boundaries between lesbianism and feminism are drawn. Unlike Cannon, who makes claims on non-womanists through her invocation of "others who care" and her critique of white dominant ethics, Hoagland does not make claims on non-lesbians through a category like "others who care." She provides a critique of heterosexualism that may raise concerns important to feminists, but in the terms of Hoagland's text, non-separatist resistance to heterosexualism runs the danger of merely reinforcing heterosexualism by recognizing it as meaningful (1988, 57). Responding to the critique of heterosexualism is important to the possibility of a feminist ethic which may include (but not determine) lesbians who are also feminists, as well as heterofeminists. If, as Hoagland argues, heterosexualism is a major axis along which the subordination of women is inscribed then the possibility of women's resistance to heterosexualism becomes critical to feminist as well as lesbian ethic.

Recognizing some of the historical problems with lesbian separatism since the 1970s, Hoagland adopts a number of strategies that resist the reification of a monolithic lesbian community or the rigidification of the separatist stance. Hoagland develops a performative understanding of separatism, which in conjunction with her efforts to include diverse lesbians within the text undercuts an essentialist reading of *Lesbian Ethics*. Thus, to be separatist is to refuse to provide labor to heterosexualism at any given moment, whether this means living on "womyn's" land or refusing to be in any way deferential to those men with whom one interacts. Hoagland refuses to define the term "lesbian" because she understands definitional impulses as imperatives of a defensive ethical stance with regard to borders. She is similarly vague in defining lesbian "community":

> I will be purposefully vague about the term 'community', but I have in mind the loose network—both imagined and existing now—of those who identify basically as lesbians. What I am calling 'lesbian community' is not a specific entity; it is a ground of our be-ing; and it exists because we are here and move on it now. (1988, 3)

Hoagland's refusal to name specifically what she means by lesbian and lesbian community allows her to recognize that the boundaries of lesbian community are in no sense stable or definitive while at the same time recognizing that lesbians constitute a social group living under specific social conditions. Hoagland also works, particularly through the inclusion of diverse lesbians in her citations and examples, to recognize the diversity of lesbians in order to resist the constitution of lesbian community as predominantly white and middle-class as has historically been the case with much lesbian-feminist organizing (Ross 1995). The refusal to define boundaries has also proven to be a point at which those who might otherwise find themselves at the margins of lesbian ethics can build relational possibilities, as for example in Elisabeth Däumer's (1992) reading of the text in relation to bisexuality.

Yet, while Hoagland recognizes diversity *within* lesbian community, as indicated by her various examples, she fails to recognize the complexity created by interrelations among economies of differentiation. In her claims for specificity, Hoagland distinguishes between the forms of oppression faced by lesbians in the United States and the forms of oppression faced by other social groups in this country:

> ... I think the form of lesbian oppression [is] distinct from other forms of oppression.
> In my estimation, lesbians as a group are not primarily targeted as scapegoats, as, for example, the oppression of jews has been constructed. Lesbians as a group are not primarily characterized as inferior and culturally backward in ways that justify enslavement or economic exploitation, as the oppression in the u.s. of blacks, japanese, and chinese, among others, has been constructed. Lesbians have not had lands stolen and then been rounded up and placed on reservations as the oppression of native americans in the u.s.

has been constructed. And lesbians are not primarily characterized in relation to others in ways that depict our identities as complete and our nature
fulfilled through subordinating our lives to those of dominant members of
society, as the oppression of women has been constructed. The *form* of lesbian oppression is not primarily a relationship.
    The society of the fathers, rather, formally denies lesbian existence. (4)

While Hoagland is careful to be inclusive of diversity in the body of her text,
including examples and quotes from lesbians in different race and/or class locations, as well as those living with disabilities, the quote above fails to overcome the difficult problem of how to be specific without being exclusionary.
Where is the place of "blacks, japanese, and chinese, among others," who are
also lesbians in the schema delineated above?

María Lugones (1990c), in a review of *Lesbian Ethics*, contrasts the multiplicity within a single inclusive community described by Hoagland with the
multiplicity of various communities. In particular, she argues that heterosexualism, the system that defines lesbian oppression, is not one single system
but a number of systems operating in different ways in different cultures, and
some of these cultures dominate others. Thus, even if a lesbian chooses to
separate from heterosexualism, she may or may not work within a singular
lesbian community, and her social location remains complex. She is not
defined by "lesbian" alone. Lugones elaborates this move as a pluralist separatism necessary to the reality of multiplicitous selves. Just as Cannon's text
alone does not represent the complexity and diversity of Black women, neither
does Hoagland's text do so for lesbians. The multiplicity of heterosexualist
systems described by Lugones indicates the possibility of multiple forms of
separation.

Although Hoagland's refusal to name lesbian community definitionally is
a move away from clearly defined and enforced boundaries, it may obscure the
fairly strong borders that are invoked by her separatist stance. To claim that
to be a woman *always* implicates one in subordination borders on an ontologi-
cal claim that undercuts her performative theory. This claim also fails to acknowledge resistances to heterosexualism on the part of "women," including
heterosexual women. One of the factors that obscures multiple resistances in
Hoagland's text is the tendency to conflate sexuality and gender in her positioning of lesbianism and heterosexualism, such that a resistance to heterosexuality equals resistance to gender. While gender and heterosexualism may
be interrelated, and thus resistance interconnected, they are not necessarily the
same.[169] Such a conflation obscures the operation of heterosexualism as a complex system of social organization, not merely a sexuality, as well as the inter-
structuring of sex, gender, race, and class.

Hoagland is reworking the problematics of the relationship between lesbian and feminist theory and practice that were in part set up by the 1970s

moves discussed in chapter 2. She explicitly rejects the reification of the "feminism is the theory, lesbianism the practice," matrix in favor of "lesbian theory" in order to recognize the ways in which lesbian exceeds feminist (theory). Interestingly, while in the 1970s, the move from feminist theory to lesbian practice had the potential to both conflate lesbianism and feminism (lesbianism as "the feminist solution") and simultaneously to assert lesbian-feminism as autonomous from (hetero)feminism, Hoagland, needs to break down this configuration in order to (re)assert the autonomy of lesbian from feminist.[170] This time the assertion takes place specifically by constituting "lesbian" as a site of theory. Nonetheless, Hoagland also maintains some parts of the relationship between lesbian and feminist as established in the 1970s. Hoagland shifts, but also maintains, the lesbian-feminist relationship between sex and gender. Binary gender difference is, in fact, central to heterosexualism, which could not even be conceived without gender. It is from this position that Hoagland adopts Monique Wittig's claim that "lesbians are not women" in order to show that lesbians work in resistance not only to the system Hoagland names as "heterosexualism," but also in resistance to gender. She also shifts but maintains some of the tensions between autonomy and alliance. She asserts autonomy, but does so in part by maintaining crucial aspects of feminist analysis (theory). The assertion of separation between lesbian and feminist is also a challenge to feminism to take the critique of gender more seriously and further. The challenge to feminism is not simply to revalue "women" and challenge women's subordination, but to do away with the category "woman/women" entirely.

Given Hoagland's continuing implication in the problematics of movement autonomy—her text recognizes diversity within (in a way that Morgan's Introduction to *Sisterhood is Powerful* does not), and yet does not articulate various forms of diversity or the complexity implicated in that diversity—the question becomes, Is it possible to rework autonomy and alliance so as to articulate both diversity and complexity? In order to do so, it would be necessary to resist both the conflation of lesbian and feminist and the conflation of gender and sexuality so as to recognize their unstable and complex interrelation. Here, a complex network of relations among lesbians, women, separatisms, and other resistances of the type suggested by Lugones seems to open the possibility of both recognizing the relative autonomy of, for example, various lesbian theories and practices and their interrelation. One step in the process of building such a network is to accept the separation of the conflated position lesbian-feminist, but also to recognize the interrelation of the two terms. The complexities of the relationship between lesbianism and feminism indicate that it is better to term such a position "lesbian and feminist," than run the risk of eliding the ways in which lesbianism and feminism exceed each other.[171] The position of lesbian and feminist recognizes both a boundary, indicated by the need for both names, and an alliance which may be internal to a particular person, group or community—one may be both lesbian and feminist—or which may connect particular persons, groups or communities; lesbian may ally with feminist. This move opens the door to the complex claim that lesbians both are and are not women. An effective feminism, one that can participate in working alliances (rather than simply desire to do so), must recognize the complexity of both parts of this claim. It also opens the door to various women's resistances to heterosexualism. For example, Sharon Welch (1990) in *A Feminist Ethic of Risk* has provided a critique of the "ethics of control" from a feminist perspective. This coincidence indicates the applicability of Hoagland's critique beyond the bounds of "lesbian ethics." Welch, however, does not name heterosexualism as a site where the ethics of control is structured, but rather concentrates on a site that she labels "Euro-American, middle-class" (14–15), thus, once again raising the issue of lesbian "closeting" within feminism and the complex interrelation among the diverse sites that structure dominations.

Reading Hoagland in relation to Cannon and Lugones also raises these issues. How is it possible, for example, to undertake work that is not only feminist and lesbian, but also anti-racist and anti-classist? To see the complexities entailed in such an alliance it is useful to read Cannon's and Hoagland's texts specifically in relation to each other.

Possibilities and Limits

In order to prevent calls for feminist alliance politics from devolving into a mere cultural pluralism, it has been necessary to delineate the sets of relationships within which feminism is implicated. The readings of Cannon's and Hoagland's texts become critically important in clarifying the position of a feminist ethics in relation to the complexity and diversity of women's moral activity. For example, feminists might be limited in their responses to these texts if they adopt either a strictly modern or a strictly postmodern stance. Feminist ethics can, however, move across but also exceed the boundaries of both modernism and postmodernism in order to claim agency and form alliances among women who are variously marginalized by both modern and postmodern social formations.[172] Even as these two texts demonstrate some of the limits of the modern/postmodern binary, they also demonstrate some of the limits of feminism. A feminist movement which is to enact its commitment to resist the domination of all women must recognize that feminism itself will not be the means by which all women undertake resistance.

The texts themselves leave a number of relational questions unremarked, however, particularly at the point of intersection between race and sexuality, the point at which the texts might overlap, but the boundaries between race and sexuality appear to create a relational silence. *Black Womanist Ethics* is basically silent on issues of sexuality. This particular exclusion is mutually constituted with the particular form of inclusion of women of color, including African American women, in *Lesbian Ethics*. My critique of this mutually constitutive inclusion and exclusion is not a critique of these two particular authors and texts, but, rather, of the ways in which this problem is symptomatic of problems in movement. These two theorists are, in many ways, leaders in articulating relational complexities. Elsewhere in her writing Cannon is strongly critical of "heteropatriarchy."[173] Hoagland is one of the few lesbian or feminist ethicists outside of religious studies to acknowledge Cannon's text. How is it, then, that these two texts were produced with this particular relational silence?

The answer can be understood by exploring the ways in which the inclusions and exclusions of these two texts are mutually constitutive. In particular, I want to explore the ways in which the form of inclusion in *Lesbian Ethics*—specifically the ways in which the drawing of inclusive boundaries, while an important step in recognizing differences *within* lesbian communities, may elide the complex relationships among the various communities within which lesbians move and act. Somewhat paradoxically, dependence on an inclusive methodology simultaneously constitutes exclusions. Since the publication of the book in 1988, critiques have been made along the lines suggested by Lugones, and Hoagland has shifted her analysis in response to these criticisms. Yet, traces of a singular lesbian community within which difference is contained remain even in the description of *Lesbian Ethics* that Hoagland (1992) provides in the "Lesbian Issue" of *Hypatia*. Hoagland states in beginning her section on differences: "So what are the possibilities of lesbian communities? One is diversity, for we emerge *from* everywhere—Palestine and Israel, Argentina and Cherokee Nation, China and India" (201, emphasis added). Her language then shifts from lesbian communities to that of living "in community," a form of living in which each individual is one among many. Some of the shift from the plural to the singular is a shift from the noun of communities to emphasize the verb of living in community, yet, it can also be read as the dominant story of coming out, "we" as lesbians emerge from (not within) our various communities which we leave in order to live in community with each other, where we are one among many. This scenario, in its failure to theorize the ways in which we live within differing communities even while we live as lesbians—we may both come out and stay in various communities—is part of what creates the mutually constitutive exclusion and inclusion, in other words the silence at the intersection of the two texts. The dominant story of coming out dis-articulates lesbian ethics from Black womanist ethics precisely through the dis-articulation of lesbian community *from* those "other" communities within which lesbians live and resistance to heterosexualism might be undertaken.

Complex Differences

These two texts work at the intersections of moral economies. This work at the intersection indicates the crucial role that complexity plays in the politics of diversity. The assertion of difference within a single moral economy will be open to recuperation as the same. In this way, as Christina Crosby (1992) points out, the 1990s discourse of "differences" functions in the same way as did "identities" in the 1980s. Without articulating the interrelations that complicate differences, normative matrices will not only deny lives at the intersections of moral economies, but will also materialize social movements which end up looking like—reiterating—the dominant public sphere that they challenge. *Black Womanist Ethics* and *Lesbian Ethics* accomplish one form of complex rearticulation—they articulate the intersections of differentiation and in so doing materialize possibilities for social movements which don't deny the complex interrelations of gender, race, class, and sexuality. They argue against a dominant ethics of capitalist independence and control and against a "woman's" morality that complements and enables dominative ethics. They complicate the terms of interrelation and articulate moral agency not in a moment of in-dependence from relation but as constituted and empowered in the context of relational and communal activity. They *work* in the intersections.

Black Womanist Ethics and *Lesbian Ethics* both recognize diversity in relation to their own materializations of identity. Cannon recognizes others who care, and in so doing, reverses the order of precedence for potential alliances between womanists and feminists. Instead of desiring that Black women join a (previously existing) autonomous feminist movement, the invitation of "others who care" works precisely to move "others," including feminist movement, toward the concerns of Black women. Hoagland works to materialize the diversity of lesbians and lesbian ethics by including extensive citations and quotes of the norm productive activity of lesbians from various locations. Thus, these texts assert both diversity and complexity in the normative materialization of identity. Yet, they accomplish one form of complex (re)articulation while, at their own margins, they mutually constitute an interstice between the two sites at which they work. There is a gap where Black womanist and lesbian ethics might be spoken together, a gap constituted at the margins of these texts. As I have suggested, this is not simply a problem for the authors, but is rather a problem constituted in movement. The economies of sexualized racism and racialized heterosexism form the context of social relations that must be addressed to respond to this problem. In particular, as Cannon states, the context formed by a dominant ideology of intersection between race and sexuality means that "At the crux of the ideology that Black women were an inferior species was the belief that Black women, unlike White women, craved sex inordinately" (1995, 49). This ideology incites a resistance that refuses the all-encompassing equation "Black women = sexuality" but that does not necessarily erase all connections to sexuality. The interstice between these two texts is further constituted by the politics of "coming out" and the assumption that one would "come out of" other movements and communities into lesbian existence. The effect of this assumption is to recognize diversity, but to deny the complexity that accompanies diversity, the ways in which lesbians might simultaneously participate in "lesbian community" and in movements that are not and cannot be fully contained within the bounds of "lesbian."

Intersections alone do not fully articulate complexity. Intersections are a necessary component of complexity given the contemporary social relations in which difference(s) are produced, and work at the intersections constitutes its own margins, producing some intersections as interstices even while normatively materializing others. This gap suggests the need for the complex articulation of intersections of social differentiation and the simultaneous establishment of connections among movements which are never in and of themselves fully "inclusive."

My suggestion for addressing complexity is not to abandon the assertion of autonomous movement or to claim that the tension between autonomy and alliance can be resolved by splitting the two and favoring only alliance. This tension will persist under the contemporary conditions in which social differentiations are produced, and it will also persist in any ethics or politics that values diversity (Mouffe 1995). Rather, my suggestion is to reverse the order of primacy, so that alliance is understood to be the necessary pre-requisite to movement. *Black Womanist Ethics* suggests that alliances across race and class may be primary to establishing an inclusive feminist movement, that to be a "feminist" one must become an "other [woman] who care[s]" about, moves toward, and works with the concerns of Black women. *Lesbian Ethics* similarly moves to rework the relations between feminist and lesbian. The text asserts that the conjunction of lesbian and feminist is an alliance, rather than a singular identity. The necessary work at the intersection between gender and sexuality cannot be accomplished by making feminism completely inclusive of "sexuality." Simultaneous articulations imply that feminism both recognize the implication of gender in (hetero)sexuality *and* the extension of lesbian ethics beyond the bounds of feminism. In these terms, the ideal feminist movement is not a newly diversified (autonomous) movement, but a movement that is built in and through alliances. Complexity implies that not identity or unity, but alliance, makes for effective moral agency and political movement.

Complexity also means that alliance challenges and continually reconfigures the boundaries of movements. To undertake alliance requires not just joining of, but fundamental change in, social movements. Each text challenges not only the margins of feminist movement, but the central constructions of feminist norms, specifically those norms that have materialized racist, classist, and heterosexist feminisms. *Black Womanist Ethics* and *Lesbian Ethics* are complex undertakings because they do not simply assert an-other identity to be lined up along with (white, heterosexual, middle-class) feminist movement in an alliance of "women's movements." Rather, these texts both demonstrate the intertwining of race and class and sex in the midst of gender, *and* they assert themselves as different from and extending beyond feminist movement, as an (ex)tensive differentiation that cannot be productively reduced to, but might be allied with, feminism (Meese 1990). In this (complex) arrangement an alliance along the lines of gender, race, class, and sexuality is both a presupposition to and an extension beyond effective feminist movement.

Black Womanist Ethics and *Lesbian Ethics* normatively materialize complex differences. They articulate norms and values that make possible lives in social spaces that have been marked out as unlivable, spaces inhabited by beings who have not been recognized as fully persons, the not yet subjects, who are always already immoral, and hence, ultimately, inhuman. Materializing life in these spaces is a complex undertaking because gender, race, class, and sex interact in ways that not only intersect but also contradict each other. The intersections have been created as interstices by dominant moral economies that materialize social relations through the reiteration of a norm and its opposition. The ab-normal secures the norm's status. Normative gender relations are based on the materialization of woman as not-man, race relations on color as not-white, class on poverty as not-work (ethic), and sex on homo as not hetero-sexual. The binary nature of these oppositions allows for two and only two positions. Black women and lesbians do not fit in gender relations where women are simply not-men. These oppositions also intersect and reinforce each other, but often in contradictory ways. "Women" do not work because they live opposed to "men" who do, and yet in Cannon's terms Black women are Blackworkingwomen, while in a third layer of complexity, dominant ideologies locate Black women as failing to live the (Protestant) work ethic. Materializing the normative possibilities of lives in these intersections destabilizes dominant oppositions and makes possible the production of norms outside the binary framework. This norm productive work empowers different possibilities which are not simply recuperable into the economy of the same. And, yet, in asserting its difference, each text creates margins that de-materialize other difference(s). Living in differences is one aspect of a complex articulation of social relations. The spaces in-between differences, even those differences materialized at the intersections of social relations, remain important sites for working alliances. The next chapter will explore the dangers of failing to articulate the spaces both in and between differences.

4 | Working the Public
Social Change in Diverse Public Sphere(s)

THIS CHAPTER CONTINUES the process begun in the last chapter of complicating the bases of feminist movement. It extends chapter 3's question of possibility—Can feminist politics constitute itself in complex relation to diverse women's movements?—to ask Can feminist politics render itself meaningful in relation to queer activism? Specifically, through an analysis of the videotape "Gay Rights, Special Rights," produced in 1993 by the Traditional Values Coalition, I explore the ways in which right-wing movements in the United States have articulated their own alliances over the spaces between gender, race, class, and sexuality. Part of the feminist stake in this case is that some women locate their resistance to domination in queer politics and that the issues of domination raised by anti-queer activity are deeply entwined with gender issues. The enforcement of heterosexuality, particularly the enforcement of heterosexual marriage, is precisely about controlling women's bodies even as it denies them the possibility to be queer.[174] Such stakes name a relatively clear site for connection between feminist and queer movement: Can feminist movement invest in the project of queer space as a means of resisting the dominative control of women's bodies?

I have also chosen this case to test and stretch the boundaries of feminist movement. "Gay Rights, Special Rights," purposefully elides issues of gender and of "women's rights." The videotape is concerned mostly with relations between (gay and straight) white men as intertwined with a politics of racialization. The question that this case raises for feminist ethics and politics is, Can feminist movement read itself in such a case where gender is not the primary axis of action or analysis? Also can the project of creating a space for bodies to be queer be configured as a specifically feminist project given both the multiple genders and gender subversions of those who might avail themselves of such a space? In such a case the boundaries named by the conjunction between feminist, anti-racist, lesbian, and queer are complicated, not by conflating feminist and queer politics, but by implicating feminism in queer movement. Even if queer names one site in which feminism finds itself, however, there remain both ways in which feminism exceeds queer and other sites, such as anti-racist politics, which exceed "feminist" and "queer" politics and at which they might intersect.

This chapter looks specifically at the space in-between the two texts of the last chapter, in-between the racialized politics of sexuality and the sexualized politics of race, in order to consider how work in differences is necessary, but insufficient, to alliances. Working in alliances requires working with the excesses of differentiation because difference is always accompanied by *différance*. Even those differences constituted in the intersections, such as those articulated in *Black Womanist Ethics* and *Lesbian Ethics*, produce their own margins and, thus, they also produce excess at the margin. As Butler points out, the excesses of differentiation also complicate the "we" internally. Those who live in the spaces "outside," who are abjected from, a particular "we" also exist "inside," as the "founding repudiation" of the subject "we" (1993, 3). Moreover, the external spaces, beyond the boundaries of a given "we" are not purely open spaces of possibility somehow outside of discourse or outside of the symbolic order, but are themselves complicated sites of interrelation between social differences (and between the discourses that articulate those differences). They are the intersections and interstices of various normative matrices. Work in these spaces between differences may open possibilities that cannot be materialized within a given normative matrix, yet the shape of these possibilities is simultaneously constrained by the normative matrices which produce them as openings, as possibilities. Thus, while the spaces between differences offer openings to materialize norms "differently" and to produce "different" norms, they are not free from the (productive and constraining) power of normativity, but are rather shaped in *relation* to multiple normativities. It is the complexities of living simultaneously in differences and in the excesses of differentiation that make for the complexities of working in alliances. The example from this chapter shows how "homosexual" functions as both (the abjected) outside of and internal (threat to) the U.S. "public."[175] In this case, the right-wing Traditional Values Coalition is able to exploit the excesses between differences, intertwining issues of race and sex so as to re-segregate African Americans and queers (from both each other and white men) and produce an alliance that ultimately articulates the position only of white men like former Attorney General Ed Meese. Through this analysis I suggest the necessity of working both within and between particular articulations of differences in order to materialize working alliances.

Queer activism presents a particularly useful case study for exploring not only the complex relationships which constitute alliances, but also the relationship between ethics and politics by exploring the relationships between norms and the bodies which they materialize. If, as Butler argues, the normative materialization of particular bodies, both individual and social, is the site for the operation of power, both productive and constraining, then norms are intimately related to the questions of power addressed by politics and social movement. This site, that connects norms to the operation of power, is the site of normativity, of the normative matrices which form moral economies as both the (productive) ground of and (constraining) limits to possibilities for action and embodiment. A primary vehicle of normative power is processes of normalization, the processes by which particular embodiments come to represent the "normal." "Hetero-normativity," for example, normalizes heterosexuality, making "hetero-sex" the normal term, the commonsensical position, unremarkable and everyday, in relation to which non-hetero-sex is queer, odd, to be commented upon, and policed. Queer activism, in its most expansive constitution, works at precisely this site of power by claiming a resistance not just to heteronormativity, but to normativity itself. For example, Michael Warner (1993) suggests, "Organizing a movement around queerness also allows it to draw on dissatisfaction with the regime of the normal in general. . . . Can we not hear in the resonances of queer protest an objection to the normalization of behavior in this broad sense . . . ?" (xxvii). Queer activism, thus, raises a crucial question about the uses of norms: Can the relationship between norms and power be reworked such that normative enactment can be in any way dis-articulated from normalization? The challenge that queer activism poses to feminist ethics and politics is whether feminism can also dis-articulate norms and normalization. Can feminism in this sense become "queer"? Conversely, feminism also raises a particularly important challenge to the claims of queer theory and politics: Is the broad claim of queer activism, the challenge to the "regime of the normal *in general*" effective or is it recuperable into a politics that dis-articulates particular differences and, thus, ultimately reasserts the centrality of those least "different" from the norm? Does queer activism, for example, primarily represent those young, urban men who initially asserted the possibility of a "queer nation" (Signorile 1994)?

This chapter explores the uses of norms in relation to the materialization of "we" as both the "we" of social movements invoked in previous chapters and as the "we" of a social body known as the "general public" or "body politic." By exploring the complex relations among these various "we's," not just among social movements but in relation to the public sphere(s) in which they move, it is possible to rethink and begin to rework both the uses of norms and the possibilities for materializing bodies, both individual and social. Thus, a reworking of the uses of norms is connected to a reworking of the body politic. Given the ways in which norms materialize bodies, the political project of resisting dominations and changing the public sphere is inseparable from the ethical project of reworking norms. Thus, this chapter demonstrates the connections between ethics and politics, showing that politics is embodied through normative materialization. Ethics and politics are not conflated; they are interrelated.

The Uses of Norms

In the Introduction to her important book, *Critique, Norm, and Utopia*, feminist and critical theorist Seyla Benhabib charts a new course for uses of norms.[176] Benhabib argues that critical theory distinguishes itself from both "neo-Kantian foundationalism" and "contemporary contextualism and post-modernism" in "its insistence that criteria of validity, ascertained via non-foundationalist arguments, can be formulated" (1986, 15).[177] For Benhabib, norms provide a means of mediating the relationships between critique and community (utopia), as well as a means of mediating across differences and through conflict. Through (rational, but non-foundational) criteria we can convince those who disagree that our vision of the world is not just an expression of our own interests, but is in fact better for us all.[178] Thus, the public is constructed as the space in which various persons and communities can participate in the project of forming and giving criteria that will guide us (as a whole) toward the future.

This space is also important to various counter-publics, those social movements that run counter to the dominations and distortions of the contemporary public sphere: "[C]ritical social theory turns to those structures of autonomy and rationality which, in however distorted and imperfect fashion, continue in the lifeworld of our societies, while allying itself with the struggles of those for whom the hope of a better future provides the courage to live in the present" (1986, 15). Here, Benhabib makes a move which is both full of hope and ultimately problematic. Through her appeal to normative criteria, Benhabib is able to hold together a space of both public and counter-public possibility. In Benhabib's (1987) terms, she is able to hold together two poles of community formation, the universality or "generalized" terms of a lifeworld (public sphere) open to all and the particular, "concrete" claims of those social movements (counter-publics) which continually challenge the dominations of false universalism in the name of the public. Thus, norms mediate the relationship between the "we" of the general public and the "we" of particular counter-publics. Despite her commitment to both the general and the particular, however, problems arise in Benhabib's construction of this relationship.

The importance of maintaining both general and particular perspectives is that the particular or "concrete" is a site of diversity. If the concrete is not maintained, is completely subordinated to the general, then the diversity of particular subject positions is lost to the shared identity of a general public. In much social theory the private sphere is the sphere of difference and needs, while the public is a sphere of equality among citizens. Benhabib is critical of this split, however, because it undercuts the public nature of moral diversity.[179]

By maintaining the public importance of both the general and the particular, Benhabib theorizes the public sphere as a social space of communicative interpretation of concrete needs. This model also allows for a certain multiplicity in terms of the "interpretative indeterminacy of action": "By 'the interpretive indeterminacy of action' I mean that human actions and the intentions embedded in them can only be identified by a process of social interpretation and communication in the shared world" (1986, 136). Social interpretation for Benhabib implies a "moral transformative process" by which concrete others speaking from their particular positions are able, through a process of communication, to transform their particular needs to generalizable needs without merely submitting to the force of dominant social actors. It is not just that in recognizing the claims of concrete others, particular interpretations of needs are transformed to recognize an already existing, but obscured, harmony of generalizable interests, but the needs themselves are transformed. Hence, generalizable interests are created through the social process of needs transformation rather than through a Habermasian commitment to the "generalized other." Thus, Benhabib uses a different approach for creating common politics than do the texts in chapter 2. In chapter 2 a common base of oppression was located in the existing structures of dominative society. For Benhabib, this commonality must be built through normative interaction. And, yet, the regulative function of the norms that Benhabib invokes ultimately serves to enact similar exclusions/problems to those enacted in chapter 2.

Although the general public is built up through the relational interaction of particulars, it also slips from this inter-dependence with the particular to function as a singular framework of (specifically western) rationality *within which* particular differences must interact. Benhabib argues that the perspectives of the general and the particular must be held in tension as two poles, and yet, at points in her texts it is clear that she constructs the general as a frame around particulars. This framing function is apparent when the tension between the general and the particular is resolved in favor of the general. In her 1992 book, *Situating the Self*, Benhabib states that general norms can "trump" the particulars of, for example, the care perspective:

> Considerations of a universalist morality do set the constraints within which concerns of care should be allowed to operate and they "trump" over them if necessary . . . ; and considerations of care should be "validated or affirmed from an impartialist perspective." (Benhabib 1992, 187, quoting Blum 1988)

Benhabib nowhere argues that care might similarly trump universalism. Thus, we find not mutual critique, but universal norms which form a framework for particular norms, delineating the constraints "within which" particulars must operate.

The usefulness of Benhabib's theory is that it allows for differences *within* the general public, differences which in traditional critical theory were displaced to the private sphere. This is an important shift in recognizing diversity, but as I have argued, it undercuts diversity that extends beyond the frame and, thereby, undercuts the complexity of working with "differences" inside and out. Differences contained within a particular discourse are relatively stabilized positions that depend on the framework of the discourse within which they exist.[180] Thus, in Benhabib's texts, western rationality maintains a dominant position as the frame of particular differences and this framework itself is unlikely to be changed by the interaction with internal differences.

Benhabib's uses of norms in configuring the relationship between the general and the particular is so crucial, because this normative relationship materializes the relationship between "the general public" and particular, diverse persons, groups, and communities "in public." Benhabib names the relationship between norms and community formation as one of materialization. Norms materialize, and are materialized by, communities:

> The perspective of the generalized other urges us to respect the equality, dignity and rationality of all humans qua humans, while the perspective of the concrete other enjoins us to respect differences, individual life-histories and concrete needs. Such communities, in my view, are not pregiven; they are formed out of the action of the oppressed, the exploited, and the humiliated, and must be committed to universalist, egalitarian, and consensual ideals. Traditional ethnic, racial, and religious communities are neither necessarily nor primarily such communities of needs and solidarity. They become so only insofar as they uphold the ideal of action in a universalist, egalitarian, consensual framework. (1986, 351)[181]

A given community only becomes a community through normative enactment. The body politic and the public "we" that it embodies are produced through norms, but problems arise, perhaps not surprisingly, at the point of the production of the "we" who is the public. Norms also adjudicate among particular communities. Thus, communities of needs and solidarity become so in Benhabib's terms only when they "uphold the ideal of action in a universalist, egalitarian, consensual framework." These norms can be used to judge "other" communities that do not fit within the framework.

Benhabib's uses of norms materialize a generalizable body politic which is the public that frames and contains within it particular bodies—particular persons, groups, and communities. Within Benhabib's understanding of norms, the creation of this "general" public is necessary because without a normative framework to materialize generalizability there will be no general criteria to mediate across differences. We will be left without criteria to choose (adjudicate) among possibilities. Ultimately, without such criteria there can be no legitimately (normatively) constituted "we," but only those communities that are produced through dominative power.

For Benhabib normative criteria and the "we" they materialize are historically (not naturally or foundationally) constituted, yet, this particular form of constituting a "we" continues to enact the "economy of the same" analyzed in chapter 2. While the perspective of the concrete "other" may challenge given embodiments of the public, particularly through counter-public social movement, when the tension between the general and the particular slips so that the general supersedes or frames the concrete, rather than remaining in tension with it, these social movements will tend to re-iterate the dominant general public. In this latter case, the women's liberation movement will make itself the subject of public import by creating an autonomous subjectivity for the social group "women." "Women" in this sense will fit into the public. They become a "difference" within the public which simultaneously reiterates the public as the "same." Possibilities for alliance formation among different (groups of) women, however, will be undercut by the demands of autonomy. In this sense the general public maintains itself as the norm by maintaining divisions among particular others. If, in order to be normatively recognized, particular movements must reiterate the general framework, then the demands of this reiteration will relate them to the general but undercut any direct relation to each other (except insofar as they mirror the general). Counter-public movements are, thus, contained: contained within the public by not extending beyond or effectively challenging its frame, and contained as units of difference separated from each other.

The videotape "Gay Rights, Special Rights" effectively shows the potential containment of counter-public movements. The videotape works to establish two minorities, "racial/ethnic minorities" and "homosexuals," that are completely separate from each other. Significantly, the video does not mention women or gender, in part, because women are themselves a majority (not a minority group). By eliding women and locating the public claims of each named group as those of a particular minority, the videotape also works to establish those who do not belong to either group—straight whites—as the normative location of the "general public." While this result is perhaps not surprising in a right-wing video, it is worth exploring further, because if Benhabib is correct in articulating the uses of norms in relation to the public, then the videotape raises the question of how the public is normatively produced in the United States. What is the relationship between the "general" public and various "particulars" in the United States?

"Gay Rights, Special Rights"

"Gay Rights, Special Rights" is a 1993 production of the Traditional Values Coalition, headed by right-wing Christian Lou Sheldon. The video is in many ways a sequel to "The Gay Agenda," which was used successfully by the Coalition for Family Values in the Colorado campaign for Amendment Two and in the controversy over "gays in the military." "Gay Rights, Special Rights" was initially used, once again successfully, in the battle to repeal the Cincinnati ordinance that prohibited discrimination against lesbians and gays. The video promotes the racist, anti-Semitic, and homophobic aspects of the Christian Right agenda, while posturing as an alliance between conservative whites and people of color. The videotape presents itself as protecting civil rights, but it ultimately portrays all anti-discrimination law as promoting "special rights." The video also promotes the (re)Christianizing of "America," in part by narrowing the legacy of the 1950s and 1960s civil rights struggles to recognize only its Christian aspects. Although the video supposedly depends on a cross-racial alliance, the reconfiguration of civil rights as "minority protections" allows principal spokesmen Ed Meese, deconstructor of affirmative action under Ronald Reagan, and Trent Lott, notably anti-civil rights Senator from Mississippi, to promote the racist aspects of their agenda, even as they decry the "homosexuals" for trying to take on "full minority status."

The entire premise of the video is that "homosexuals" want the same rights that "racial/ethnic minorities" were granted in the civil rights legislation of 1964 and 1965. The video argues, however, that to grant "homosexuals" these rights would be to grant "special rights." This logic effectively implies that the Voting Rights Act and Civil Rights Act also granted "special rights." The video reasserts white, heterosexist Christian supremacy by positioning rights which are not "special" as those rights which articulate a general public (that has no need of anti-discrimination protections). The video constructs an opposition between racial/ethnic "minorities" and "homosexuals" in order to establish Ed Meese as the representative of this (general) public. This opposition is normatively materialized through the establishment of a legitimate minority, which simultaneously de-legitimizes other, specifically "homosexual," minorities. Once they are normatively constructed in this manner, both counter-publics are effectively contained so that there can be no cross-over between them or between "minorities" and the "general public."

An analysis of the narrative structure of the video will demonstrate this construction of the general public. The video is structured into four parts: The first establishes people of color as members of legitimate racial/ethnic "minorities" and de-legitimates claims to civil rights by "lesbians, gays, bisexuals, and transgenders" (in other words queers) because they do not appropriately embody "minority status." Here we see a multi-cultural array of people of color (presumably straight) contrasted with a virtually all-white array of queers, mostly white gay men, many of whose bodies are out of control—disrobed, acting sexual, screaming, or simply marching and dancing.[182] This first section establishes the clarity of the opposition between the two counter-publics, implying that there is no confusing diversity within or between these two groups. There can be no such thing as a legitimate, "homosexual" person of color. Lesbian and gay people of color appear only half a dozen times in the entire video (Ed Meese alone appears four) and the placement of each reinforces the idea that these persons have been deluded by the larger (read: white) "gay community," thus, establishing that they have crossed over from one category to another, rather than that there is overlap between the categories.[183]

The opposition is enacted in the very opening of the video as the disembodied voice of Dr. Martin Luther King, Jr., is heard giving part of the "I Have a Dream" speech at the 1963 March on Washington, followed by a visual of the 1963 March and then a visual of Larry Kramer at the 1993 March for Lesbian, Gay and Bi (march organizers purposefully omitted the "sexual") Equal Rights and Liberation. Thus, the 1963 Civil Rights March leading to civil rights legislation, is set up to contrast with the 1993 March and the possibility of a Lesbian and Gay Civil Rights Bill being passed by Congress. This contrast establishes the framework for the double containment of "minorities" which the video accomplishes. Once we see Dr. King and the assembled crowd at the march, we see what a legitimate minority looks like, and it doesn't look like Larry Kramer. In fact, Kramer's body dissolves into King's, while we are told that "out of pure logic," "it was wrong to discriminate against Black people simply on the basis of color." This use of Larry Kramer's body also enacts the anti-Semitism of the videotape as the Jewish Kramer dissolves into the Christian King, re-enacting Christian supersessionism and implying that "true" minorities can be recognized by the general public through a shared Christianity.[184] Thus, not only are legitimate minorities marked as Christian, so is the general public. The videotape thereby reduces the history of civil rights struggle to its Christian aspects and (re)Christianizes "American" history in general. The narration further establishes containment by promoting a conservative reading of Civil Rights struggle. Racial domination is reduced to discrimination. Moreover, this discrimination occurs "on the basis of color," signaling the video's obsession with race as skin color and skin color alone. The focus on the visibility of "skin color" works to establish the "marked" status of legitimate "minorities," thus, distinguishing legitimate "minorities" from both illegitimate minorities and the general public.

The "general" public is not visibly marked, and "other" counter-publics, which are marked only by their behavior, are both illegitimate and particularly insidious because you can't tell who they are unless you catch them in the act (one of the services the video provides to the unsuspecting general public). The distinction between visible marking and behavior is further secured by a conflation between ethnicity and race as representatives of the "Hispanic community" and "The Chinese Family Alliance" argue that ethnicity, unlike homosexuality, does not constitute a "behavior-based group." By implication in this configuration, ethnicity like race is conflated with visible marking. Thus, in this first part of the video racial/ethnic groups may be "deserving" in their claims to (special) rights, but they are never fully public. Significantly, the question of rights in relation to gender discrimination and the inclusion of gender in civil rights legislation is never engaged by the video, because to do so would complicate the opposition between racial/ethnic "minorities" and "homosexuals." "Women" are part of both groups, and an additional focus on women would threaten to highlight the minority status of white men, rather than allowing them the assumed majority status of the norm(al). Thus, once again the video is drawing on multiple meanings of the word "normal"—the normal as norm, the normal as unmarked, and the normal as common, as what most people are/do.

This section not only separates the two counter-public "minorities" from each other, it establishes the difference between (counter-public) "minorities" and the (majority) general public. At the end of this section, Ed Meese proclaims that "As a white male I have no rights whatsoever." Meese concludes after a pause, "other than what is shared with everybody else." Of course, all civil rights are shared by all citizens. Meese has the same protections against race and sex discrimination as all citizens. "As a white man" he is just less likely to experience such discrimination. Yet, the initial mis-statement of the law (by the former Attorney General) is crucial to the argument of the video as a whole, because it constructs civil rights as special rights, as special protections for those persons and groups awarded "full minority status." Thus, from the beginning of the video not only "gay rights," but all civil rights to freedom from discrimination are constructed as "special rights" and racial/ethnic "minorities" are established as a particular group (granted "full minority status") distinct from the general public (that has no rights).

The videotape is direct, if not blatant, in its construction of civil rights as special minority protections, and people of color are the initial spokespersons of this point of view. Cheryl Coleman, listed only as "Public Affairs Representative" and one of the only African American women to be granted a speaking role, states while standing in front of the U.S. capitol building, "This Civil Rights Act amendment would completely neutralize the Civil Rights Act of 1964. What it will do is that it will say is that anyone, anyone with any type of sexual preference, which would include everyone would be protected under this law, so therefore there would be no protections for minorities specifically." The implication once again is that civil rights "protections," rather than being available to all citizens, are handed out by the government specifically to minority groups. Here the distinction between racial/ethnic "minority" and behavior-based "group" is brought crucially into play, as Raymond Kwong, listed as President of the Chinese Family Alliance states, "The Government has no business putting its stamp of approval on a behavior-based group, let alone elevating it to full minority status." Rev. Lou Sheldon, listed as Chairman of the Traditional Values Coalition (the group which produced the video), puts the final cap on this section stating in reference to "homosexuals," "They want to be elevated from a behavior-based lifestyle to a true minority status that would give them special rights."

Interestingly, Sheldon, who is white, is shown standing in front of a group of African American men, thus, signaling the next major move of the video-tape. The authority of the white spokesmen who populate the following sections of the video is built up (in part by dependence upon, in part by the contrast with) the people of color who open the video. Perhaps most tellingly, people of color are only visible in the first quarter of the videotape. Having used a multi-cultural alliance to establish the legitimacy of white, male authority in the persons of Ed Meese and Trent Lott, we see only two token people of color as representatives of authority after the first nine minutes of this forty-minute videotape, while there are thirty-five appearances by white male authorities, and two by the token white female. Lou Sheldon depends on people of color to do the labor of establishing racial/ethnic "minorities" as in need of special protections granted by the government. He depends on people of color to establish his authority to say his lines, just as the United States has historically depended on the labor of people of color to establish "white" culture and society. It is, however, the contrast between the special rights granted by "minority status" and the lack of (a need for) civil rights claimed by Ed Meese that ultimately establishes the white men as "representative" of the general public. Thus, I would suggest that the visual use of people of color in the beginning of the videotape is something more than a hypocritical dependence on token people of color to validate the racist positions of white men (although it is that). The segregation of people of color in the beginning of the tape is in line with the ideology of the tape as a whole which attempts to locate people of color as a particular minority separate from the general public represented by white men (in the government).

The containment of racial/ethnic groups is furthered in the following sections of the video as the public role of straight, white men takes center stage. The second part of the video is still rhetorically directed at de-legitimizing "lesbian, gay, bisexual, and transgender" claims to civil rights as a minority, but it visibly concentrates on the bodies of (supposedly straight) white men who represent the public in contrast to the still out of control bodies of mostly white gay men. Here the apparent obsession which powerful, supposedly straight, white men have with gay white men is played out once again. Just as with the debate over "gays in the military" where Sam Nunn and colleagues focused on white male officers in the shower, when in the Marine Corps African American lesbians were discharged at twice the rate of white gay men (Schulman 1994, 269), so also the video turns its attention to white men when queer people of color and white lesbians are less protected by economic privilege and, thus, more likely to suffer from discrimination on the basis of sexual identity and to need access to civil rights claims.

Class issues are brought into the tape in the form of a series of economic contrasts purportedly intended to show that gays and lesbians have not suffered real discrimination. Gays and lesbians have, for example, never been denied voting rights and reportedly have not suffered job discrimination, but rather have high levels of income (contradicting the following section of the videotape which advocates protecting the right of the business owner to discriminate against "homosexuals" in hiring practices). Here traditionally anti-Semitic tropes of a small minority with undue economic (and political) power are invoked. The use of this trope effectively erases working-class queers, particularly people of color and white lesbian and bisexual women who face race and gender segregated labor markets. To point out the particular import of this trope is not to equate domination based on sexuality with racial domination (a mistake which, as I will argue below, lesbian and gay movements often make, just as they have too frequently accepted and made use of marketing reports which focus on the "high" incomes of some gay men), it is rather to show that the real concern of the videotape is with privileged gay men who might insidiously replace straight white men as representatives of the public.

The third part of the video, thus, heightens the stakes of argument, claiming that gays aspire not just to legitimate status as a counter-public, but to take over the public. Here the demands of the 1993 March are listed, but the focus is also on the possibility that white, male "homosexuals," sometimes visually indistinguishable from straight white men, might take over. We begin to see the threat to society as a whole if minorities, in this case white gay men, are not controlled. In the fourth and final section, this potential threat is connected to the threat already posed by racial/ethnic "minorities." In this section the authoritative representatives of the general public point out that "gay rights" would simply extend the problems faced by white men as a result of racial/ethnic claims to civil rights. Ed Meese argues that small business owners might actually have to go against their (Christian) values and hire "such people." The "economics expert," Grover Norquist, speaks of just "one more reason" to sue the beleaguered business owner on the basis of discrimination, and Trent Lott claims that moral values would be "*further* degraded" by any more anti-discrimination restrictions. Thus, the video concludes that the real threat of civil rights is to the natural rights of white men. In fact, one authority argues that the real problem with anti-discrimination education in the public schools is that young boys who naturally prefer boys to girls, might mistake this natural inclination for the unnatural attractions of homosexuality. Thus, at the end of the video the construction of the unmarked general public is established not only on the basis of the visual opposition between race and homosexuality, but also on the need to contain both "minorities" for the sake of society "as a whole."

Thus, the video promotes the racist, homophobic, and anti-Semitic aspects of the Christian right agenda by reasserting Christian whiteness, specifically straight, white maleness, as the only form of embodiment which is unmarked and, therefore, representative of the "general public." The video materializes the general public through the three-party interaction I described above as establishing the "normal." The representation of Ed Meese contrasts with that of racial/ethnic minorities, not simply because Ed Meese is different from them. If that were the only basis of contrast, Meese's position could itself be named as particular and as openly racist. By opposing racial/ethnic "minorities" to another "minority," however, Ed Meese "as a white male" is removed from the direct opposition which could name his position as particular and "white male" becomes instead representative of the general public without any (particular) rights.

In "Gay Rights, Special Rights," public norms are materialized by disciplining and containing "minority" bodies. Through this action Ed Meese becomes the representative of normal, unmarked embodiment and the normative public. The uses of norms to tie the materialization of the normal to the normative is particularly effective in relation to a liberal public structured by tolerance. In this situation the Christian Right claims to be both a normative public and a counter-public in need of tolerance. Whenever opposition to the Right is raised by a particular counter-public, an opposition which appeals to dominant culture to stand against intolerance, the Right positions itself as a counter-public which is oppressed by intolerance. In this way the liberal public is paralyzed, because it cannot distinguish among counter-publics which it is to "tolerate." "Gay Rights, Special Rights" articulates the other side of this strategy. The Christian Right positions itself as the public by materializing oppositions among other bodies—in this instance, people of color and lesbians, gays, bisexuals, and transgenders—and claiming to be the voice of those few values which the liberal public has left. Here the "Christian" part of the Christian right is brought into play as those white, middle-class liberal Christians who fear that tolerance has evacuated all possible values are reassured by the possibility that the public is normatively structured after all. Thus, the video effectively sutures the relationship between norms, normativity, and the normal, so that the very possibility of public norms is presented as dependent upon control of those marked as abnormal. With such a tightly stitched seam between norms and the enforcement of the normal, the power of normativity becomes fundamentally constraining of those bodies it materializes. The video needs racial/ethnic bodies (at least at the beginning) to establish the white public, just as the United States has always used the labor of racial/ethnically marked bodies to establish white culture and society, but it reassures the "public" that these and other bodies can be contained. The effectiveness of this strategy is that it repeatedly induces white, Protestant, middle-class America to accede to this program without having to acknowledge itself as the voice of intolerance. Rather, middle America is simply asked to ensure that no one gets "special rights."

Publics and Counter-Publics

Although the construction of the public in "Gay Rights, Special Rights" is obviously a right-wing appropriation, it is important to analyze because its assumptions, particularly its assumptions about the general public and "minorities," are found not only in right-wing discourses. Unfortunately, as strategized by the national lobby groups which were its primary sponsors, the 1993 March on Washington for Lesbian, Gay, and Bi Equal Rights and Liberation accepted the two primary assumptions that I have criticized in the agenda of the Christian Right: that the public is the general space inhabited only by those who can aspire to the phantom status of unmarked (in)visibility and that legitimate counter-publics are inhabited by visibly marked "minorities." Videos of the March produced by the major national lobby groups based in Washington, "Prelude to Victory" by the Human Rights Campaign Fund (now Human Rights Campaign) and "Marching for Freedom" by the National Lesbian and Gay Task Force, display precisely these assumptions in virtually the same manner as does "Gay Rights, Special Rights": dependence on people of color to establish the authority of white activity, containment of these same people of color to reassure the "general" public, and a reinforcement of, in this case through an aspiration to, the unmarked status of the general public (read: white and middle-class). Once these assumptions about the public are accepted, then racially marked bodies can at best claim the contained space of a counter-public minority, while white lesbian and gay bodies can aspire to the public only by denying the particular difference of queerness and acceding to the unmarked categories of the white, middle-class family.

The March organizers focused on entrance into the status of the "general" by developing a media strategy of mainstreaming which promoted white, middle-class family lesbians and gays as the true, but invisible, face of "lesbian, gay and bi" sexual identity, while downplaying those visible queers which the media had focused on in the past. As with the Christian Right, this strategy is intertwined with a dependence on the legitimating power of the 1963 March on Washington and a simultaneous containment of people of color as a (legitimate, but contained) "minority." All of these elements are present in the beginning depiction of the March in "Marching for Freedom." The first shot of the March itself is of the assembled crowd on the Mall before the main stage in front of the U.S. Capitol. We see a sea of predominantly white arms (in close up only white people are visible) swaying to the freedom song "Woke Up this Morning with My Mind on Freedom." Here the major themes are established. The legitimation for the March is the 1963 Civil Rights March on Washington, but what is legitimated is civil rights for mainstream, white gays and lesbians who are just like the "general public" (but for their sexual identity).

The video then fades into marchers in the street and a series of brief interviews with Marchgoers explaining why they came to Washington follows. The order of the interviews in conjunction with the statements replays the dominant tropes. The first three interviews are with young white men, the first two of whom are visually virtually indistinguishable—baseball caps, shirtless, with rainbow paraphernalia. They say, first, "I've been looking forward to this for a whole year"; and then, "[I'm] looking forward to a lot of positiveness channeled out throughout the whole United States because of the March"; and when the third man is asked, "What are you marching for today?" he answers, "Full civil rights for gays and lesbians . . . definitely." Civil rights for gays and lesbians are here tied to the aspirations of average (indistinguishable) white gay men. The next interview with two lesbians who are pushing a baby in a stroller brings home the mainstream point: "We're normal people, we pay taxes, we go to work every day, have families, go bowling and, you know, we're regular people and that's what we need to show the rest of the country." Most importantly, gays and lesbians are normal people; they match the norm, which is tied directly to middle-class family values. This series shows that gays and lesbians do not even challenge dominant gender norms: The men are young and single, average guys visible on almost any college campus, and the women continue to form families and have children. Having, thus, established white gays and lesbians as the (general) norm, the video can then return to the legitimating presence of African Americans, now clearly representing a "minority." Two African American lesbians are shown next articulating their (the video makers'?) hopes for "community" and a "unified march": "I'm looking forward to a lot of positive energy, large numbers, we love the community, we're glad to see the people out, and it's going to be a unified march." African Americans are a minority, but they are also no different than the representatives of the (general) community. They too are "looking forward to positive energy," and they in no way articulate a difference that would challenge a community and unity built on this dominant representation.

The containment of people of color is furthered by a construction of "diversity" as referring to mainstream white people. For example, in the video "Prelude to Victory," by the Human Rights Campaign Fund, Tori Osborne, then Director of the National Gay and Lesbian Task Force, proclaims "look at our great diversity," and the videotape cuts to a white man. In the series that follows tokenized people of color are represented but always contained between representations of white people. Thus, these videos present a tokenized representation of people of color in the national or "general" movements similar to that used in the right-wing video.

This sequence shows how "diversity" conceptualized only as within a group can be recuperated. Osborne is declaring that "we" are a diverse community, but the framework of the community and the meaning of diversity is established through a re-iteration of the general norm. Diversity may be found within this frame, but it does not challenge the structure of the frame—neither the community nor the general frame which are ultimately the same, white and male. Thus, we see how "diversity" can, under these circumstances, come to mean "the same." With the media strategy of mainstreaming, the assumption is that the media has focused on those visible "queers" who are "different" from (and thus interesting to) the general public. The "true" diversity of the "lesbian, gay, and bi" community, then, is represented by those who are most "like" the general public. As with *Sisterhood is Powerful* the "problem" of diversity is not getting diverse persons to join a pre-existing, predominantly white, middle-class movement, the problem is the constitution of a dominantly white, middle-class, and in this case male movement out of the diverse participants in queer politics.

The question of norms is central to this problem. If movements cannot work with diverse and complex norms, then the uses of norms to materialize simultaneously the normal and the normative will produce this type of dominative social relations within the moral economy of the same. A similar strategy of containment was used with regard to queer visibility which might challenge the family-like appeals to white, middle-class norms, including norms of disembodiedness with regard to sexuality. The clearest example of this containment was the shortening of "bisexual" to simply "bi" in the official name of the March, the 1993 "March for Lesbian, Gay and Bi Equal Rights and Liberation."[185] Despite this strategy of downplaying sexuality, the producers of "Gay Rights, Special Rights" attacked the March both for excessive sexuality *and* for appealing to conservative ideals of family. Thus, the strategy of containment is not necessarily more effective in resisting right-wing appropriation and attack, and yet it does work to deny both the differences (queerness) *between* "lesbians, gays, bisexuals, and transgenders" and the "general public" and *within* counter-public social movements as diversity devolves to "normal."

Having thus aspired to inhabit the general public by forefronting unmarked lesbian and gay bodies, the March relied heavily on analogies between lesbian and gay oppression and racial oppression, particularly on analogies with the 1963 Civil Rights March, in order to establish counter-public claims for minority group oppression and the need for a lesbian and gay civil rights bill. Thus, for example, in the portion of Larry Kramer's speech shown in

"Gay Rights, Special Rights," Kramer paraphrases King to say that one day men and women will not be judged by their "sexual desire," but by the content of their character. In using this analogy in this way, Kramer accedes to the conservative reading of "civil rights," appealing to those norms which make the general public a social space inhabited only by those who can (un)mark themselves by proclaiming that "sexual desire" shouldn't matter.[186] Simultaneously, Kramer depends on the visibility of bodies marked by racial difference to promote the claim that sexual identity, like race, should be a "protected category." There is a lot going on here, and just as with civil rights, there is more to Larry Kramer than this conservative point. It would be dangerous to define Kramer or queer movements, including ACT UP which he helped to found, by this moment alone, which "Gay Rights, Special Rights" clearly wants to do.[187] The analogy with race, however, not only erases the historical differences between racism and homophobia, as well as anti-racist and anti-heterosexist struggle, but accepts the assumption that race is a protected category (a site of special rights)—as if to be racially marked in the United States is somehow to be protected. Perhaps even more problematically, once conservative assumptions about the public are accepted, particularly the assumption that the body politic is constituted by overcoming the particular embodiments of race and sexual identity, then racially marked bodies can at best claim the contained space of a counter-public minority, while white lesbian and gay bodies can aspire to the public only by denying visible queerness and acceding to the unmarked categories of the white, middle-class family.

Although the ideology of race promoted by "Gay Rights, Special Rights" is itself racist and distorting, it is successful in part because it taps into existing racism within lesbian and gay movements. One way to challenge both the racism and homophobia of "Gay Rights, Special Rights" and of lesbian and gay movement is to challenge the notion that civil rights movements are necessarily about inclusion within a framework established by the dominant white, middle-class society. All of these videos use this problematic notion of inclusion to contain "minorities" so that there is no threat to the structure of the dominant society. The videos are quick to undercut any potential threat to or call for change in the structure of the "general public." In "Marching for Freedom," for example, civil disobedience is contained within the category of "individual expression" and is presented through digitized effects of video production which obscure both the bodies and their actions. Civil disobedience can work as a crucial element in struggles for civil rights, however, because it is a form of activity which through its embodied disobedience challenges the status of the general public as disembodied and all encompassing. By graphically demonstrating those bodies which are excluded from the general public, it names that general as a particular which is not normative for all. A march focused on full inclusion in the general public would require a change in the structure of the "general" itself, so that the "general" could sustain the multiple forms of diversity denied by these videos, including differences between "queers" and the current construction of the general public and the diversity that might constitute a movement as "queer."

Thus, when considering how to fight the type of distortions used in "Gay Rights, Special Rights," it is not necessarily useful for movements to try to distance themselves from the "radical" implications of their claims. While we are often told that such a strategy is necessary for "effective" politics, it may simply play into the racist and homophobic assumptions of the U.S. public sphere. Such a move undercuts effectiveness both by replicating the dominations/dominative practices of the public (thus, lesbian and gay movements are susceptible to charges of racism because they are constituted on racist premises), and by undercutting potential for alliance formation. Rather than effective alliance building, movements working with these assumptions tend simply to re-iterate the tokenism of the public sphere.

The alternative (and perhaps ultimately more "effective") strategy is to rework queer movements so that they are constituted in alliance with and among the radical aspects of civil rights struggles and other movements for social justice. This alternative implies a shift in movement agendas from issues focused on reiterating lesbians and gays as the general public to issues which are constituted primarily in alliance (in other words where alliance precedes or guides the issue). For example, contemporary debates over "gay marriage" are often formulated in precisely this manner: Lesbians and gays should have access to the same "benefits," such as access to employee health insurance plans, that accrue to married couples. Yet, there are other ways to formulate the issue triggered by the unequal distribution of benefits. Obviously, a health care system that made health care and/or insurance available to the entire "public" would shift the debate dramatically. But, even if the issue of benefits were framed in the relatively conservative terms of access through employment, lesbian and gay movements could focus on "benefits" that were designed so that a working person could include another person, not necessarily their spousal equivalent. Then, these movements would, for example, address working people who are responsible for elder care in circumstances where their elders do not have health insurance, as well as "domestic partners." This type of strategy could articulate with feminist critiques of marriage as an institution which constitutes "family values" as patriarchal values in support of the state, and, thus, connect to the activisms of "straight" women who are working to create alternatives to marriage. Not only does this move start from a position of alliance, rather than defining queer issues "autonomously" and then hoping for alliance, it also provides a site for working to fight internal class hierarchy and racism as enacted in the assumptions of queer movement. This move could connect queer issues to those of "normal" (non-queer) people, while demanding full inclusion in the public sphere, but it does so by resisting, not replicating, the constraints of that public.

Norms and Politics

Returning to Benhabib, she argues that feminist or lesbian or queer or anti-racist or any other politics requires normative criteria which may be developed in dialogue among particular persons, groups, and communities, but which can also be used to adjudicate among the particular norms which regulate these individuals or groups.[188] The examples of this chapter, both right-wing and progressive, suggest, however, that this conceptualization of the relationship between general and particular norms may materialize both a general public and particular movements that cannot sustain diversity and complexity, but instead reiterate dominative practices. Is this really a problem of norms, however? Perhaps the examples of this chapter are just bad enactments of norms which are otherwise sound. In other words, could this be a problem of politics separate from norms, where we can never expect the realities of politics to live up to the ideals of ethics? The fact that both right-wing and progressive movements share these practices suggests that it is not simply a matter of political commitment or intent. The political commitment to racism such as that displayed by Ed Meese and Trent Lott is not necessarily shared by lesbian and gay political organizations like the Human Rights Campaign and the National Lesbian and Gay Taskforce, but the question remains, are we faced with a problem of norms as well as politics? Would, for example, reasserting the normatively general nature of the general public effectively resist the right-wing appropriation of civil rights as special rights? In other words, is it enough to correct Ed Meese and point out that he too shares civil rights protections? This correction would reassert the tension between the general and particular—in making an anti-discrimination claim a person or group is both citing their place in the general public as entitled to civil rights and acknowledging a particular location as the object of discrimination on the basis of, for example, "gender."

I would also suggest, however, that it is the slippage between the two conceptualizations of the general and particular—the two held together in tension versus the general as framework for and adjudication of the particular—that "Gay Rights, Special Rights" effectively exploits. The representation of Ed Meese depends on both meanings of the general. In saying that "as a white male I have no rights," Meese is also saying that those who represent the general do not need special rights and in this sense the general public supersedes, is distinct from and above, particulars. In concluding "except for those shared by everyone else," Meese is also claiming that the general is fully inclusive of all particulars. Thus, any challenge to the general from a particular perspective can simply be contained within the general, or if it cannot be so contained, it can be judged as outside of or below the general, as a "special" interest group—a particular that cannot also represent the general in the way that Ed Meese in his (particular) embodiment "as a white male" can.

This embodiment of the general public is a materialization of a similar slippage at the normative level as exemplified by slippages in Benhabib's texts. At the normative level the "we" of moral agency slips between a "we" who is the universal ideal of western norms and a "we" who is formed in the particular context of western rationalism and from this context judges "others." Although for Benhabib general norms come out of the negotiations among/between different particulars, these negotiations can take place only within the framework of modern, universalist rationalism.[189] When Benhabib states that "interactive universalism is the practice of situated criticism for a global community" (1992, 228), the word "universalism" performs this framing function for an otherwise situated or contextual interaction. When she says, "[communities of needs and solidarity] become so only insofar as they uphold the ideal of action in a universalist, egalitarian, consensual framework" (1986, 351), the norms that she lists are not simply a part of, or representative of a party to, these negotiations—they are its frame, and the simultaneous inclusion and exclusion which constitutes the "general" is repeated in relation to "other" norms.[190] "Other" norms become differences *within* this frame—a pluralism of particular (communities) who share the general norms of universalism, egalitarianism, and consensuality and, thus, who do not fundamentally challenge the frame—while any excess, any exteriority which exceeds this framework is an "other" to be judged.[191]

Benhabib would argue that the challenge to the shape of the general is precisely what is available through the questioning and reflexivity of universal rationalism. But the slippages in her texts crucially undercut this claim. How do we "know" whether a challenge to the general is an "other" to be judged or a difference to be incorporated through change in the shape of universalism? We know only through the public process of reason giving and needs transformation within the terms already established by the framework—universalist rationalism. Benhabib grounds this knowledge in a distinction between true and false needs. Previous critical theorists restricted the realm of needs to the private sphere because of the difficulties presented by attempts to distinguish between true and false needs. Without such a distinction, individual needs were configured as personal preferences, the site of differences, to be removed from public discourse. Benhabib argues, however, that a distinction between true and false needs is possible if needs are considered not to be individual impulses, but "fundamentally linguistic and social in character":

False needs would then be viewed as those aspects of inner nature which resist verbalization and articulation, leading instead to distorted communication and action. . . . Epistemically, we cannot say that *all* needs that permit linguistic articulation are true, but only that those which do *not* permit linguistic articulation cannot be true. (1986, 338)

I have argued at length elsewhere (Jakobsen 1995b) that this formulation addresses domination through practices of silencing but fails to address domination effected through inducements to speak in dominant terms. In other words, this model of "truth as articulation" fails to acknowledge the effects of the inducement to speak generally, in the terms already established as general. And, yet, as the examples of the past several chapters have shown, it is this inducement which is the motor for the dominant "economy of the same" that leads diversity to devolve into similarity. It is the inducement to articulate themselves in these already established terms that leads "lesbian, gay, and bi" movements to articulate themselves as mainstream and normal/normative. Thus, ultimately, Benhabib cannot sustain both her commitment to diversity and her commitment to adjudication in the terms of western rationalism.[192]

This failure raises a number of questions about reworking the normative relationship between the general and the particular. What if we were to maintain the tension between the concrete and the general, even at the point of diversity and conflict? Would, then, the norms that materialize particular bodies be general as well as particular public norms? I am not suggesting that we give up on the idea of the public, or of general norms, but rather that we should not give up on multiple, particular norms or their publicity by consigning them to a position in which they can be trumped by the general. Then, perhaps the problem with giving up on the framework which Benhabib finds necessary is not so much that we will be criterialess, but rather that we will have more criteria than we know what to do with. Thus, the hierarchy of the relation when the general slips to become the framework of the particular is subverted, and perhaps more importantly, this subversion opens the possibility of specifically social relations which do not require hierarchy to maintain their sociality. In other words, if the general need not subsume the particular in order to constitute society, then hierarchy is not necessary to the possibility of social relations. Moreover, the general is not a coherent site of unity, but rather the location of a network of (potentially contradictory) interrelations. This move dispenses with the necessity of containing or even denying contradiction for the sake of social relations, because if generalization is possible despite contradiction then so is sociality.

Benhabib enacts the slippage which resolves the tension between the general and the particular because without a framework of general norms we would be without determinative criteria at the point of moral diversity and conflict—the point at which she turns to adjudication. Are, however, the two central terms of this formulation—the need for a moral framework and the move to adjudication—the only, or even the best, possible understanding of and response to moral diversity and conflict? In "Gay Rights, Special Rights," the opposition between the two "minorities" establishes the space outside of and above their conflict at the site of the "normal," both in the sense of the norm, that which judges the others, and in the sense of unremarkable, that which is unmarked. The "minorities" then stand out as marked(ly) different from the norm, as different in a particular way, while the norm is not marked as particular. Similarly, it is this contrast between the unre-mark-able norm and the marked difference that presents western rationalism as a universal that is not also particular, while "other" universalisms are rarely recognized as universals at all. For example, while Benhabib considers multiple "universalistic ethical theories" within the European tradition (1986, 332) she nowhere considers Cannon's work or its (particular) universalism.

Assumptions about adjudication in relation to conflict are similarly problematic. The imposition of a single set of criteria is configured as the necessary and reciprocal response to violent conflict, and thus, the potential violence of this imposition is masked. Also masked are the ways in which the requirement/necessity of a singular framework may induce conflict, constituting individuals (whether persons or ethics) as holders of competitive claims to be adjudicated within that framework. The claim that individuals must submit to adjudication within a singular framework may itself incite violence as individuals prove unwilling to sacrifice sets of norms for the sake of the unifying demand of singularity.[193] Moreover, other possibilities for non-violent conflict resolution are masked. For example, the contemporary turn to mediation rather than adjudication in some civil disagreements indicates the ways in which adjudication does not provide the only means of conflict resolution. Competitive struggle within the singular framework of "the law" does not provide the only means of resolving disputes, and may not even provide the most non-violent means of so doing. In particular, mediation is a methodology which does not necessarily place the various "sides" to a given conflict within a singular overarching framework which provides for a single set of adjudicative criteria. Rather, mediation works in between the various sides of conflict. Agreement or acceptance is built in this space rather than enforced through the ordering power of the frame.

The question that remains is how power relations operate, and specifically, how to resist dominative power. Benhabib suggests that this resistance can only be effectively enacted through a normative commitment to egalitarianism, universalism, and consensualism which can "trump" other norms which might be the site of domination. Chantal Mouffe (1995) suggests alternatively that domination is resisted by the joining together of those who have less social power, while recognizing that social relations will always institute some asymmetrical forms of power and, thus, history and antagonism will never be completely "resolved."[194] Mouffe's alternative opens the door to recognition of the ways in which the norms that Benhabib lists as regulative are themselves historically implicated in relations of domination. It implies that resistance to domination is dependent not on norms alone, but on the constitution of relationships. Yet, because relationships are materialized by norms, to place the issue of power in its relational context is not to sever norms and power or create an ethical vacuum. It is to recognize that norms do not fulfill a function where they simply regulate power. Rather, norms are implicated in power just as power is implicated in norms.

In this configuration, the space in-between particular norms is not a space of moral impossibility, a normless vacuum which leaves room only for arbitrary "decisionism." Because this space is created specifically (rather than arbitrarily) between moral traditions, it is not a space of complete openness or unlimited proliferation, but simply the underdetermined space of relational possibility. It would be a completely arbitrary space only if the space "between" traditions were not also implicated in the space "within." The space of moral possibility is underdetermined because no tradition or normative matrix is completely closed off to any other, rather differences exist within, permeate and complicate the historical development of any tradition, and these differences within are connected to differences among, the without, outside, or external differences with which each tradition must interact. Connections and complications lead interactions to have effects within any tradition implicated in the interaction. If moral traditions were completely closed off from one another then alliances, except as confluences of interests, would be impossible. There would be no way to build connections among traditions or movements which internally implicated the movements with each other. Thus, social movements might stand shoulder to shoulder in the horizontal line-up of interests, but they would not be able to link arms to open themselves to connections where parts of one movement were inside "others." Movements would also be unable to form on-going relationships that could work to change the structure of the public in which they operated. As the examples from this chapter show, movements that do not form complex alliances are likely simply to advocate for their particular interests within the public.

The moral task in a social world marked by diversity and complexity is not necessarily to choose among particular ethics, but to work in the midst of diverse and complex norms and values. For example, the necessary relational work highlighted by resistance to the constructions of "Gay Rights, Special Rights" would be in and between lesbian, gay, bisexual, and transgender movements, movements for racial justice, and women's movements, work which would need to make visible those lives and bodies at the intersections and interstices of these constructions of social movement. Unfortunately, the politics of visibility pursued in the 1993 March on Washington, like the politics of autonomy described in chapter 2 is most likely to produce movement in which those "queers" who are least marked are also the most visible—white men. "Gay Rights, Special Rights" purposefully does not talk about women because to do so would undo the minoritizing move of the video and because of the binary investment that powerful white men have in their gay counterparts, who could be like them except for their sexuality. Within the logics of male dominance and white supremacy "these guys are everywhere" and they could take over. Although the March on Washington was undertaken in the name of "lesbian, gay, and bi" its politics of visibility plays out these same complicated dynamics of the marked and the unmarked. Assuming that "lesbian, gay, and bi" names an invisible minority that simply needs to be made visible in the context of a U.S. public in which unmarked white men are all that we see, means that privileged white men are likely to become the site of visibility for the movement, and the alliance named through the listing practice devolves to "gay." Thus, for the same reasons that Robin Morgan's assertion of autonomy for women's liberation in order to make sense within the U.S. public produced white women as the center of women's liberation, neither "Gay Rights, Special Rights," nor a "gay" politics of visibility makes visible to us anything but the narrowest range of queer women. Whether it is the tokenized white spokeswoman and the tokenized and eroticized few examples of bare-breasted women in "Gay Rights, Special Rights" or the mainstream white lesbians with a baby at the beginning of "Marching for Freedom," it is all too predictable that in a politics of visibility we won't see many women, and we almost definitely won't see women who are queer in any number of ways.

This predictably dominative outcome shows the need for a feminist politics which is both allied with and implicated within queer movements. The assumption that queer movement can proceed autonomously from feminist movement allows for a dis-articulation of particular power relations, among for example gender, race, and sexuality. Invocation of such a dis-articulated "queer" politics can materialize an unmarked and uncomplicated subject, a "queer" subject who is normal in all ways but sexuality. For example, despite the ways in which "queer" politics is supposed to create movement possibilities that were not tied to the constraints of identity indicated by "gay, lesbian, and bi," it is not clear that the enactment of "queer" movement is significantly more diverse in terms of race and class than the feminist theory presented in *Sisterhood is Powerful. Fear of a Queer Planet: Queer Politics and Social Theory* (Warner 1993), the anthology in which Warner makes his claim for the broad meaning of "queer," does present relative gender parity with articles by men only slightly outnumbering articles by women, but it presents only a "somewhat diverse" (Roof 1995) picture of race and class with one article on class and a few on race, and it demonstrates little diversity in terms of sexuality with no articles on bisexuality, transgender, or transsexual politics, or a broad conception of "sexual minorities." This re-iterative dis-articulation of diversity even under the name "queer" shows that work with the complexity of interrelations is necessary to realize the stated desire of queer politics to challenge not just hetero-normativity, but the various and multiple regimes of the "normal." The relationship between particular normative matrices and the "regime of the normal in general" would have to be reworked to accomplish the "broad" meaning of queer invoked by Warner (1993).

Yet, if feminist movement does not also recognize the ways in which queer politics can be implicated within women's movement, a similar dis-articulation can take place. Gender can be dis-articulated from sexuality so as to mystify the ways in which the hetero-sexist discourse of "Gay Rights, Special Rights" also constitutes male dominance—men represent both the general public and the primary threat to the public, once again rendering women publicly irrelevant. Thus, working to materialize feminist politics at a site where women are not particularly visible and gender is not the first axis of analysis and action is important not simply to address a potentially gender dominative politics of sexuality, but also to articulate an effective feminist politics. "Gender" is also reconceptualized as it is articulated in and through the analysis and activism. The meaning of gender is constituted in its relation to race and sexuality. Perhaps more importantly, a potentially queer feminist activism works to pull "gender" out of the binary context of the male-female opposition. In this sense, alliance politics changes the very basis of feminist movement. The primacy of a politics constituted as resistance to gender oppression becomes a politics dedicated not just to ending the domination of all women, but also all of the dominations that women face. The allied activism required by such a politics is resistant, in part, by shifting the very terms—"gender," "race," "sexuality"—through which both domination and resistance are articulated, meaning that the basis of feminist politics is itself moving. Social movement, if effective in making change, must also (repeatedly) change itself.

In so doing, counter-public movement can also remake the public within which it works, and as I have suggested, may even subvert the distinction between the "public" and its opposite, the "counter-public." In arguing for the need to rework the relationship between the general (public) and the particular (counter-public), the fundamental shift I am suggesting is from an understanding of the uses of norms as ultimately building a normative *framework* to one of building a *network* among diverse and complex sets of norms, bodies, and publics. The image of the network delineates several key conceptual features— the possibility of diversity which is simultaneously interrelation: the multiple centers of activity (sites) and various types of connections (links) among centers; the complexity of interrelation as various sites are linked in multiple non-linear ways; the ways in which working with any specific relationship or set of relationships invokes other relationships, sometimes unexpectedly; the potential of on-going contradiction as the links cross each other which can nonetheless be sustained by the network "as a whole"; the links (the spaces in-between) as of equal importance in forming the network as are the sites which are linked; the possibility of on-going gaps, openings, and spaces; the dynamic behavior of the network, the potential for mobility, the on-going possibility of making, changing, or undoing specific links/connections/relationships. Because of this dynamic quality, the model of a network also invokes the labor which is implied in social activity and, particularly in social movement and alliance building. Links among various sites of social activity and movement must be built, maintained, and addressed or changed over time. On this reading, norms don't provide a framework for moral decision making, they provide a network of moral possibilities. The social relations articulated by this network do not constitute spaces of complete freedom because norms in their materializing capacity are constraining as well as empowering. Neither, however, is moral possibility completely determined by a single method of framing which delimits all but the "right" action.

This shift from conceptualization of the "public" as a singular framework *within which* diverse communities interact to the connections *between* those communities which can be built in a variety of ways opens the door to a radical "plurality of subjects" and a "proliferation of radically new and different political spaces" (Laclau and Mouffe 1985, 181). Constituting the public through new relational forms also opens the door to new versions of moral diversity, specifically to the possibility of a *complex pluralism*, where diversity neither devolves to singularity, nor is maintained, as it is in liberal pluralism, as individual units of "difference." Rather, normative diversity is also the site of complex interrelation, and it is in these relationships between and among different normative traditions and enactments that the work of on-going critique and change, the production of new norms and values, takes place. Thus, the public sphere is not necessarily a single sphere of civil society in relation to a single nation-state. It is instead a network of public spaces connected to each other in various ways.[195] These various publics can relativize the role of the state, and they also relativize each other. No single person or group represents the "general public," but also no "particular" person or group is fully self-representative. Persons and groups as subjects of activity are constituted in relation to each other, and these relationships invoke various norms and values. The fear of this relativizing activity is that the various norms and values could incite conflicts that are not subject to resolution or at least not to non-violent resolution. Here the adjudicatory role of the state is presented as necessary. I have argued, however, that adjudication within the state is just one means of resolving conflict, and that it is not a site of non-violent conflict resolution, but is, rather, frequently appealed to precisely because it is the site of legitimated violence.[196] Because the state is a site where violence is central, social movements must continually question the forms of legitimation for that violence. Ultimately, the state does not form an all-encompassing framework for politics. The state then provides only one such site of democratic activity. What the relativization of multiple publics provides is sites of interaction, including conflict resolution, in addition to adjudication within the state. Yet, this interaction will not consist only of conflict resolution; rather conflicts at various sites must themselves be seen as part of the process of democratization among diverse and complex publics. Not all conflicts are violent, nor are conflicts simply disturbances to be resolved.[197] Rather, conflicts are productive of democracy.

In-Between Differences

The examples from this chapter show the dangers of a politics of "differences" where diverse "differences" and the normative economies which produce them are conceptualized as clearly distinct from one another. A politics of sexuality, lesbian or feminist or queer, that fails to articulate with an anti-racist politics opens the door to right-wing articulations which, in this case, connect the racism of some forms of lesbian and gay politics with a homophobic, anti-Semitic, and ultimately racist agenda. This example shows that the spaces produced between differences are very important political spaces where connections that determine the meaning of social relations can be made. It also shows that in order to work effectively in these spaces it is necessary to work with both categories of difference and the excesses of "*différance*," the difference which exceeds, but is also internal to a given category in the way that, for example, race exceeds but is also internal to sexuality or sexuality exceeds but is also internal to race. The mutually constitutive silence of the last chapter was indicative of the space between these two sites, between diversity within and diversity without, between difference and the *différance* that always accompanies differences. This complexity suggests the need for social movements to articulate spaces between movements without completely over-writing them. The attempt to fill the gaps completely would be an attempt to completely suture the social, to establish a permanent fixed set of relationships with a (single) determined meaning. The examples from this chapter show how this gap is a space of possibility. It is shaped by the production of those differences that constitute its boundaries, but it is also underdetermined, and thus open to activity that can fix relations among differences in a number of ways. "Gay Rights, Special Rights" worked in this space to establish a set of connections that serve a right-wing Christian agenda. Lesbian and/or feminist and/or womanist and/or queer activists might also work in these spaces to create a different set of connections, ones that challenge the current relations of production of differences as domination.

These gaps or openings are multiply located. They exist not only between the moral economies that produce differences, but also between the norm and its reiteration. Drucilla Cornell in "What is Ethical Feminism?" (Benhabib et al. 1995, 86) argues that feminism works in the gap between the cultural construction of "Woman" and the materializations of "women's" lives. The possible imaginings of women's lives, of their activisms, is limited by the construction of Woman, but this limit is not a complete determination. If it were, there would be no institution of social regulation and control. This gap is the space for iterations of women's activity, which are "original" in the sense of different. Cornell also suggests that the exposure of the limit of meaning is one possible strategy for expanding its boundaries. Because the boundary is a horizon of meaning it recedes as we move toward it: "As the boundary recedes, we have more space to dream and re-imagine our forms of life" (95).[198] Moreover, I would argue that this boundary is not a single boundary. Woman invokes a series of interrelated binaries, hierarchies and regulations which suggest that there is not a single, structural definition of the limit, gap, or space inbetween.[199]

Cornell's example points to the continuing need to work "in" as well as "between" norms and their materializations. Social movements are not working in a completely open social field, but are working in *and* between norms and materializations that both empower and constrain activism. For effective social movment, it is necessary to interrogate the particular forms of empowerment and constraint enacted through different normative matrices. To focus only on "between," to do away with "in," is once again to undercut both diversity and complexity. Such a move fails to recognize the particular materializations, the particular relations, that form the in-between and, thus, it loses sight of the particular differences and their complicating excesses with which movements must work. The complications between "differences" remain as reminders that these particular relations are produced through reiterative materializations and, thus, that they can change.

5 | Conclusion
Work-ing Alliances, Net-working Democracy

WHENEVER ONE THEORIZES about moral diversity the "question" of universalism or the "problem" of relativism is inevitably raised. The last two chapters have suggested that the question of universalism and relativism is not about a binary opposition, where the universal names that which is generally normative and the relative names norms which are particular to a specific group or locality. Chapter 3 suggests that universals may themselves be specific, developed in a particular location, and yet, simultaneously articulate universal claims. These particular universals are not necessarily "false universalism." After all stark relativism is itself based on the universal claim that universals are always false (Pfeil 1994, 224). Rather, the question is the relation between the particular and the universal and the implication of any given universal. Chapter 3 shows that Black womanist ethics is a specific ethics in relation to universal struggles, while chapters 3 and 4 suggest that western rationality is also a specific or particular universal, developed in a specific location, tied to a particular set of hopes and dreams, but dedicated to a universal equality and respect for all human beings. Those hopes and dreams have not been realized in modern social formations. Chapter 4 also suggests that the "problem" of relativism, the need for criteria to choose among ethics, may be misplaced; the moral question posed by diverse and complex ethics is not how to "choose" or to "judge" among them but how to work in and with that diversity and complexity.

The "problem" of relativism is often posed as if the fact that various ethics are relative to one another means that they are indistinguishable, they are all the same, equally valid and valuable and hence there is no way to choose among them. Chapter 4, however, suggests another possible interpretation of relativism. If norms or moral traditions are relative, they are relative to one another—relativism names a site of relation. Thus, I suggest that ethical relativism is about relational work in and among diverse ethics, including diverse universals. I am not suggesting that ethical universals should be eschewed, but I am suggesting that they be relativized, in other words that the intertwining of the universal and relative be recognized. My hope is twofold: 1) to challenge, through a reading of relativism as relationalism, the facile nature of the charge of relativism (a charge which is frequently made as if the term "relativism" required no specific explanation); and 2) through this re-reading, to challenge the usefulness of the opposition between universalism and relativism and, thereby, open the door to new understandings of universalism as well. Because the critique of relativism is the major critique of moral diversity, a critique which is maintained, albeit in different forms, by both conservative critics and progressive critics, it is necessary to first consider these concerns directly before moving on to reinterpretation.[200]

In her groundbreaking book *Moral Boundaries: A Political Argument for an Ethic of Care*, Joan C. Tronto (1993) argues in relation to Anthony Cortese's (1990) advocacy in *Ethnic Ethics: The Restructuring of Moral Theory* of " 'a pluralistic theory of moral development' " (Cortese 1990, 92, quoted in Tronto 1993, 94) that "two problems confront a simple claim for pluralism against the universalism boundary." In delineating the problems, Tronto succinctly lays out two sides of what is frequently articulated as the "problem of relativism":[201]

> First, to make a claim for moral pluralism sidesteps the difficult problem of relativism. If there are many sets of moral values, how does one decide among them? Second, and in some ways a related problem, to suggest the desirability of moral pluralism is to ignore the relative power of different moral conceptions. If the powerful maintain that moral universalism is the only true morality, then when subgroups call for moral pluralism they seem necessarily to be calling for the preservation of a lesser type of moral theory. (94)

Cortese, however, is not making a simple claim for pluralism. He is making a set of claims which advocate pluralism and question universalism, but which also question whether modern moral reasoning misses the most important aspects of moral life. He argues, "Relationships, not reason nor justice, are the essence of life and morality" (157). Tronto would certainly agree with this final point, but she believes that an ethics of care can incorporate universalism, whereas for Cortese, recognizing a substantive moral life, implies similarly recognizing moral pluralism.[202] Cortese comes to this conclusion by questioning a number of issues and assumptions which are crystallized in claims for ethical "universalism" through a history of the intertwining of ethical, social, and psychological theory from Kant through Durkheim, Marx, Weber, Piaget, and Kohlberg to Habermas.[203] Various characteristics—rationality, autonomy, and equality—are all invoked in modern claims for universalism. This configuration of issues works to manage a series of ambiguous meanings founded in fundamental splits—between subject and object, between the individual and society, between the individual as similarly equal to all other individuals and the individual as uniquely different from all others.[204] Thus, relativism, in the terms of contextualized pluralism advocated by Cortese, is read by critics as if it also invokes social determinism over against the freedom of agency. Heteronomy is opposed to autonomy, multiplicity to singularity, and, completing the circle, relativism to universalism.

This matrix is precisely the type of circular, loosely structured web of binary oppositions described by Catherine Bell (1992) as structuring a worldview based on hierarchies inscribed in the binaries. This worldview is itself a specific, historically produced ethical tradition, which as Bell suggests, appears within its own terms to be both natural and necessary, but outside the particular tradition or historical conditions is neither. Suggestions, like Tronto's, that it is necessary to rationally "decide" among moralities, work to protect the moral agent from heteronomy, to construct the agent as free from the determinism of arbitrary decisionism. Most importantly, the invocation of the necessity to "decide" operates to reinforce the entire set of binaries connected to universalism-relativism as necessary. Cortese argues alternatively, that the location of agency in rational decision-making attempts to make coherent a complex matrix of gaps and slippages between the social and the individual, freedom and determinism through a rationality which both constrains behavior and produces the supposedly autonomous individual, an individual who is simultaneously the subject of agency and subjected to the discourses through which she is produced. Both rationality and moral agency are not free from, but remain implicated in, the histories and contexts that produce them. Placing morality fully within the context of relationships does not do away with rationality, but it does shift the meaning of ethics and opens the door to contextualized pluralism, what I have termed a "complex pluralism."

Consider the second side of Tronto's criticism: "Second, and in some ways a related problem, to suggest the desirability of moral pluralism is to ignore the relative power of different moral conceptions. If the powerful maintain that moral universalism is the only true morality, then when subgroups call for moral pluralism they seem necessarily to be calling for the preservation of a lesser type of moral theory" (94). Tronto here assumes that "subgroups" will not be calling for moral universalism, an assumption which *Black Womanist Ethics* challenges. Yet, Tronto's claim can also be read as if moral pluralism in and of itself undermines the possibility of criticizing dominative power relations—if each plurality carries the same claim to "truth," then the critique of domination has no more claim to truth or legitimacy than the enactment of domination. The possibility that relativism undermines the critique of dominative power relations is one which a number of progressive critics take up. Yet, as Cannon's and Hoagland's texts show, the critique of domination can be carried out from particular perspectives and is perhaps most effective when those perspectives are allied.

The question is whether the critique of apolitical or politically ineffective pluralism that Tronto wants to make must turn only (and seemingly irresistibly) back toward some type of unity or universalism. For example, Fred Pfeil (1994) raises these same issues.[205] Pfeil's concerns are also laid out around two points of potential difficulty. The first is that persons and movements will be trapped *in* difference. He worries that the invocation of differences establishes unbridgeable chasms of difference, thus, reinforcing the inability to talk to, with, or about an-other. These chasms imply that those who place a primary value on "difference" will not be able to respond either ethically or politically to situations where difference is engaged. On the other hand, Pfeil is also concerned along with Nelly Richard (1987/88) that an uncritical postmodernism can accomplish this devolution by integrating the other back into a framework which absorbs all differences and contradictions, where "differences" lose any specificity and operate in the (undifferentiated) space of absolute difference. This concern reflects the loss of diversity if the space *between* differences is the only site of activity. For Pfeil unity and universalism appear necessary to address these problems. Thus, he quotes approvingly Sabina Lovibond's call for a unity that leads to the "eventual convergence with those of all other egalitarian or liberationist movements" (Lovibond 1989, 28, quoted in Pfeil 1994, 224). Does the call for eventual convergence fully articulate the complexity of relations "in-between"? If the spaces in-between difference and unity, relative and universal go unarticulated and, hence, ineffectively practiced, the potential to articulate an entire series of (complex) relational possibilities is lost.

Complicating Terms

Diversity can be variously articulated in relation to universalisms, and the complexity of these articulations delimits the possible political effects of the invocation of universal (or particular) norms. Andrée Nicola McLaughlin (1990), for example, suggests that Black women's "quest for human wholeness," is part of a universal resistance to domination based on the diversity of meanings of Black politics in the contemporary post-colonial situation. McLaughlin delineates the various meanings of Black politics and the differences among African-American, Afro-Caribbean, South Asian, and Black British "subjects" as just some of the pluralities necessary to common political struggle against domination. Alternatively, Joan Scott (1995) suggests that there are multiple (at least two) universalisms—universalisms which are both contradictory and interdependent—operating within the enlightenment universalism historically constituted through the French Revolution and French republicanism. The universal equality of individuals which republicanism claimed to be predicated upon, but which was simultaneously the product of republicanism, intertwined with notions of the universality of difference. Because the very meaning of the "individual" was based on the differentiation of one "individual" from another, "individuality required the very difference that the idea of the proto-typical human individual was meant to deny" (3–4). This difference, which abstract individualism simultaneously depended upon and denied, could be used to exclude those marked as different from the "universal" rights of citizenship.[206]

Claims for the singularity of modern universalism are also made through a narrative of historical "progression" (that matches a supposed logical progression) in which all universalisms "other" than the "one" universalism of modern rationalism are located simply as traditions over against modernity. Here tradition is assumed to precede and be superseded by modernity.[207] This progress narrative is, then, one means of eliding the complexity of the relationship between universal and relative as well as modernity and tradition. Naomi Schor (1995) argues, however, "speaking from a strictly logical perspective, particularity does not always *precede* universalization. . . . what appears to be a prior cause (i.e., particularity) is in fact a subsequent effect" (22, emphasis in original). On this reading particularity is not prior to and superseded by universalism, but rather, particularity is produced by the need of universalism to distinguish itself. Moreover, the examples from the various chapters of this book, show the historical relationships among "traditions," including modern universalism, to be variable. So, for example, Black womanist ethics is a tradition which draws on historical elements preceding modernity (in terms of African "survivals"), elements in critical relation to modernity (the critique of capitalism), and non-modern elements co-temporal with modernity (the specific universalism of the struggle for human wholeness as articulated by the Black Church). Lesbian ethics, alternatively, can be conceptualized as reversing the order of relation. If one accepts the argument that gay and lesbian "identity" developed out of the modern period, lesbian ethics is a tradition which proceeds from (and supersedes?), rather than preceding, modernity. Linda Zerilli (1993) suggests that it is the work of lesbian theorist Monique Wittig precisely to write lesbians into the space of the universal as "the trojan horse of universalism."[208] The move on the part of Wittig to write lesbians into the universal is so powerful, as was Sojourner Truth's similar move to speak herself into the universal, because Wittig and Truth do not simply draw on the tradition of modern universalism, working simply to expand the already existent universal to include them within its normative boundaries, so that the universal continues to subsume the particular. As Schor points out, while Wittig's universal is claimed in relation to traditions of French thought, in claiming the specifically lesbian as the site of the universal, it challenges the traditional construction of French universalism which Scott argues is based on a masculinity which in its monogamous heteronormativity is contrasted to "primitive" cultures and, thus, secures French imperialism. Thus, Wittig challenges the normative shape of the universal, moving it to new locations and complicating the relationship between the universal and the particular.[209] These examples show that the relations between traditions and modernity are not structured by historical development, but by historical and contemporary conflict and on-going relational possibility. Modernity does not contain the conflicts of various particular traditions within its frame, but is rather a participant in conflict. The shape of the space in-between traditions and modernity and the work which it allows will determine in what ways this conflict is productive.

In sum "relativism" is a problem because it assumes that any moral configuration other than modern universalism leaves a pluralism in which all moral claims carry equal value. An alternative to either this liberal (in its most conservative sense) pluralism or modern universalism can be constructed by reworking the meaning of "relative." To be "relative" is not to be the "same," but to "have a connection or be pertinent to," "to result from or depend on a relation," to be "intelligible only in relation to," "to refer to, relate to or qualify" (Funk and Wagnells). Thus, for norms and values to be relative is not for all norms and values to be the same or equal, but for them to exist in relation to other norms and values, just as I have suggested modern universalism exists in relation. In this sense, relativism is not a problem, but the context of moral activity. This context appears to be a "problem" because autonomous individualism has a "problem" with relationships which threaten to determine it, to leave the individual in the grip of socially determined multiplicity (heteronomy). I would suggest, however, that to locate morality in relationships opens rather than determines moral possibilities. Relationships among diverse and complex persons and communities create possibilities for critique of existing social relations, for the knowledge that life could be otherwise, for the possibility of change. Yet, these possibilities are not the straightforward actions of the autonomous individual, the determinations of a completely free will. Rather, they are always the complex possibilities of moral agents working in the context of relationships.

Articulating morality through complexity opens moral possibilities, in part, because the more connections among specific social units, the more complex the interactions, and the more complex the interactions the more opportunities for freedom.[210] Because complexity challenges the containment of diversity within clearly bounded "units" it frees space for various interactions beyond the bounds of such containment. Thus, complexity provides an important alternative starting point for the theorizing of freedom and democracy. In contrast to liberal economic and political theory where freedom is located precisely in the separation of clearly bounded individuals, in freedom from attachments, this view suggests that freedom can be located in the complexities of interrelation. Placing complexity at the center of analysis implies that solidarity rather than identity is constitutive of public life and that diversity and its accompanying complexity can be the source of (rather than threats to) public activity and democracy. This possibility suggests that working political alliances, rather than simply being the result of brokered interests among individual units of activity, can become sites which transform particular needs and interests and reconstitute the "public" (Benhabib 1992, Fraser 1989). Craig Calhoun (1993) argues for "taking difference seriously while trying to avoid relativism and speak generally" (41). If, however, relativism is relationalism, is the sets of relation in, between, and among different sites of ethical and political activity, then relativism is not opposed to the generality which is supposed to define the public sphere, but is in fact the very discourse through which publicity is built, while *différance* remains the limit to that publicity, the horizon which reminds us that no relationship can ever be fully articulated and, thus, the public can never be closed. Democratic contestation will always be necessary, and the ground of the public is the risky ground of decision in the face of ultimate undecidability.

Complexity, Alliance, and the Public

Complexity may provide a means of moving between the two poles which I have thus far considered in the terms of ethics—universalism and relativism. Some version of these poles also appears in theories of alliance politics or coalition formation. In her book *Justice and the Politics of Difference*, Iris Marion Young (1990) argues that justice entails a "heterogeneous public and group representation" (183).[211] While Young argues for "the justice of recognizing both specific needs of a group and rights of full participation and inclusion in the polity," she also identifies two poles of possibility for the question of how to accomplish the equality entailed in justice: "Those seeking social equality disagree about whether group-neutral or group-conscious policies best suit that goal and their disagreement often turns on whether they hold an assimilationist or culturally pluralist ideal. . . . I argue for the justice of group-conscious social policies" (173). This choice is detailed in Young's description of an ideal coalition:

> The idea of a Rainbow Coalition expressed a heterogeneous public with forms of group representation. The traditional coalition corresponded to the idea of a unified public that transcends particular differences of experience and concerns. In traditional coalitions diverse groups work together for specific ends which they agree interest or affect them all in a similar way, and they generally agree that the differences of perspective, interests, or opinion among them will not surface in the public statements and actions of the coalition. This form ideally suits welfare-state interest-group politics. In a Rainbow Coalition, by contrast each of the constituent groups affirms the presence of the other as well as the specificity of their experience and perspective on social issues. In the Rainbow public Blacks do not simply tolerate the participation of gays, labor activists do not grudgingly work alongside peace movement veterans, and none of these paternalistically concede to femi-

nist participation. Ideally, a Rainbow Coalition affirms the presence and supports the claims of each of the oppressed groups or political movements constituting it, and arrives at a political program not by voicing some "principles of unity" that hide difference, but rather by allowing each constituency to analyze economic and social issues from the perspective of its experience. This implies that each group maintains significant autonomy, and requires provision for group representation. Unfortunately, the promise of the Jesse Jackson campaign to launch a viable grassroots organization expressing these Rainbow Coalition ideals has not been fulfilled. (188–89)

There is, however, in Young's articulation of a heterogeneous public and group representation, no articulation of the complexity within and among groups. In her description of the Jackson campaign's instantiation of the Rainbow Coalition, Young eschews principles of unity and promotes groups' autonomy within the coalition but offers no description of what links them together as a coalition, nor of how their interrelation affects group or identity formation within the coalition. In this coalition, "Blacks" work with, they "do not simply tolerate" the presence of, "gays," yet, Young's description does not articulate how they work together, or how they challenge the interstice constituted by naming the autonomous groups "Blacks" and "gays." This interstice is produced and maintained precisely through a politics of difference or diversity that does not adequately articulate its correlative complexity. Thus, finally Young does not analyze why the Rainbow Coalition could not fulfill its promise. Once, again we are left with a call for (in this case) coalition politics which does not fully account for its historical failure (it is simply "unfortunate"). Specifically, Young's reading does not account for how persons and groups become "allies." Thus, Chantal Mouffe is critical of Young's description of coalition because it "is still conceived as a process of dealing with already-constituted interests and identities" (1992, 380) and, thereby, does not fully challenge the relations of production of "difference." If difference is produced as hierarchy and domination, then justice can never be achieved without changing these relations. As I have argued, persons and groups become allies through the activity of working in and through alliances. This constitutive process of alliance formation in which allies do not precede, but are rather the product of, alliances implies that individual and group identities do not necessarily dissolve but do change in becoming allies. Alliances fail, in part, because the work required by this process, the work of constructing (our)selves as allies in the spaces in-between identifications, is not adequately theorized.

Ernesto Laclau and Chantal Mouffe (1985) contribute by theorizing articulations, the connections between movements that are both necessary to sustain alliance or coalition and that partially fix the meaning of activisms which are otherwise underdetermined. "Gay Rights, Special Rights" is, in part, a contest over the meaning of civil rights struggle. Whether civil rights struggle is articulated as "minority protections" or "social justice for all" depends on whether civil rights is articulated with capitalist individualism or other struggles for social justice. If the meaning of (not special) "rights" is connected to capitalist individualism, then any rights claimed in relation to group oppression are special protections. If, however, the meaning of rights is articulated as fundamentally about social (not individual) justice, then civil rights legislation is about equal, not special rights. Ed Meese works to fix the meaning of rights in the former sense by locating legitimate rights as the purview of the unmarked individual. The analysis in chapter 4 suggests that his articulation is possible, in part, by dis-articulating connections among issues that civil rights legislation addresses, and that social movements could more effectively work to fix the meaning of rights in the latter sense by making connections among both issues and movements. Moreover, Laclau and Mouffe recognize that making connections not only shifts the meaning of activisms, but also the identities of moral and political actors. For example, I have suggested that connecting anti-racist and anti-homophobic movement shifts and complicates the meaning of "lesbian community" and, hence, of "lesbian" in lesbian ethics described by Hoagland.

Laclau and Mouffe identify two poles around which contemporary politics works—autonomy and hegemony—poles which materialize the logics of difference and equality. Mouffe (1995) summarizes as follows:

> Between the project of a complete equivalence and the opposite one of pure difference, the experience of modern democracy consists in acknowledging the existence of those contradictory logics as well as the necessity of their articulation: articulation that constantly needs to be recreated and renegotiated, since there is no final point of equilibrium where a final harmony could be reached. It is only in that precarious space "in-between" that pluralist democracy can exist. (43)[212]

Despite their focus on the connections between movements and activisms, Laclau and Mouffe spend very little time theorizing the space in-between autonomy and hegemony, which they identify as a space of "alliance" (141), in part because they use the narrow definition of alliance as only based on "given interests" (184). While they recognize that movements based on autonomy, alliance, and hegemony are all politically necessary, they value hegemony because it creates a new reality, a new "common sense" which partially fixes meaning for all the different elements of a social formation and, thus, (momentarily) secures a progressive meaning to the various terms (now moments): "For, nothing can consolidate anti-racist struggle more than the construction of stable forms of overdetermination among such contents as anti-racism, anti-sexism and anti-capitalism which, left to themselves, do not necessarily tend to converge" (141). Thus, Laclau and Mouffe argue for the formation of a new "common political identity" as the ideal outcome of articulatory practices. Mouffe later defends the need for this "common identity," because "The political community, as a surface of inscription of multiplicity of demands where a 'we' is constituted requires the correlative idea of a common good, but a common good conceived as a 'vanishing point,' a 'horizon of meaning,' something to which we must constantly refer but which can never be reached" (1995, 36).[213]

Is, however, convergence and commonality the most useful conceptualization of the matrix which would materialize the type of social formation that they invoke as connecting "anti-racism, anti-sexism, and anti-capitalism?" Mouffe (1995) is herself critical of Habermas's "regulative ideal of free unconstrained communication" as "something that far from providing the necessary horizon of the democratic project, in fact, puts it at risk. . . . Any understanding of pluralism whose objective is to reach harmony is ultimately a negation of the positive value of diversity and difference" (44). The question is whether convergence and commonality are a necessary horizon, or whether they also ultimately operate to negate the positive value of diversity. At the very least, the focus on convergence leaves under-theorized the space "in-between," the space in which we currently work. It is unclear, for example, whether the various aspects of articulated movements must be grounded in a common sense or whether the network of connections can enable movements to work together without a common sense. The question is whether a common political identity or a hegemony will be able to protect diversity as Laclau and Mouffe intend, holding together in tension the poles of difference and equivalence. They wish to challenge the relations of production that currently produce "differences" and instead advocate a politics that shifts and reworks and remakes identities from those differences. But, what of the correlative complexity that accompanies diversity? Is a new "common" political identity the only possible site of a politically progressive and radically democratic "we"?

Laclau and Mouffe argue specifically that connections among multiple movements are made through a logic of equivalence. Equivalence works through the displacement of norms from one site of struggle to another. In the "equivalential-egalitarian logic" the norm of equality is displaced from its initial site identified by Laclau and Mouffe as the European democratic revolution—equality among citizens—to other sites of democratizing movement. So, for example, Mary Wollstonecraft "displaced [democratic discourse] from the field of equality between citizens to the field of equality between the sexes" (154). Gender subordination which was legitimate before the displacement is, through this activity, made illegitimate; women are claimed to be equal to men, just as all citizens are equal to each other. This move also makes social movements equivalent to one another. If women are equal to men just as citizens are equal to one another, then women are also equal to citizens and the movements for democracy (equality for citizens) and women's rights (equality for women) are equivalent. For Laclau and Mouffe, it is on the basis of this equivalence that links among movements can be established, giving the logic of equivalence its power in articulating a progressive meaning for social movements: "For the defence of the interests of the workers not to be made at the expense of the rights of women, immigrants or consumers, it is necessary to establish an equivalence between these different struggles" (1985, 184).

The power of claiming equivalence is evident in the social movements—feminist, civil rights, human rights—which have time and again been founded upon it.[214] In practice the logic of equivalence has allowed claims for equality and rights to circulate among movements, but it has not been fully effective in connecting movements. As I argued in chapter 2, white feminist movements in the 1970s used the claim to equivalence as Laclau and Mouffe suggest, to displace the "equivalential-egalitarian" logic onto the terrain of gender relations. This displacement was used to extend equality to "women," to make "women's liberation" a topic of political movement, and to establish a (relatively) autonomous feminist movement. Yet, in part because it was a displacement of the logic of other movements, "women's liberation" failed through this move to (re)connect to the movements—civil rights and socialist or left—whose logic it displaced. The displacement that allowed the formation of autonomous movement simultaneously dis-articulated the work of persons whose work was articulated in more than one movement. Claiming equivalence did not make equivalent movements, nor did it connect movements to each other.

Laclau and Mouffe argue for the ideal of a radical and plural democracy, claiming that the norm of equality and the norm of liberty are mutually limiting terms, and thus, that the logic of equivalence must always be limited by a logic of autonomy: "[T]otal equivalence never exists; every equivalence is penetrated by a constitutive precariousness, derived from the unevenness of the social. To this extent, the precariousness of every equivalence demands that it be complemented/limited by the logic of autonomy" (184). Simply limiting equivalence by autonomy does not, however, articulate the complexity of relations among movements.[215] It does not fully theorize the complex space of relationship in-between autonomy and equivalence, the space of alliance. What type of links are necessary to connect movements in a radical and plural democracy, to articulate (in both senses of the word) the ways in which movements are both equivalent and remain different? It also fails to articulate the multiplicity of norms (in addition to equality and liberty) or "social logics" which are implicated in these relationships.[216] Thus, it fails to articulate relations among movements that do not trace their tradition (of norms and activities) to the (European) democratic revolution in the same way that Laclau and Mouffe do. As the examples from the chapters show, the logic of European democracy is not the only logic which can circulate as part of articulatory practices. In chapter 3, for example, womanist and lesbian ethics/movements could be connected around the (different) critiques of western individualism that each offers.

By further theorizing the space of alliance it may be possible to articulate links among movements that are not constituted by the logic of equivalence. Such a move also opens the door to forms of political identity and movement that can be constituted between autonomous differences and a common identity.[217] In this sense, connections can be distinguished from commonality, so that while articulatory practices, the practices that produce connections, open the door to shifts in identities (and differences) they do not necessarily produce commonality. Articulations produce the possibility for shifting identities, but by being articulated these identities do not necessarily form a common political identity.[218]

Nonetheless, because a common political identity is often held to be ideal or, if not ideal, to be necessary for political effectiveness, the shift away from unity is experienced as a loss. Naomi Schor, for example, describes the loss she finds as feminism has moved away from understanding itself as a movement founded in relation to commonality: "Now while some would argue that this commonality never existed except as a (false) universalism, I would argue that such a commonality, however contested, however limited in its geopolitical sphere of application, did exist in the early days of feminism and did make possible some of its greatest gains" (28).[219] She emphasizes the loss experienced in the shift away from this commonality as a loss of the ability of women to speak as the universal (relegating them forever and unnecessarily to the particular), and she also hopes to reinstate the hope of universalist movement with a "new" rather than "old" universalism. Schor articulates this hope by (re)articulating a series of issues that could be connected as "necessitating" a new feminist universal: "Determining what might constitute a specifically feminist universal for our time—which would, it appears, have something to do with a certain freedom of determination by women regarding what is done to their bodies (rape, sati, clitoridectomy, enforced sterilization, and enforced reproduction are some of the dubious practices that come to mind as necessitating a feminist universal to be combated)—presents a far more daunting challenge" (41). This is a complicated claim.[220] The list works to specify the conditions "necessitating a feminist universal," and it achieves the type of displacement which Laclau and Mouffe describe as claims to equivalence, where bodily integrity or lack of bodily integrity (rather than inequality) is the term of equivalence. Such movement has been powerful and has led to gains for feminist movement. Certainly, for example, second-wave U.S. feminist movements to resist violence against women have been extremely powerful and made important gains—battered women's shelters, rape crisis intervention, women's self-empowerment, sexual abuse survivors movements. And, yet, attempts to make these issues the issues of equivalence—the issues which all women share and which therefore form a basis of unity—led not to commonality, but to a splintering along a number of vectors, including across race and class lines, and in the (themselves sometimes violent) battles termed the "sex wars" (Jakobsen 1995a). Schor's list also exhibits the problems of such claims to equivalence. Schor is suspicious of some French feminist claims to universalism because "it is deeply informed by the particularity of French universalism and its ingrained inhospitability to differences" (41), an inhospitability tied to the history of colonialism and imperialism, and yet, this list is tied to precisely the same history.[221] Part of the problem here is the direction of displacement as it establishes movement from rape, thus constituted as the "center," to sati the "margin" made equivalent to the center. A certain type of power *is* lost by shifting from commonality to diversity and complexity, and for those women whose lives and issues are/were articulated by any given commonality, this loss would be a displacement from a center of power to the margins of that center. But, de-centering is not always dis-empowerment. As, Laclau and Mouffe argue, displacement can be a means of articulating power relations in new ways. I am suggesting that through alliances based not on commonality, but on diversity and complexity, other centers of power can be built, sometimes through displacements which work in different directions than the chains of equivalence described by either Laclau and Mouffe or Schor.

Diversity and complexity work in the space in between Young's description of a politics of difference where the differences are already given and simply need to be represented and Laclau and Mouffe's ideal of a common political identity constituted through chains of equivalence. Diversity articulated in and through complexity addresses the space of interrelation between the two poles. Complexity recognizes how identities and differences are constituted through relational activity and, thus, how they shift and change as a result of interaction. Complexity is a language that can also articulate the unevenness of the social. Inderpal Grewal and Caren Kaplan (1994) suggest that under contemporary conditions where the social is not either fully modern or fully post(modern) "The question becomes how to link diverse feminisms without requiring either equivalence or a master theory" (19). Thus, they argue for "scattered hegemonies" as a way to describe the openings and inconsistences in the social which are "the effects of mobile capital as well as the multiple subjectivities that replace the European unitary subject" (7). These multiple subjectivities must be engaged if alliances are to be formed. Yet, if the rainbow coalition or any other alliance is to sustain itself for any period of time, it must also be able to articulate the links which can be constituted in-between these differences. The process of building these links will undoubtedly shift the meanings and norms of different traditions, and yet, the telos of a new common identity can threaten to write over the spaces and gaps in-between which are precisely the sites of alliance building. Thus, links can be built only by engaging the complexities of diversity and the limits of *différance* within, between, and among traditions and movements.

The focus on links between movements and subjects suggests a correlative shift in focus away from the search for community which has frequently marked both feminist movement(s) and theories.[222] Neither community nor the solidarity of collective action can be located in either a pre-existing common identity or in an overarching normative framework that holds together (contains within it) various differences. Iris Marion Young (1994) in her more recent work on "gender as seriality" suggests the need for conceptualizing "women" as the subject of feminist movement at different levels of relation. For example, by "gender as seriality," Young means women as an "amorphous collective" defined by "the fact that in their diverse existences and actions they are oriented around the same objects or practico-inert structures" (728). "Practico-inert structures" refers to a sedimented history of the production of gender difference. Feminist movement, however, is a grouping of women, specifically "in order to change or eliminate the structures that serialize them as women" (736). These distinct levels of collectivity show that the solidarity of feminist movement does not depend on, nor is its goal necessarily the creation of, a community of all women. Feminist movement may refer to the serial collective of women, but this collective is not an all-encompassing community. It is, rather, a series of subject positions created by relations and histories of the production of gender difference and resistances to that production. Young concludes, "This is why feminist politics must be coalition politics" (737).

The point of theorizing these different levels of connection is to dis-articulate solidarity from community and from identity. While community may be a result of solidarity, it is not a necessary pre-requisite to nor telos of movement. Analogously, solidarity does not depend on identity, nor is identity the necessary product of movement solidarity. Moreover, if a serial collective, a collection of locations in social histories which are also potential sites of identificatory practices is the referent for movement, then a specific identity is not necessary to the activity that is movement. Thus, what is required for movement is not an overarching community or a pre-existent identity, but action which creates articulations, which makes connections. Here we find the power of Ada María Isasi-Díaz's now famous statement (as quoted by Susan Thistlethwaite 1989, 25):

> In a lecture at Chicago Theology Seminary, Ada María Isasi-Díaz was asked by a black woman in the audience, "How can women of color trust white women?" She replied that she had learned to trust white women who would "cover your back."

Isasi-Díaz is emphasizing relational action, not consensus, understanding, or shared community or identity as the basis of political alliance.[223]

The connections, the spaces in-between, not the ground or frame, then, become the crucial sites for the action of making movement. These spaces can also be the site to de-stabilize normative regulation. While norms materialize identities and communities, the spaces in-between complicate and challenge the claims to coherence of norms, traditions and their materializations. For example, alliances can complicate the relationships among norms of "equality, liberty, solidarity," or "universalism, consensualism, egalitarianism," by placing these lists in relation to the "struggle for human wholeness," or "autokoenony." These complications re-make traditions and produce new values without necessarily re-solidifying, permanently fixing, a new normative tradition or establishing once and for all the value that is a "common good." Complications remain, as does diversity. Alliances shift locations and interests, and these shifts produce complicated and boundary-blurring relationships. Thus, alliances can do the work of pulling persons and groups out of their specific interests and identities and into newly articulated meanings and positions, while simultaneously maintaining commitments to and materializations of diversity and complexity.

Agency as Alliance, Alliance as Agency

In the past several chapters, I have argued against the logic of political movement that makes the formation of autonomous movement primary to the establishment of alliances. The assumption that an autonomous movement will precede alliance is part and parcel of the western logical assumption that singularity is the origin of diversity and of the enlightenment assumption that autonomy is the basis of moral agency. I have argued that diverse women's movements and activities preceded an "autonomous" predominantly white, middle-class, and heterosexual women's suffrage or women's liberation movement. It is this precedence which explains the diversity of *Sisterhood is Powerful*, the collection of which precedes the writing of the Introduction. I have also argued that diversity precedes autonomy in the sense that women and social movements are constituted in and through multiplicity. Singularity comes out of and remains intertwined with diversity, and the task of feminist ethics is to learn to work with this diversity and its accompanying complexity at the level of norms and values.

On this reading, alliance becomes the primary site for the construction of both moral agency and political effectiveness, thus, fundamentally shifting the site of agency from autonomy to alliance. Alliance is agency because that which both incites and enables agency is fundamentally relational. Engagement with "others" can create the initial disjunctions which form the incitement to agency, the desire to move toward an alternative future. Such disjunction opens the door to reworking a given moral tradition in its relationships to others and the normative matrices that it engages.[224] The realization of any alternative future is further dependent on relationships to effectively materialize it. For example, Angelina Grimké was moved to leave her Southern home, not simply because of high moral ideals, but, in part, because her engagement with others in the context of witnessing the brutality of punishment meted out to slaves created a disjunction with the gentile mores of her race and class position, opening up for her the possibility that there was something morally wrong with her own society. Yet, her ability to act in relation to this disjunction and her eventual production of moral agency as an abolitionist was dependent on relationships at a number of points. It was only through the opportunity to participate in Quaker communities and to join Sarah in Philadelphia and then to form alliances with African Americans that she was able to effectively act in relation to this opening and work for abolition. She was only able to act on the initial disjunction when she participated in a community that formed her as an ally, and some of the limits of this community formation also established her limits to be fully effective as an ally—the limits set by the "chord of prejudice" in white abolitionist movement.

Thus, the process of subject formation, of developing agency, also depends on others, on alliances. So, for example, second-wave feminist agency often developed out of "consciousness-raising groups" where the process of women coming together to discuss their situations as specifically social situations enabled individual women to change and feminist movements to form. Nelle Morton (1985) has termed this process "hearing into speech" in order to indicate the formation of (an individual woman's) speech as based on the social act of hearing (rather than an individual speaking the pre-existent truth-of-the-self which the group then "heard"). Agency is also constituted relationally, as a multiplicity, not as a unity. In this case, agency is constituted through solidarity that connected women's stories into social movement(s). Solidarity, thus, provides a way of constituting agency on the basis of diversity, so that both agency and diversity can be maintained. In choosing this way, the possibility of change and critique is located in several (diverse) places, thus, undercutting the narrative of a singular path to liberation, but also opening new opportunities for resistance and change that do not depend on access to such a path.[225]

The primacy of alliance is often resisted because it is supposed to be ineffective—complex and cumbersome, lacking clarity (Lugones 1994), and difficult to materialize. And, yet, the arguments of this book indicate that it is precisely those practices dedicated to unity and clarity, or to diversity without complexity, that can make U.S. social movements ineffective in their stated goals. Such practices, for example, led 1970s feminism to be unable to sustain alliance with civil rights movements, made contemporary lesbian and gay politics open to the right-wing appropriation of "Gay Rights, Special Rights," and led feminist movement to founder on its inability to represent women. In each of these cases, problematic practices within movement led to an inability to form working alliances. Autonomous or coherent subject formation is often seen as the key to both moral agency and the possibility of social movements. As Cannon, Hoagland, and feminist theorists like Sharon Welch (1990) and Catherine Keller (1986) have pointed out, the assumption connecting autonomy and agency is itself tied to capitalist norms and an ethics of control. Thus, they suggest that a moral agency that effectively challenges these dominative norms must be grounded in relationships. The last several chapters have similarly suggested that the assumption connecting autonomy and movement is tied to the moral economy which produces the general public, and hence autonomous movement may only be effective in reiterating the general norm. Alternatively, connections or articulations among movements may be the key to reworking the "public" effectively. Thus, those who argue that a coherent identity is necessary for either moral agency or political effectiveness, who argue, for example, that "women" must constitute a coherent unit for feminist movement to be effective, miss the ways in which alliance is the basis of agency.[226] Diversity does not undercut agency, it complicates it.[227]

The shift I am suggesting is not just that solidarity stands at a site between the two poles of "unity" (understood as coherence) and "diversity" (understood as unrelated differences), but also that solidarity shifts the site of agency away from identity and to alliance. At the end of his essay, for example, Pfeil suggests solidarity as a "way *through* difference" (225, emphasis in original), and he appeals to working together as the practice of constituting this solidarity. In this alternative understanding, solidarity is the precondition for an "I" who can work with others. The "I" who is an ally becomes so only in and through the process of working together ("with others"). Pfeil is here referring to some of his own experiences of working with alliances. My own education in alliance politics took place doing anti-apartheid work at the Washington Office on Africa. It was this work in a multi-racial, multi-national alliance that produced me as an ally. Thus, for example, before working at the Washington Office on Africa, "I" had absolutely no knowledge which was useful to "my" South African allies. It was only in and through working with them that the knowledge which I had (previously), for example, of white church-going constituencies *became* knowledge useful to them ("the others I work with").

In returning to the question I raised in the Introduction of producing "I" and "we" as subjectivities that name allies and alliances, the process that makes it possible for "us" to be allies, begins not with the assertion of an autonomous "I" who can then join a "we," or with a particular "I" who is subsumed by a general "we." Rather, the production of "ourselves" as allies begins with the sets of interrelations within which we work and is enabled through the process of building particular sets of relationships. Thus, it is the articulations, the sets of relationships, that determine the possibilities for any given subjectivity, "I" or "we." For example, the production of a feminist movement that could challenge the sexism of left movements in the 1970s can be read as a process of shifting alliances, rather than as a process of asserting autonomy. Toni Cade reports such a shift as the move that enables Black women's struggles for liberation: "What characterizes the current movement of the 60's is a turning away from the larger society and a turning toward each other. Our art, protest, dialogue no longer spring from the impulse to entertain, or to indulge or enlighten the conscience of the enemy; white people, whiteness, or racism; men, maleness, or chauvinism; America or imperialism . . . depending on your viewpoint and your terror. Our energies now seem to be invested in and are in turn derived from a determination to touch and to unify. What typifies the current spirit is an embrace, an embrace of the community and a hardheaded attempt to get basic with each other" (7). Thus, the subject of liberation is not pregiven, but is formed through the process of building particular relationships, and as Cade's list indicates such relational work, even if focused on a subject named singularly as "the community," always invokes diversity and complexity. Any such singular is built up out of and remains constituted by the relational plural.

The question in making alliances the subject of agency is how to understand this multiplicitous subjectivity. Amy Mullin suggests five methods of responding to multiplicity in the self, a multiplicity which is in part fueled by the diverse and contradictory norms, which the "self" embodies.[228] Mullin names four of the methods as "assimilation, compartmentalization, toleration and negotiation" (1995, 10). Interestingly, she does not name the fifth alternative, the one that she advocates. She does describes it as "the possibility in which confrontation, dialogue, and self-examination can lead to change in each aspect of the self" (9). Mullin provides a critique of each of the first four methodologies. Assimilation works to eradicate differences through hierarchical power relations that subsume or even eliminate those qualities deemed less good, central, or essential. Compartmentalization tends to assume that all "units" of difference are themselves coherent or homogeneous wholes, leading to the potential for a never-ending fragmentation. Toleration can accompany compartmentalization where each part manages its co-existence with the others, precisely by limiting contact and interaction among parts. Negotiation opens the door for interaction among the parts. It allows for commitment to a process of interaction, a commitment which enables ethical responsibility without the need to control the outcome through the institution of "one stable center of command, one voice with the final say" (18) (or in Benhabib's terms, one overarching set of criteria). For Mullin, the problem with negotiation is that it depends on pregiven, in some sense coherent, if not homogeneous, entities to participate in the negotiation.[229] Mullin argues instead that a version of multiplicitous persons formed in and through social interaction is more helpful.

My suggestion of a name for Mullin's fifth option is "alliance." Alliance involves response-ability, contestation, and negotiation, but it is not fully articulated by any of these interactions. If even individual subjects of agency are formed from alliances, then alliance invokes not the coherent units of difference(s), but the complexity of relationships at the intersections of normative matrices. So, for example, the relationships between anti-racist and anti-homophobic movements described in chapters 3 and 4 are not negotiations between two clearly separate and bounded movements. The assumption of such separation fuels the iconography of "Gay Rights, Special Rights," that claims "people of color" are straight and "gays" are white men. If people of color names an alliance that, for example, connects but does not conflate race and ethnicity, that includes gay, lesbian, bisexual, and transgender people and an alliance like "queers" connects, but does not conflate, radical sexualities and people of various races and ethnicities, then a much more complicated picture than that named simply by "negotiation" arises.

Complexity means that alliance is not the complete undoing of autonomy any more than it is the complete enactment of hegemony. Alliance is not the conflation of identities, as, for example, in the conflation lesbian-feminism which developed out of Johnston's initial attempts to ally women's and gay liberation, but led to the subsumption of lesbians under feminism that Hoagland resists with her (re)assertion of lesbian autonomy. Movement back and forth between autonomy and alliance will persist. Because alliance is located both in and between "identities" and "differences," it does not necessitate the abandonment of autonomy for alliance, but rather demands the maintenance of complexity. In the Introduction I mentioned the need for Women's Studies programs to engage with sites that exceed the boundaries of the category "women" if they are to fully engage the diversity and complexity of women's lives and activisms. The analysis of this book does not suggest, however, that this engagement is best addressed by merging programs or departments into a super-department of "other" studies that incorporates the various, currently distinct, areas of ethnic and cultural studies, or by "mainstreaming" women's studies so that it exists only in "general" departments. It should be noted that such moves are often umbrellas under which to cut administrative support, faculty lines, and other resources to programs that challenge traditional curricula. This outcome should not be surprising, not only given the current conservative climate of educational budget cutting, but also for reasons suggested in the examples in this book. The attempt to subsume particular sites of study under general rubrics (whether the "main"stream or the "other") undercuts diversity and complexity in precisely the ways outlined in chapter 4, where those least marked by particularity are most empowered to represent the general. Thus, we could easily find a "cultural" studies, once again dominated by privileged white males as the "general" representative of diverse areas of study, including ethnic and women's studies. The alternative to the attempt to find a general rubric under which to combine areas of study is to work to develop a network of interrelations through which to connect and ally diverse areas. In this arrangement the various sites of study are nodes in the network and work must be undertaken to build articulations, work that will change, but would not necessarily merge, the nodes themselves. It could, ultimately, break down current boundaries and administrative divisions, but merger is in no way the ideal outcome. Rather, the ideal is to both maintain diversity and work through the complexities of making connections.

Working Alliances, Moral Economies: Politics and Ethics

Normative matrices materialize moral economies within which differences are produced. Intertwined identities and differences are produced through re-iterations of the norm, reiterations that materialize the norm, giving it embodiment. Normative reiterations are productive, they produce the possibilities of subjectivity, but they are also constraining and constrained by the relations of production. The coercive demand to produce oneself as, for example, a gendered being is not under contemporary relations of production avoidable. Materialization of any norm is never complete, however, and it simultaneously produces excess. This excess creates the need for social enforcement, but it also opens the door to play on the "original" norm, the space of originality that is new and different. Play does not mean a space of total freedom from constraint, but it is a site of struggle over norms and possibilities for change. Play is, thus, serious business, but it also materializes imagination and creativity. Social movements, meaning movements of and for different enactments, create possibilities for changing the shape of a normative matrix or producing new norms. Thus, empowerment, constraint, and change can exist simultaneously, delineating a site of moral labor named "agency."[230]

Under contemporary relations of production, differences, along lines of gender, race, class, and sexuality are produced as dominations. Moral economies are relatively autonomous, overlapping, and interrelated, thus, they create the complexity and contradictions of inter-locking dominations that simultaneously institute segregations and gaps in social relations. Within these relations of production, moral economies of differentiation are linked as hierarchical binaries to a dominant moral economy that produces the "general public." So, for example, the economy of gender produces women as different from men and in so doing also produces men as normatively "general." The general is reproduced across moral economies as (repetitive) hierarchical binaries, the effect of which is a loose network of binaries where each binary both is separate from and reinforces the others. These conditions, the simultaneity of interrelation and segregation, make for the complexities of social movement. As the reading of Sojourner Truth points out, the domination against which African American women work is produced by shifting among binaries. For example, at points, African American women, Sojourner Truth among them, were denied a claim in the gender economy; they are not normatively women, and thus must be shifted to the economy of race, but at the moment of enfranchisement they were not normatively raced and are shifted back to gender, pinned to the identity of disenfranchised women. This structure induces social movements both to struggle separately, addressing themselves only to single binaries, and to reiterate, and thus reinforce, the general norm. Marginalized groups focus only on the "center" and claim a place for themselves in the center, and relations among marginalized groups are ignored, producing the sites at which moral economies intersect as interstices, gaps, or silences. Thus, as analyzed in chapter 2, in order to constitute itself as an autonomous movement, women's liberation replicated the dominant economy of the same, thereby erasing Black women's movements as *women's* liberation and failing to form connections to movements of poor and working-class women or to materialize the gay/feminist alliance, despite the expressed longing for connection.

These conditions make for the difficulties of producing working alliances and the ineffectiveness of repeated calls for alliance formation that do not take complexity into account. Alliances have been invoked in the context of a liberal politics of diversity or a more radical, but still flawed, feminist politics of "differences." Both liberal diversity and feminist "differences" fail to address the economies within which differences and the complexity of relationships among differences are produced. Because norms both empower and constrain the material possibility of subjectivity or agency, the political project of producing working alliances is also a project in ethics.

In order to build alliances, one must be able to work with the complex interrelations among moral economies so as to produce intersections as articulations, connections among struggles, and as resistances. One must also be able to work with the diverse and complex norms produced by "communities of resistance and solidarity" (Welch 1985). Chapter 3 investigated different moral traditions that have been produced at the intersections of moral economies. *Black Womanist Ethics* names the moral tradition of African American women's struggles at the intersection of gender, race, and class to "prevail against the odds with moral integrity" (Cannon 1988, 2) and to actualize "an inclusive human community" (169). *Lesbian Ethics* names the work of lesbians producing values, making choices under conditions of constraint, and taking the relational risks to make a "moral revolution." Despite the intersections between these two texts given the ways in which sexuality is racialized and race is sexualized while both are gendered and classed, the differences represented by these traditions cannot be resolved through an assumption of unity or some singular focus on oppression.[231] Nor is such a resolution or unification either necessary or desirable for the work of effective resistance to domination to which they are committed. As chapter 4 demonstrated, working alliances require working with the excesses of differentiation, work that occurs in-between, rather than being contained within, particular differences.

Working in the spaces in-between makes room for the type of interaction among groups that changes norms and identities, interaction which is not accounted for in the "Rainbow Coalition." As Ranu Samantrai (forthcoming) points out in her study of Black British politics in the 1980s,

> Conflicts between constituencies cannot be resolved through either assimilation or multiculturalism, both of which presume that norms defining communities remain undisturbed as groups encounter one another. . . . A pluralism capable of addressing the complexity of contemporary British racial and gender politics would recognize the value of dissent which interrupts attempts to consolidate boundaries and maintain stable norms. Such a pluralism would build upon conflict in order to challenge the inclusions and exclusions through which majority and minority constituencies, and the resulting norm of a fundamentally white Britain, are maintained.

Working in-between is the labor necessary to materialize possibilities for a complex pluralism, a pluralism that recognizes the complexity of interrelation between the poles of unity and diversity.

Working in-between is both a means of living in and amongst social change and of creating room for on-going change, affirming a commitment to "a world that needs changing" (Bammer 1991). The question of ethical method is not one of finding the overarching values which frame all others, but one of reworking the multiple values of the various traditions in and between which we work. In this sense, ethics is a language for an on-going way of life, not for a single answer to a moral dilemma. These questions are part of social processes which create moral knowledge by articulating rather than naturalizing "the politics of ethics."[232] Ethics, thus, works to enable rather than foreclose political struggle. The priority of ethics shifts from resolution of conflict to creation of new possibilities for communities and relationships. Yet, ethical language is always limited by social conditions. Thus, constructing feminist ethics is only one part of a complex set of resistances addressing the nexus of ethical discourse, political practice, and social conditions.

How does one undertake this work, however, without either re-iterating a telos of eventual unification or abdicating ethical responsibility for the direction of activity? A shift in ethical conceptualization from responsibility to response-ability may go some distance in explaining how one can work in alliances without being trapped either in or between these two poles.[233] Because the language of response-ability is not a moral perspective, but a language of interaction, it allows for recognition of partiality and openness to others without having to protect its coherence. Response-ability names the skill of working in relationships, of responding to moral claims made from various locations while also recognizing the normative power of one's own (diverse and complex) commitments. Response-ability names the on-going process of working to resist and contest dominations and the responsibility of producing new norms and articulating democratic values under conditions of constraint.

The conclusion of this book is, thus, not an end, but a starting point, a point from which to move forward with new ways to understand the work we are doing and to formulate questions about what work we should do in the future, work in the spaces in-between that can produce us as allies. "We" can be connected without being identified. We can work together.

Notes

1. For useful explorations of alliance building and women working together across differences see Reagon (1983), Narayan (1988), Albrecht and Brewer (1990), and Hirsch and Keller (1990), particularly Childers and hooks's contribution.

2. bell hooks uses the term "feminist movement" to break down the supposed singularity of movement indicated by the use of the definitive article in "*the* feminist movement." See for example, Childers and hooks (1990).

3. Both Nancy Fraser (1989) and Seyla Benhabib (1986, 1992) have usefully argued that needs and interests are developed through processes of social interaction.

4. See, for example, the various positions adopted in Benhabib et al. (1995).

5. See Gardiner (1995) for summaries of contemporary debates over "agency."

6. I would like to thank Laura Berry for clarifying these issues for me through e-mail communication.

7. These challenges come from a variety of movements which have articulated "different" moral voices—feminist, womanist, *mujérista*, and lesbian to name a few (Gilligan 1982, Cannon 1988, Isasi-Díaz 1993, Hoagland 1988)—as well as from postmodern critiques of modern conceptions of subjectivity and agency (Benhabib et al. 1995). The relationships among and between these various perspectives and their critiques are hotly debated. For example, Mohanty (1994, 163, fn 4) reads the "earlier political analyses of Third World feminists" as "prefiguring" postmodern challenges to modern assumptions of unity, while Lugones (1994) reads the two sites as producing different types of analysis. Lugones argues that "postmodern literature . . . goes against a politics of identity and toward minimizing the political significance of groups"; while her position, one which can also be seen in "the literature on mestizaje, affirms a complex version of identity politics and a complex conception of groups" (475).

8. This coincidence of the modern western enlightenment, which promises emancipation, and a historical period of domination provokes the suspicion that these two historical processes are co-implicated. For a full consideration of this question see Jakobsen (1995b).

9. My analysis is obviously indebted to Iris Marion Young's (1990) *Justice and the Politics of Difference*. In particular, Young offers a definitive critique of liberal pluralism and its inability to take into account asymmetrical power relations. While there have been numerous critiques of pluralism as a mere reinforcement of status quo "differences," I am particularly concerned with the avoidance of responsibility which Young identifies as implied in such pluralism, "interest-group pluralism allows little space for claims that some parties have a responsibility to attend to the claims of others because they are needy or oppressed" (119). As María Lugones (1994) points out, however, Young's text must be extended in (at least one) different direction(s) in order to fully theorize the complexity of persons and groups constituted in and through "interlocking oppressions" (471-73).

10. Spillers reports, "For instance, in my attempt to lay hold of non-fictional texts—

of any discursively rendered experience concerning the sexuality of black women in the United States, authored by themselves, for themselves—I encountered a disturbing silence that acquires, paradoxically, the status of contradiction" (1992, 74).

11. Ellen Messer-Davidow (Gardiner 1995) provides a useful definition of discourse in her theory of agency. A discourse is a systematic set of social relations made up of both linguistic and extra-linguistic activities. Thus, a discourse is not simply another word for language, but additionally refers to a variety of practices and their institutional and social contexts. These activities and the relations which form their context—in other words a "discourse"—establish meaning. As Messer-Davidow points out, "kicking a ball down the street and kicking it in a football game may be similar actions, but their meanings differ because the actions are integrated within different systems of relations" (Gardiner 1995, 31). Although discourses are systems, they are never fully stable either internally or in relation to other discourses. While meanings may be partially fixed through "articulations" (Laclau and Mouffe 1985, 113) which link elements of a discourse together into a system, these linkages depend on social conditions which are contingent and variable.

12. Bell explains the semantic theory behind this claim as follows: "In this semantic universe, every sign is an implicit set of contrasts and every contrast invokes another. Yet despite the continued juxtaposition of nearly equivalent oppositions, the contrasts are orchestrated so that some come to appropriate, reinterpret, or qualify others. On the one hand, the semantic system evoked is a closed and endlessly self-deferring circular system; on the other hand, the hierarchical orchestration of the contrasts and deferrals generates the sense of a universal totality, a unified and authoritative coherence informing the whole scheme of things" (1992, 101).

13. Claims to enact a "difference feminism" have now become a strategy of various conservative political organizations who are dedicated to "separate but equal" roles for men and women. In this case "difference feminism" is opposed to "gender feminism" which supposedly wants to erase all distinctions between men and women. Alternatively, conservative arguments can also be articulated so as to make gender differences the site of a "radical feminism" in contrast to a mainstream feminism directed toward similarity between men and women. In this version, any differences between men and women signal that women's social subordination is the fault of those who are "different."

14. This apparently arbitrary list—where, for example, are south Asian studies "located"?—names the various studies programs instituted at the University of Arizona as of 1996.

15. See Mohanty (1994, 149–51) for a brief history of some of these struggles.

16. Elizabeth Spelman (1988) analyzes the problem of "women and minorities" as the "ampersand problem" for feminism. In order to address the problem, she turns to a strategy of specificity, advocating that feminists should specify the particular genders which are articulated in and through race and class, etc. Shane Phelan (1994) extends this strategy, arguing for a complex version of specificity.

17. Susan Shapiro (1994) is also critical of the politics of *différance* alone as reinforcing the ways in which the "West" uses the "Other" to signify "*différance* within a system opened endlessly (nomadically) internally," while "differences" which could "rupture [the West-Other relation] from within or without . . . are deferred, erased, effaced" (190).

18. Drucilla Cornell (1993) points to the example of Derrida's attempts to work in these spaces in-between by writing a "choreographic text with polysexual signatures," which "still involves designating masculine and feminine voices at the same time that it tries to blur the traits and lines of thought traditionally associated with the gender opposition" (91–95). It is interesting to note that Cornell is developing a feminist reading of Derrida's

texts specifically in response to feminist critics of this aspect of Derrida's work. These criticisms indicate problems in Derrida's work and also the difficulty of working in the spaces in-between.

19. I have elsewhere analyzed this multiplicity and ambiguity as "ambi-valence" (Jakobsen 1995a).

20. As Drucilla Cornell points out, "one can never know for sure whether any attempt to shift the boundaries of meaning and representation through a reinvention of language is in complicity with or breaks with existing ideology" (95).

21. See, especially King's (1994) chapter 2, "What Counts as Theory?" on this history.

22. In responding to this suggestion, Card (1995) points out that Frye shifts many of the concerns which are traditionally considered ethical to the political.

23. Grosz goes on to state, "Ethics is a response to the recognition of the primacy of alterity over identity. Ethics, particularly in the work of Emmanuel Levinas, is that field defined by the other's needs, the other's calling on the subject for a response. In this case, the paradigm of an ethical relation is that of a mother's response to the needs or requirements of a child. Ethics means being called by and responding to the other's otherness. It thus defines a long-term goal for feminists seeking autonomy for both sexes. Only when each sex is recognised as an independent otherness by the other is an ethical relation between them possible" (1989, xvii). The paradigm of mother-child relations indicates how the (singular) focus on "otherness" can become implicated in traditional (feminine) ethics. I would argue alternatively, that the intertwined constitution of alterity and identity through normative enactment are necessary for a full "definition" of ethics.

24. Norms and values are variously divided and interrelated in both monographs and anthologies on ethical theory. In his book *Morality*, Bernard Gert (1988) argues that "impartial rational persons advocate acting in accordance with moral rules" (75), whereas to create goods is not necessarily required by reason, rather a good is that which no reasonable person would avoid (50). Thus, there can be moral disagreement about the ranking of goods and evils, but not about the moral rules (xxix). Alternatively, the editors of *Ethics: A Feminist Reader* (Frazer et al. 1992) cite the "classical understanding of ethics," in emphasizing questions of values and the good life, although they see the answers to these questions as governed by norms: "ethics is the theory of the good life (both for individuals and for societies), and it involves the study of value—not just the empirical question of what people *actually* value, though no moral philosopher can be indifferent to this, but the normative question of what it is *right* or *appropriate* to value" (1, emphasis in original). Sometimes these divisions follow the traditional distinction between "morality," from the Latin *mores*, carrying more of an implication of codes of conduct and "ethics" from the Greek root for ethos, which tends toward a way of life (Singer 1994, 5). Divisions don't always follow these lines, however, and ethics and morality are now frequently used interchangeably (Pojman 1989, 1).

25. Butler's full description of the materialization of "sex" is:

> "[S]ex" not only functions as a norm, but is part of a regulatory practice that produces the bodies it governs, that is, whose regulatory force is made clear as a kind of productive power, the power to produce—demarcate, circulate, differentiate—the bodies it controls. Thus, "sex" is a regulatory ideal whose materialization is compelled, and this materialization takes place (or fails to take place) through certain highly regulated practices. In other words, "sex" is an ideal construct which is forcibly materialized through time. It is not a simple fact or static condition of a body, but a process whereby regulatory norms materialize "sex" and achieve this materialization through forcible reiteration of those norms. That this reiteration is necessary is a sign that materialization is never quite complete, that

bodies never comply with the norms by which their materialization is impelled. Indeed, it is the instabilities, the possibilities for rematerialization, opened up by this process that mark one domain in which the force of the regulatory law can be turned against itself to spawn rearticulations that call into question the hegemonic force of that very regulatory law. . . . "Sex" is thus, not simply what one has, or a static description of what one is: it will be one of the norms by which the "one" becomes viable at all, that which qualifies a body for life within the domain of cultural intelligibility. (1993, 1–2)

26. Even Joan C. Tronto (1993), who courageously recommends boundary crossings, shies away from the implication that such crossings might also subvert the boundaries which contain moral diversity. I consider her criticism of Anthony Cortese's (1990) *Ethnic Ethics* for failing to address "the difficult problem of relativism" (94) in the Conclusion.

27. Cannon's and Hoagland's theories will be considered in depth in chapter 3.

28. See Gardiner (1995), King (1994) chapter 6 "Global Gay Formations and Local Homosexualities," and Tsing (1993) for readings that complicate the relationship between determinism and agency.

29. I refer to these dislocations as "non-modern," being mistrustful of the linear implications of postmodernism and the various relationships to modernity which it elides.

30. This meeting was inspired by the epilogues which conclude a number of recent books, particularly in women's history, which reach toward these types of questions. At the end of books like Peggy Pascoe's (1990) *Relations of Rescue* and Lori Ginzberg's (1990) *Women and the Work of Benevolence*, there are five- or six-page epilogues or afterwords where the authors consider the implications of their historical arguments for the contemporary situation, frequently for contemporary feminist movements. Peggy Pascoe, for instance, calls hers "A Legacy to Ponder: Female Moral Authority and Contemporary Women's Culture."

31. This move is also undoubtedly informed by my (inter)disciplinary training in a program in "Ethics and Society" where we learned both to read ethical theory in the context of the sociology of morality and religion; and where we were trained to make ethical theory in relation to a sociological understanding of institutional practice and social change.

32. Luce Irigaray (1981a, 1981b) has made a crucial contribution to understanding how it is that a capitalist economy and liberal democratic polity, supposedly based on "difference" or "diversity" among commodities or ideologies, actually devolves into a "hommosexual" economy among men—an "economy of the same" in which exchange relations take place only among men and in which women are the objects of exchange. Within this economy men must ultimately be "the same." As Elizabeth Grosz (1989) summarizes, "Exchange relations to date have posited a basic universality or sameness of the agents of exchange, thus guaranteeing the commensurability of exchanged objects" (148). Similarly, the modern ethical ideal of universal respect posits an ultimate similarity among moral agents based on a universal(ly similar) rationality.

33. For example, in her study of Rochester, New York, Nancy Hewitt (1984) reports that African American women formed the first female anti-slavery society in Rochester in 1834 and a second society, the Union Anti-Slavery Society in 1850 (42). White women in Rochester founded three anti-slavery organizations from the 1830s to the 1850s: Female Anti-Slavery Society, Western New York Anti-Slavery Society, and Ladies Anti-Slavery Society. For histories of women's anti-slavery societies in New York, Boston, and Philadelphia see Yellin and Van Horne (1994) and Hansen (1993).

34. Some feminist theorists (Butler 1990b) have suggested that there is a great need for the proliferation of women's positions as a strategy of resistance necessary to undermine culturally hegemonic ideas of woman. This task is an important one, and one of the pur-

poses of this chapter is to show just a few examples of this proliferation in one historical period. Given the complexity which accompanies diversity, however, simply documenting diversity or promoting proliferation is insufficient to the subversion of discursive dominance.

35. When I refer to women's "moralities," I am using the term in a broad fashion which includes both speaking and enacting morality. Actions can "speak" moralities just as speaking can enact them. For example, street demonstrations or acts of civil disobedience can be powerful public statements of moral and political positions. Speech acts can actively establish the boundaries of a moral community, for example, by naming who is "us" and who is "them." The interactive nature of moral speaking and acting does not necessarily occur without contradictions, however. Thus, it is important not to merely subsume one under the other. Elsa Barkley Brown (1989) uses this broad connotation with respect to womanist consciousness which includes both statements and activities.

36. Hewitt (1984, 11) argues that these contradictory values often served as a barrier to women's solidarity across races and classes. This problem is particularly evident in the relationship between bourgeois social reformers and the lower-class women they purported to "help."

37. By "moral labor" I mean all those undertakings which contribute to the development and maintenance of moral relationships and moral communities. In order for moral relationships to exist, norms must not only be produced, but also maintained and reproduced. In addition moral labor may be undertaken to change the specific norms and enactments of a particular relationship or community. My use of the term "moral" to describe a relationship or community is not to pass a particular value judgment, but to imply that the parties to a relationship or members of a community have normative expectations of themselves, of others, and of the relationship or community itself. These expectations may vary, or be in conflict, but given the governing power of norms, moral labor will be necessary to the existence of that relationship or community. Thus, all the work that goes into establishing a relationship and developing an understanding of that relationship as a moral relationship with a set of normative expectations of parties to the relationship and of the relationship itself, is moral labor.

38. As Joan M. Martin (1996) points out, "The relation of women to work is historically embedded in patriarchal, racist, and classist understandings that the essential biological, emotional, and spiritual nature of woman defines the nature of her labor. This is generally true in three interrelated aspects of social life: the so-called public world, the community, and the home (the domestic or 'private world'). In the public world, the work that women of diverse backgrounds and socially constructed groups undertake is nearly always poorly rewarded financially in proportion to that of all socially constructed groups of men; in the community, it is seen as voluntary 'service'; and in the home, it is unpaid work of no monetary value to a nation's gross national (economic) product and is often subject to conflicting and hypocritical moral valuation" (321).

39. For an example of a contemporary natural law theorist see Fuchs (1983). Because natural law theories deny that norms are produced at all, feminist challenges based on the social location and interests of those (men) who discovered the moral laws found in nature are irrelevant.

40. For an example of a social constructionist theory that maintains common meanings within a society, thereby, also failing to acknowledge the possibility of divided moral labor see Walzer (1983). An argument for the "common" structure of norms within a given society also renders irrelevant the question of which persons within the society carry the social power necessary for publicly recognized norm production.

41. The term "complicity" may itself imply a level of intentional action that is better understood as "implication" in structures of domination.

42. See, for example, Cannon (1988), Hoagland (1988), Welch (1990). My project is to try to work through the complexities of a historically situated agency.

43. Sarah and Angelina Grimké were not only some of the first women to speak to mixed audiences in public, they were also the subject of one of the first dissertations in women's history done in conjunction with second-wave feminist movement by Gerda Lerner in 1967 (Kerber et al. 1995). They have since been the subject of extensive historical investigation (Friedman 1982, Bartlett 1988, Ceplair 1989). Both Sojourner Truth and Catharine Beecher have similarly been the subjects of early and extensive feminist history (Sklar 1976, Sterling 1984, Boydston et al. 1988, Joseph 1990, Omolade 1994, Stetson and David 1994, Painter 1994, 1996a, 1996b). Women in abolition movements, slave narratives, and women's spiritual and political activisms have also been the subject of extensive work (Lowenberg and Bogin 1976, DuBois 1978, Harley and Terborg-Penn 1978, Hersh 1978, Raboteau 1978, Sterling 1979, Giddings 1984, Jones 1985, Andrews 1986, Gates 1987, Jacobs 1987).

44. For the published documents of the Grimké sisters see Ceplair (1989), Barnes and Dumond (1934), Angelina Grimké (1838a, 1838b), Bartlett (1988).

45. For Catharine Beecher's position I look specifically at two of her texts, *An Essay on Slavery and Abolitionism with Reference to the Duty of American Women* (1837) and *Treatise on Domestic Economy for the Use of Young Ladies at Home and at School* (1841). Although these works were published some years apart, Kathryn Kish Sklar (1976, 136) reports that Beecher began working on the *Domestic Economy* directly after finishing the *Essay* and there are clear connections between the two documents. For example, the material on women's subordination in the *Domestic Economy* (2–3) almost directly mirrors this material in the *Essay* (98–100). For additional letters by Catharine Beecher see also Boydston et al. (1988).

46. Because Sojourner Truth did not write her documents, there are no extant documents which are not recorded by an intermediary. Thus, the major available source is the *Narrative of Sojourner Truth* (Gilbert 1970) first published by Olive Gilbert, a white abolitionist, in 1850 and then reprinted in 1878 under the name of Sojourner Truth and including the *Book of Life*. See Jeffrey C. Stewart's Introduction to the Schomburg Library edition (Truth 1991) for this publication history. Stewart argues that it is "unclear whether [Truth] was truly illiterate" (1991, xxxix). Additional letters written for her by friends and relatives are published in Dorothy Sterling (1984, 399–401).

47. See Jean Fagan Yellin's chapter "Angelina Grimké" in *Women and Sisters: The Antislavery Feminists in American Culture* (1989, 29–52).

48. Friedman argues that white abolitionists accepted (to some degree) antebellum white middle-class ideologies which depicted "the Negro as at once a carefree, impulsive, immature child and an innately untamed, uncivilized, sexually threatening savage" (1982, 169). While the child required supervision and instruction on the part of white missionary-reformers, the savage required separation and restraint.

49. One of the more dramatic examples of African Americans' eventual impatience with white abolitionists, and of whites' continuing paternalistic response to African American independence, was William Garrison's dispute with Frederick Douglass over the founding of Douglass's independent anti-slavery newspaper *The North Star* (Friedman 1982, 187–95). See also, chapter 2, "Black Militancy Confronts Militant Abolitionism," in Allen (1974).

50. The "Pastoral Letter to the General Association of Massachusetts to the Congregational Churches Under Their Care" was authored by Rev. Nehemiah Adams and issued on July 28, 1837 (Lerner 1971, 189). Angelina is clear in her letters to Weld that it is this attack against them, not their desire to promote their own issue, that has made women's rights of central importance to the battle for abolition: "These letters [written by the Grimkés and

published in *The Spectator*] have not been the means of *arousing* the public attention to the subject of Woman's rights, it was the Pastoral Letter which did the mischief" (Angelina Grimké to Weld and John Greenleaf Whittier August 20, 1837, Barnes and Dumond 1934, 428, emphasis in original).

51. Class position is one of the striking differences between the Grimkés and Catharine Beecher. Given that she did not marry, Beecher's middle-class background did not provide her with the economic security to know that she could support herself. Making a living for herself is one of the central issues with which she struggled. For Beecher the one position which would have allowed her a podium for public speaking and financial support, that of a minister—the option provided by her father's example and adopted by her brothers—was closed to her. Rather than challenging this difference with claims of sameness—a position which would have presented her with serious material problems—Beecher sublimated it, claiming that the self-sacrifice of women's subordination provided them with a superior moral voice. While other middle-class women did not follow Beecher's choice of strategies, it seems clear that her economic concerns were one factor influencing her decisions.

52. Daniel Scott Smith in "Family Limitation, Sexual Control, and Domestic Feminism in Victorian America," in *A Heritage of Her Own: Toward a New Social History of American Women* (Cott and Pleck 1979) argues that "Nearly all feminist abolitionists . . . were, in effect, domestic feminists. Because of the persistent importance of the public/private distinction, most domestic feminists, on the other hand, could not be public feminists" (240). This would explain the Grimkés' acceptance of women's domestic roles, while Catharine Beecher maintained an adamant refusal of women's public political roles.

53. Beecher (1841, 4–7) adapts her argument from Alexis de Tocqueville (1945), who in *Democracy in America* argues that the American liberal democracy is successful because it is surrounded by a set of republican institutions which are indirectly supportive of the public sphere by creating citizens with mores to counterbalance the corrosive competitiveness of the economic and political process. Tocqueville's argument has also been the basis of contemporary "communitarian" positions such as that presented in *Habits of the Heart* (Bellah et al., 1985).

54. The correspondence between Catharine and Lyman that documents the conversion struggle is collected in *The Autobiography of Lyman Beecher* (Lyman Beecher 1961).

55. In his *A Plea for the West* (1835), Lyman ties the work of ushering in a Christian society to America's role in ushering in the millennium. Catharine, like many of her contemporaries, accepts that the success of U.S. democratic institutions is tied to the ushering in of the millennium, a theme which runs through the "Introduction" to the *Domestic Economy* (1841, 1–14). In contrast to Lyman, however, she wants to highlight women's role in this process.

56. For example, in the *Essay on Slavery and Abolitionism*, Beecher writes passionately about the potential break-up of "the community" over the question of slavery (1837, 136–37).

57. Even in the material quoted from Tocqueville, he speaks of the "voluntary surrender" of a woman's will as something in which the women of America take pride (1841, 6). Once again, this reference is to the domestic relation, but Beecher ultimately connects domestic submission to political freedom through moral superiority.

58. The position of women's moral superiority gained through chosen self-sacrifice was contradictory not only with the argument from nature, but with social reality. For example, Catharine's "choice" of life work was structurally imposed in that she could not follow the example of her father down the path to the ministry, a path which was taken by all of her brothers.

59. Interestingly, Catharine's sister Harriet Beecher Stowe with whom she worked on various editions of the *Domestic Economy* took a similar position in the tremendously popular *Uncle Tom's Cabin*, arguing that the evil of slavery was ultimately best addressed through domestic maternal morality (Fleischner, 1994).

60. Carol Gilligan's (1982) ethic of care is the most well-known contemporary ethic that makes the maintenance of connection a primary norm. Gilligan refers to "false attachments" as a means of criticizing connections and relationships that are abusive, but I have argued elsewhere (Jakobsen 1996) that this distinction between true and false connection is inadequate to the complex task of building relationships.

61. As she grew older she began to argue for women's right to financial independence despite her continuing rhetorical commitment to domestic economy. For example, whereas her initial arguments for the importance of women to the teaching profession had included self-sacrificial rhetoric to the effect that women would teach for half the wages demanded by men since teaching was a prelude to marriage, in her later work Beecher advocated higher wages for women so that they could support themselves should they so choose (Sklar 1976, 269).

62. "Present throughout her life, but increasingly pronounced in her later years . . . was a fear of the brute force of males and of the social, sexual, and physical vulnerability of women. Only at their very great peril did women challenge men's power directly" (Boydston et al. 1988, 231).

63. In analyzing the contradictions of both the Grimkés' justice paradigm and Catharine Beecher's woman's "different voice," I am not suggesting that the two perspectives are necessarily equally problematic from the point of view of contemporary feminist ethics or alliance politics. I am stressing that the Grimkés' position cannot be fully analyzed separately from Beecher's or vice versa.

64. In her early experiences as a slave Isabella understands God as "master," who resides in the sky, but who answers her prayers (Gilbert 1970, 27, 33, 41, 46, 59). After attaining her freedom and then after her conversion while working in New York City, her understanding of God is an immanent one—"God revealed himself to her, with all the suddenness of a flash of lightning, showing her, 'in the twinkling of an eye, that he was *all over*—that he pervaded the universe—and that there was no place God was not'" (Gilbert 1970, 65). In 1843 she is led to become an itinerant lecturer out of her disillusionment with millennialist preacher Robert Mathias, articulated by both an economic analysis—"the rich rob the poor, and the poor rob one another," and by a call from the spirit (Gilbert 1970, 97–102). Upon recovering from a serious illness in 1875, Truth reported that "She feels for some special purpose her life has been spared. . . . She says, 'My good Master kept me, for he had something for me to do'" (Gilbert 1970, 252).

65. The *Narrative* reports that she did internalize white ideologies, viewing her master as a "god" and beating her own children for stealing from him (Gilbert 1970, 33–34).

66. Sojourner Truth left New York City to begin the "pilgrimage" which resulted in her public speaking career and adopted the name Sojourner in 1843.

67. After leaving New York City and taking up the name Sojourner in 1843 she initially followed the Millerite preaching circuit. Millerism was a brand of millennial theology that enjoyed great popularity in the early 1840s. Because of her great effectiveness as a speaker, she was then recommended to other non-Millerite gatherings (Painter 1994, 146).

68. See also Andrews (1986).

69. On the formation of African American women's consciousness, see Patricia Hill Collins (1990) *Black Feminist Thought*. Collins argues that Black feminist thought derives from a combination of African survivals in Black women's traditions and the particular po-

sition of African American women in the U.S. political economy as "inside/outsiders" (19–40). African American women have been positioned as workers at the heart of white society (e.g., as domestics in white families), hence they know white society "from the inside" while also maintaining a critical distance. Collins recognizes that such a positioning could (and sometimes did) result in an internalization by Black women of white ideologies, but Afrocentric traditions can also provide the leverage to maintain critical distance.

70. Giddings describes some of the contradictions resulting from these pressures as "Black women activists traversed a tricky and sometimes contradictory path in responding to the challenge. On the one hand they agreed with the fundamental premises of the Victorian ethic. On the other, they opposed its racist and classist implications. At the same time they were conscious of the pressure on free Blacks to prove they could be acculturated into American society. Because of their alleged inability to do so, organizations like the American Colonization Society, which included some of the most influential White liberals in the country, were stepping up efforts to repatriate free Blacks to Africa. For Black women, *acculturation* was translated as their ability to be 'ladies'—a burden of proof that carried an inherent class-consciousness" (1984, 49 emphasis in original).

71. This led some literary societies to adopt membership requirements that included statements of moral character and relatively high dues structures (Winch 1994).

72. See Riggs (1994), chapter 2, "Roots of the Present Dilemma (1800–1920)" for a description of the complex and contradictory forms of social stratification within the Black community. See also Boylan (1994) on the connection between membership issues for antebellum literary societies and status distinctions. On some of the implications of standards of "respectability" for both dominant projects of nation-building and resistance movements see Mosse (1985).

73. See also Jacqueline Jones (1985, 59–60).

74. Painter writes, "In the nineteenth century, this process [of making her individuality into directly grasped symbol] made Sojourner Truth = "the Libyan Sibyl" = black exotic, and in the twentieth century, it made Sojourner Truth = Ar'n't I a woman?" = strong (black) woman" (1996a, 288).

75. The proceedings of this meeting are reported in a letter to William Lloyd Garrison from William Hayward dated October 1, 1858 (Gilbert 1970, 137–39).

76. Painter provides a detailed reading of photographic portraits of Sojourner Truth which, like the *Narrative*, she sold to support herself. The original caption read, "I sell the Shadow to Support the Substance. SOJOURNER TRUTH." Painter argues that Truth had control over the production of these images in terms of pose, clothing, and props and that she is always dressed in tailored clothes and pictured with indicators of intelligence, maturity, and respectability. "In none of these portraits is there anything beyond blackness that would inspire charity, nothing of the piteous slave mother, chest-baring insolent, grinning minstrel, or amusing naif" (Painter 1996a, 285).

77. For letters dictated by Truth describing these activities, see Sterling (1984, 251–56).

78. This description is presented as "Another journal speaks of Sojourner Truth's presence at this [Women's Suffrage Association, Women's Rights Convention] meeting thus." There is no attribution to the specific journal.

79. A report of an 1872 talk reads as follows: "As to woman suffrage she declared that the world would never be correctly governed until equal rights were declared, and that as men have been endeavoring for years to govern alone, and have not yet succeeded in perfecting any system, it is about time the women should take the matter in hand" (Gilbert 1970, 247).

80. Truth's support of the "Exodus" to Kansas also marked another difference be-

tween her and Frederick Douglass, who took a stand against the Exodus, arguing that African Americans needed to stay and fight for their rights in the South despite whatever violence and oppression they experienced there (Painter 1976, 247–50).

81. For more on womanist consciousness and moral voice see Cannon (1988, 1995), Grant (1989), Sanders et al. (1989), Townes (1993), Townes, ed. (1993), Williams (1993a), Douglas (1994), and Riggs (1994).

82. Susan Thistlethwaite (1989, 12) analyzes this strategy as "truth-in-action." Thistlethwaite argues that truth-in-action militates against abstract notions of truth by focusing on experience and activity, but it also militates against an uncritical reification of the category of experience as the arbiter of truth. Rather, truth-in-action represents an unstable notion of truth which continually questions "experience" against the available discourses (25). Thus Sojourner Truth points to her experiences to subvert dominant discourses of womanhood and women's morality, using the "truth" of her experiences as critical leverage to draw upon or subvert dominant discourses for her own purposes in enacting her moral claims for changes in the system of power relations which order her experience as an African American woman. This activism, in turn, forms continuing experiences from which to critique prevailing discourses.

83. James H. Evans (1990) has identified a similar relationship to traditions as central to African American Christianity which "renders a prophetic critique of the present political order not because they completely reject the past or uncritically embrace a novel future (as does modernism) but because they seek and embody the creative conflict and possible community between the new and the old, between the past and the future" (215–16).

84. Michel Foucault (1984a) used the category of "dangers" to indicate skepticism that any action is either wholly good or bad. Any action runs particular dangers, some more pressing than others. This category allows one to evoke the polyvalent and context-determined nature of any action without abandoning judgment altogether. Thus, for Foucault the primary moral task is to determine which is the "main danger" (Foucault is particularly concerned with dominations) and resist that danger: "My point is not that everything is bad, but that everything is dangerous, which is not exactly the same as bad. If everything is dangerous, then we always have something to do. So my position leads not to apathy but to a hyper- and pessimistic activism. I think that the ethico-political choice we have to make every day is to determine which is the main danger" (343).

85. On "interstices" see Spillers (1992). Critical race theorist Kimberlé Crenshaw's (1989, 1992) work has also been crucial in demonstrating the need for a theory and practice that works at the intersection, in showing how intersections become interstices, and in articulating the complexity of intersection.

86. On "economy of the same," see Irigaray (1981a, 1981b).

87. Rebecca Chopp (1989) describes this hierarchical relationship between the central and singular One and the multiple "other(s)" as recognizing at most two subject positions— the inside or central position of "order" and the outside or marginalized position of "disorder." As with the binary opposition of gender, this binary opposition of order—between the "One" and the "other(s)"—is also hierarchical and subjugating. Disorder (often signified by "woman") becomes the "difference" upon which order depends for its dominance. Also as with gender, this opposition excludes true diversity as "difference" becomes a collective singular which only reflects the One to which it is opposed.

88. Similarly, in 1975 The Furies published *Lesbianism and the Women's Movement*, also a collection of essays written beginning in 1972.

89. The essay most frequently attributed with defining "lesbian-feminism" (Phelan 1989), is "The Woman-Identified Woman" by the Radicalesbians which appeared in 1971.

90. Interestingly, the role of lesbians or the importance of the movement for gay free-

dom developing out of the homophile movements of the 1950s and 1960s and sparked by the 1969 Stonewall rebellion is less frequently mentioned in descriptions of the historical roots of feminism. Gutiérrez (1993, 56–61) does mention the important role of lesbians in Chicano/a movements, but primarily in the 1980s.

91. In her book *Around 1981: Academic Feminist Literary Theory*, Gallop (1992) does consider *The Black Woman* as it appears in the bibliography to *Images of Women in Fiction* (Cornillon 1973). She points out that to take seriously Cade's question in the Introduction to *The Black Woman*, "And the question for us arises how relevant are the truth, the experiences, the findings of white women to Black women?" (Cade 9, as quoted in Cornillon 384, as quoted in Gallop 95), would be to seriously shift the meaning of "women" in the claim to theorize images of "women" in fiction. Given the theoretical import of this question, the citation of the mid-1980s as the moment at which "race" entered feminist theory seems difficult to sustain except as indicative of a form of forgetting.

92. The texts to which Frankenberg refers in the last sentence are Bernice Johnson Reagon's "Turning the Century," a speech given in 1981 and published in *Home Girls: A Black Feminist Anthology* (Smith 1983) and *This Bridge Called My Back* (Moraga and Anzaldúa 1981) and the Statement of the Combahee River Collective (written in 1977, initially published in Eisenstein 1978 and reprinted in Moraga and Anzaldúa 1981 and Smith 1983). Frankenberg's rendering of this story raises the important question of why *This Bridge* is a foundational text (as it should be), but *The Black Woman* is not.

93. Also, what of bell hooks's 1981 *Ain't I a Woman? Black Women and Feminism*?

94. Iris Marion Young's (1994) version of this story, because of the care with which it is told, raises similar issues: "Recent discussion among feminists about the difficulties of talking about women as a single group. . . . These discussions have cast doubt on the project of conceptualizing women as a group, arguing that the search for the common characteristics of women or of women's oppression leads to normalizations and exclusions" (713). "Doubts about the possibility of saying that women can be thought of as one social collective arose from challenges to a generalized conception of gender and women's oppression by women of color, in both the northern and southern hemispheres, and by lesbians. Black, Latina, Asian, and indigenous women demonstrated that white feminist theory and rhetoric tended to be ethnocentric in its analysis of gender experience and oppression. Lesbians, furthermore, persistently argued that much of this analysis relied on the experience of heterosexual women. The influence of philosophical deconstruction completed the suspension of the category of 'women' begun by this process of political differentiation. Exciting theorizing has shown (not for the first time) the logical problems in efforts to define clear, essential, categories of being" (714). Then Young reviews "some of the most articulate recent statements [of critique]," Spelman (1988), Mohanty et al. (1991), and Butler (1990a). Young is clear that issues of difference and dominance have been raised repeatedly and are not just "recent" developments. That her references are from the late 1980s and early 1990s does indicate, however, that another layer of founding texts has been added. Her story, because it does not subscribe to the narrative of historical progression, raises important questions: Why is it necessary to do this work again and again? What social processes lead to it being necessary?

95. I agree that, as Cheryl Clarke succinctly puts it, the 1980s represent "a watershed of multicultural feminist publishing" (1993, 218). My argument is, however, that the narrative told about the ways in which feminism was transformed in the 1980s is not a complicated enough story. It does not tell us how it is that the feminism "transformed" in the 1980s was initially constituted as a predominantly white, middle-class, and heterosexual feminism. This narrative also projects the problem of constituting a dominative feminist movement into the past, as a problem which is being, or even has been, solved. Thus, the issue of the

continual re-enactment of dominative practices and hence re-constitution of dominative movements is lost. In fact, I would argue, as does Katie King (1994, 124–37), that the telling of the story of feminism can itself be one of those practices that erases women of color and (re)constitutes women's movement as if it means "white, middle-class and heterosexual" (unless otherwise noted or transformed).

96. What was happening "until recently" in women's liberation when Morgan herself lists as the first act that explains "why a women's liberation movement now?" (1970, xxiv) Ruby Doris Smith Robinson's 1964 paper on the position of women within SNCC? What happened between 1964 when women's liberation could be located within civil rights movement and 1970 when women's liberation is predominantly white and middle-class, and where is the place of Ruby Doris Smith Robinson in the movement described by Morgan? How has she been dropped from the picture after her originary gesture and how would she or other African American women be returned to a place in "the movement" as race bias is "beginning to change"? Interestingly, more recent history (Evans 1979) indicates that Smith Robinson did not write the paper, but rather that although she participated in early discussions, the paper was written by two white women, Mary King and Casey Hayden, and the paper was submitted to the November 1964 SNCC staff retreat with "the authors' names 'withheld by request'" (Evans 1979, 85). The speculation about authorship that ensued focused on Smith Robinson, in part, because of her powerful position within SNCC. Evans concludes, "Thus white women, sensing their own precariousness within the movement, held back from direct engagement on the issue of sex roles and instead raised it anonymously, thereby inadvertently drawing on the growing strength of black women" (1979, 85). This complex history of the "origins" of feminist movement within SNCC and in Morgan's attribution of these origins to Smith Robinson indicate the ways in which singularity can be narratively constituted out of diversity.

97. Morgan writes this sentence in the middle of a deeply ambivalent passage:

> [W]omen from working-class backgrounds have been alienated from what has seemed to be a middle-class women's movement. Only recently, people have begun to discover that the women's movement *is* diverse in class origins. One reason for the previous image was that working-class women are of course compelled to strain after middle-class values (what mothers call "marrying well," and sociologists call "upward mobility"), and to act middle-class. We all began to discover that a large percentage of the movement comes from working-class backgrounds. (xxx–xxxi, emphasis in original)

The slippages among "women from working-class movements," "people," and "we all," and among "image" and "discovery" indicate Morgan's ambivalences about who is the subject of "women's movement." These ambivalences sometimes prove productive, however. New possibilities are opened up by small group consciousness-raising practices that showed that "Class oppression clearly was alive and well within the movement itself, and a number of groups took definite steps to confront and change this process" (xxi). Here the site of differences is shifted from that between movements, for example, women's liberation in distinction from welfare rights organizations, to within women's liberation itself.

98. "When the experts (white or Black, male) turn their attention to the Black women, the reports get murky, for they usually clump the men and women together and focus so heavily on what white people have done to the psyches of Blacks, that what Blacks have done to and for themselves is overlooked, and what distinguishes the men from the women forgotten" (8).

99. There is some disagreement about the spelling of Frances Beale's name: It appears as Beale throughout *The Black Woman*. It appears as Beal in *Sisterhood is Powerful*. It appears as Beal in an article appearing in the *Black Scholar* (1981, reprinted from 1975). Katie King provides the following history: "Frances Beale's essay 'Double Jeopardy: To Be Black

and Female' appears in several locations, unchanged, with a slight, but interesting variation in attribution and with differing spellings of the author's name. Three anthologies edited by white women spell the name 'Beal' and Toni Cade (and Alice Echols) spell it 'Beale.' In *Liberation Now!* (1971) the essay is copyrighted under the author's name (as in all other reprintings) but also together with 'SNCC Black Women's Liberation Committee' " (1994, 15). I follow my standard practice of reiterating the name as it appears in the text that I am reading.

100. In terms of this anthology, these multiple centers are about multiple issues more so than about multiple geographical locations. The contributors to the anthology come predominantly from New York (sixteen of twenty-seven contributors are listed as residing in New York), just as New York is the center for a number of these texts including *Sisterhood is Powerful* and *Lesbian Nation*.

101. The story does display an almost casual heterosexism. When talking of educated Black women, Reena says, "For the few eligible men around—those who are their intellectual and professional peers, whom they can respect (and there are very few of them)—don't necessarily marry them, but younger women without the degrees and the jobs, who are no threat, or they don't marry at all because they are either queer or mother-ridden. Or they marry white women" (32). This heterosexism is perhaps not surprising given that it is a pre-Stonewall text, but 1962 is also the year in which James Baldwin published *Another Country*. Thus, perhaps especially given that it is a pre-Stonewall text, it is interesting that the line is present at all, a trace of anxiety which requires "queers" to be mentioned even as they are pushed out of the picture relevant to Black women's struggles. Cheryl Clarke (1993) says, "The dialectic of Blackness and homosexuality was too subversive in the heterosexist Black consciousness movement of the late 1960s. Eldridge Cleaver, among others, attacked Baldwin for his homosexuality in *Soul on Ice*, which became the sacred (male) text during the Black Power Movement" (215).

102. See Riggs (1994) on class issues within African American women's reform movement.

103. Here Lindsey articulates what was to become the classic formulation "All the Women Are White, All the Blacks Are Men" to which Gloria Hull et al. (1981) added, "But Some of Us Are Brave."

104. Morgan does exhibit in her gesture toward alliances the assumption that alliances are necessary in order to build connections from white, middle-class feminism toward other movements. Speaking of second-wave feminism in relation to the suffrage movement Morgan states, "I fear for the women's movement's falling into precisely the same trap as did our foremothers, the suffragists: creating a bourgeois movement that never quite dared enough, never questioned enough, never really reached out beyond its own class and race" (xxv–xxxvi). Here the phrase "its own class and race" could refer to a suffrage movement which had already been constituted as bourgeois, and yet, because the assumption is that the movement produced by "our foremothers" was (always) already white and middle-class the term can also slip to describe the second-wave women's movement. The issue, thus, posed by Morgan for the suffrage movement is not that it enacted racism, but that it did not move beyond its (natural?) origin. These assumptions erase portions of the history of both suffrage and second-wave movements and the work of working-class women and women of color.

105. A methodology focused on equivalence remains prevalent in both contemporary theory and practice and, thus, investigating its effects as employed by Morgan remains a worthwhile endeavor. Laclau and Mouffe (1985) have suggested that creating chains of equivalence is the methodology for establishing a progressive (over against a neo-conservative) hegemony in the contemporary politics of radical democracy. I give further consideration to their concept of equivalence in the Conclusion.

106. Thus, it does not address the ways in which lesbians both are and are not women.

Lesbians are not defined in relation to men as "wife, mother, etc.," and yet lesbians may also make specifically feminist claims on women's liberation because, for example, they are located as women in gender-segregated labor markets. At another point, Morgan produces a similar list—this time of alternatives to women's oppression—in which sexuality and "homosexuality, or bisexuality" figure prominently:

> No one, clearly, has any answers yet, although a host of possibilities present themselves to confuse us all even further. Living alone? Living in mixed communes with men and women? Living in all-women communes? Having children? Not having children? Raising them collectively, or in the old family structure? The father and/or other men sharing equally in child care, or shouldering it entirely, or not being permitted any participation? Homosexuality as a viable political alternative which straight women must begin to recognize as such? More—homosexuality, or bisexuality, as a beautiful affirmation of *human* sexuality, without all those absurd pre-fixes? Test-tube birth? Masturbation? Womb transplants? Gender control of the fetus? . . . Parthenogenesis? Why? Why not? (xxxvii, emphasis in original)

This list, however, performs much the same function as the first. Any difference articulated by homo- or bisexuality is reduced to "absurd pre-fixes," and the central issues of women's liberation are those of (hetero)sexuality—whether to live with men or not and how to conceive, bear, and rear children.

107. By emphasizing disagreement with each other Morgan is arguing against any single-voiced representation of "different" women, resisting a tokenism which would make any one "Black woman," for example, stand for all Black women. Morgan elsewhere argues against this type of tokenism: "There are three articles by black sisters in this book written specifically about the oppression of black women; it was important to have more than one or two voices speak for so many sisters, and in differing ways. (This is also the reason for there being three different short pieces on high-school women, and two on female homosexuality. These are all areas in which the movement is only beginning to explore itself, and it is of vital importance that we not take a simplistic view about *any* group of women, including ourselves)" (xxx). Florence Kennedy's piece is here excluded from the count of three apparently because her piece on "institutionalized oppression" is not "specifically" about Black women. The pieces on Black women and high school women are here sectioned off, as is the unmentioned piece on "The Mexican-American Woman" that appears in a section called "Colonized Women: The Chicana." This section also includes a piece on women in China. The two pieces on lesbians by Gene Damon and Martha Shelly are not sectioned off in this way, but are placed in a section called "The Invisible Woman: Psychological and Sexual Repression." And finally, who is Morgan referring to when she states, "including ourselves?" And, yet, while this resistance to tokenism (a resistance which is frequently ignored in the decades since the publication of *Sisterhood is Powerful*) is important, it is not clear that a section within a general anthology (in which white women, for example, are not similarly sectioned off) effectively addresses the issue. For a late 1970s critique of these sections of *Sisterhood is Powerful*, see Simons (1979, 390–91).

108. It is more than a little ironic, that a claim which, because of its erasure of history, angered many African Americans—that sexism is also enslavement—was for Morgan a gesture toward alliance.

109. The assumption here is that one is a woman before one is Black or brown, the problem of which Elizabeth Spelman (1988, 144–46) graphically demonstrated in her example of how differently people are categorized if forced to choose whether to go through the "gender" door, before the "race/ethnicity" door or vice versa.

110. I want to thank Miranda Joseph for clarifying these issues in e-mail communication.

111. Roof (1995) attributes this economy of the same operating in Morgan's Introduction to *Sisterhood is Powerful* to its (re)enactment of a dominant modern narrative of hetero(sexual) conflict: The narrative in which feminism is victorious "is a version of the heterologous (and overtly heterosexual) conflict conjoinder pattern by which most modern narrative is already defined: it is a 'marriage' plot where two 'sides' of a binary opposition encounter conflicts and delays on their way to ultimate joinder and successful reproduction (of a child, of narrative, of satisfaction, of a less oppressive world)" (58).

112. Beal raises the question of whether there are "any parallels between [the white women's liberation movement in the United States] and the movement on the part of the black women for total emancipation" (393). Recognizing that "the white women's movement is not monolithic" (393), she argues that "one must always look for the main enemy—the fundamental cause of the female condition" (394) and that "If the white groups do not realize that they are in fact fighting capitalism and racism, we do not have common bonds" (394)

113. Ong states, "In a recent paper, Marilyn Strathern (1987) notes that feminists discover themselves by becoming conscious of oppression from the Other. In order to restore to subjectivity a self dominated by the Other, there can be no shared experience with persons who stand for the Other. Thus, necessary to the construction of the feminist self is a nonfeminist Other . . . generally conceived of as 'patriarchy.' But Strathern also cautions that if women construct subjectivity for themselves, they do so strictly within the sociocultural constraints of their own society. This paper will suggest the problems feminists experience in achieving the separation they desire when it comes to understanding women in the non-Western world" (1988, 79).

114. There are disagreements among Duberman's narrators about the particular role of lesbians in the events that began the uprising.

115. The invocation of the metaphor of the "nation" is often taken as precisely the site of this reduction. Certainly the title of the book *Lesbian Nation: The Feminist Solution* accomplishes much of both the reduction and conflation of lesbian movement to a particular type of feminism that the book is read as doing. But, this attribution can also be a reductive reading of the book. The editors of *Nationalisms and Sexualities* (Parker et al. 1992) state, for example, "it is telling that Jill Johnston's *Lesbian Nation* remains anomalous in its apparently *unironic* choice of the nation as the image of an all female erotic community" (8). Given that the tone of the book as a whole is nothing if not ironic, it seems unlikely that the choice of the "nation" metaphor was unironic. Also, Johnston uses the term only a few times in the text of the book; the term "Gay/Feminist" is much more frequent. Nonetheless, it is the case that the ways in which "lesbian-nation" is taken up as the icon of a movement raises interesting questions. In discussing the implications of the "highly politicized term 'nation,' " Becki Ross (1995) argues that although in the 1990s "nationalism" evokes militaristic and even totalitarian images, "Over twenty years ago, a kind of North American lesbian nationalism inspired by Jill Johnston's book *Lesbian Nation* (1973) embodied a much more innocent, even quixotic, notion of non-violent militancy, feminist utopia and the power of women-only collective agency" (1995, 15–16). Yet, given that one of Ross's major critiques of LOOT's enactment of lesbian nationalism is "the normative 'whiteness,' unexamined class assumptions, ageism, and ableism that hobbled lesbian feminism in the 1970s," it is useful to ask whether the consolidating metaphor of "nation" contributed to the containment of diversity.

116. Johnston's participation in post-Stonewall Daughters of Bilitis indicates that Stonewall did not represent an immediate break with 1950s–1960s homophile organizations and that Daughters of Bilitis was not completely separate from "radical" lesbian politics. Her location in terms of feminist movement as described in the book is episodic, tied to

encounters with particular movement leaders—Ti-Grace Atkinson, Kate Millet, Gloria Steinem, Betty Friedan—and particular events and lectures

117. And she does state that "all women are lesbians" (68) (dropping a qualifying "if you agree" by the middle of the book).

118. Johnston states, "The solution is getting it together with women. Or separatism. The non-separatist woman who is not included in the common conception of the feminist solution may be viewed as a co-opted part of the problem inasmuch as every sphere of government and influence is controlled at the top by the man; thus the essential separatist solution is operative at present in theory and in consciousness and at the local manifest levels of communal fugitive enterprises. The lesbian feminist's withdrawal as far as possible from the source of oppression can in no way be construed as a political cop-out. On the contrary it is at this point that the confluence of the personal/political (articulated but not significantly explored by feminists as a whole) attains the dimension of imperative reality to the lesbian" (1973, 181).

119. John D'Emilio's (1983) essay, "Capitalism and Gay Identity," made a distinction between "activity" and "identity" central to lesbian and gay theory.

120. "The lesbian has experienced male prejudice within gay liberation and heterosexual fear within women's liberation" (184).

121. The ambivalences of seeking a single base and also trying to articulate connections among movements are expressed in the following passage:

> Gay revolution addresses itself to the total elimination of the sexual caste system around which our oppressive society is organized and through which distinctions of class and race are reinforced and maintained. The target remains the same—the ruling class male, and the ruling class aspirations of every other male, but not by the old definition of that target as simply economically oppressive. It is now recognized that any Marxist-Socialist analysis must acknowledge the sexist underpinnings of every political economic power base. Gay liberation cannot be considered apart from women's liberation. Gay liberation *is* in reality a feminist movement. The oppression of women is pivotal in the strategy and goals of the gay sexual revolution. The more overt discrimination and persecution of the male homosexual makes this point clear. I mean that the hatred of the gay male is rooted in the fear of the loss of male power and prestige. . . . Gay liberation emerged out of women's liberation and through the critically intermediate figure of the lesbian the two liberation fronts unite in a Gay/Feminist movement. . . . The lesbian is the key figure in the social revolution to end the sexual caste system, or heterosexual institution, for she is the clearly disenfranchised of the four sexes. (182–83)

122. "i didn't understand it and didn't want to know from it. i thought i had the last word in feminism and that was that i was an up front lesbian" (118). Later in the book, after her disheartening encounter with the "uptown feminists" in the gay-straight consciousness raising group, Ti-Grace Atkinson is the one feminist with whom Johnston still identifies (234).

123. In the essay, "The Myth of the Myth of the Vaginal Orgasm" (164–73), Johnston also validates the use of dildoes as a central part of lesbian sex. Dildoes were another site of critique of "male-identified" sex as anti-feminist. See Samois (1987 [1981]) on these arguments.

124. One such reference to analogy directly follows the passage quoted. This reference also shows the intertwining of ambivalence about responding to the claims of anti-racist movements while using those movements as a basis for political standing: "My initial reaction to the black movement was hey wait a minute I didn't *choose* to be born white, and let me tell *you* about the problems of a white homosexual female in . . . et cetera. Now I suggest

you go up to a black person and say White People Have Problems Too and see what kind of response you get. I'm going on record here to notify every heterosexual male and female that every lesbian and every homosexual is all too aware of the problems of the heterosexuals since they permeate every aspect of our social political economic and cultural lives" (137). See also 139, 144, 145, 185, 249.

125. The history of relations between lesbians and feminist movement is both quite complicated and disputed. Echols argues that the "gay-straight split" in the early 1970s "crippled the movement, ending long-term friendships, partnerships, and groups" (1989, 204). Whittier, in her study of feminist movement in Columbus, Ohio, argues for a relatively continuous presence and importance of lesbians and lesbian issues within "the women's movement": "There were some tensions between lesbians and heterosexual feminists, to be sure, but the 'gay-straight split' in Columbus was much less intense than the conflicts other authors have described" (1995, 20). Taylor and Rupp (1993), also basing much of their research in Columbus, Ohio, similarly argue for the on-going centrality of lesbian activism to feminist movement. King (1990) meanwhile argues specifically for the complexity of any mapping of the term(s) "gay/straight" in constituting "feminism."

126. For descriptions of this type of encounter see Ross (1995), particularly chapters 7 and 8 on "Coalition Politics."

127. The contributors to *Sisterhood is Powerful* tend either to connect personal experiences of work to Marxist analysis or to make Marxist analysis the basis for understanding women's oppression. Part of this difference undoubtedly lies in a difference in site of analysis. Judith Ann in the "Secretarial Proletariat" is analyzing her experience working in corporate structures, while the members of The Furies are analyzing the continuation of "class behavior" in a movement setting which has already to some extent removed itself from corporate work structures, and yet, class conflict among the members continues.

128. The essays generally refer to a four- or five-fold distinction: "lower class" or "poor," "working-class," "middle-class," "upper-middle-class," and "rich."

129. Bunch and Myron write:

> Class distinctions are an outgrowth of male domination and as such, not only divide women along economic lines but also serve to destroy vestiges of women's previous matriarchal strength. For example, women in peasant, agricultural, and lower class cultures are often called 'dominant' because they retain some of that matriarchal strength. Male supremacist societies must try to eliminate this female strength. The primary means of doing this both in the US and in other countries is through the domination and promotion of middle class values, including an image of the female as a passive, weak, frivolous sex object and eager consumer. The class system thus not only puts some women in a position of power over others but also weakens all women. Analyzing these and other ways that patriarchy, white supremacy, and capitalism reinforce one another is crucial to the future of feminism. (8)

Note, however, that the primacy of gender oppression slips as this passage moves along. Economic arrangements are the site of destroying or maintaining vestiges of "matriarchal strength." "The *primary* means" of establishing male supremacy and eliminating female strength is the class system and the domination of middle-class culture.

130. It should be noted that while the essays in *Class and Feminism* take up race as an issue, Bunch and Myron admit in the Introduction that "The Furies, is a lesbian/feminist organization composed of white lower, working, and middle class women" (1974, 7).

131. Both Coletta Reid's essay, "Recycled Trash," and the joint essay by Reid and Charlotte Bunch, "Revolution Begins at Home," are concerned with such failures in alliance.

132. It should be noted that Myron is critical of particular types of feminist activity

around class as reinscribing rather than resisting the class system. For example, "One of the most horrifying responses in the women's movement today is that of the 'political' woman who actually goes out and works in a factory so she can look at the working class women and talk to them and maybe drop a little socialism now and then. You don't get rid of oppression just by merely recognizing it. This patronization is outrageous and every woman in the place is sure to smell the stench a mile off" (40). This type of cross-class field work is one of the methods used in discussion of class in *Sisterhood is Powerful*. See "Two Jobs: Women Who Work in Factories" (Morgan 1970, 127–36).

133. "While in some circles 'sisterhood was powerful,' for the Chicana, perhaps, it was not" (Gutiérrez 1993, 50); Bonnie Thornton Dill also questions the widespread applicability of sisterhood while simultaneously exploring "prospects for an all-inclusive sisterhood": "The cry 'Sisterhood is powerful!' has engaged only a few segments of the female population in the United States. Black, Hispanic, Native American, and Asian American women of all classes, as well as many working-class women, have not readily identified themselves as sisters of the white middle-class women who have been in the forefront of the movement" (Dill 1983, 131). See also María Lugones and Elizabeth Spelman, "Have We Got a Theory for You! Feminist Theory, Cultural Imperialism and the Demand for 'The Woman's Voice'" (1983) and María Lugones in collaboration with Pat Alake Rosezelle in "Sisterhood and Friendship as Feminist Models" (1992). Ellen Carol DuBois and Vicki L. Ruiz (1990) similarly make use of and challenge the metaphor in the title to their women's history anthology, *Unequal Sisters*. Judith Roof (1995) has criticized the metaphor of sisterhood and the anthology *Sisterhood is Powerful* as consolidating feminist movement within a family narrative that "not only tends to complete the erasure of positional differences among women (and all issues relating to position), but also . . . invokes all of the power disparities of intrafamilial squabbles whose resolution is usually a return to a status quo" (57).

134. Some of these tensions are evident in Stein (1993). Walters (1996) argues that "queer" theory and politics are often set up in contradistinction to 1970s "lesbian feminism." Although she relates a story of boring, flannel-wearing lesbians over against pomo, drag-loving queers (844), she doesn't cite any specific sources for this story. Moreover, she tends to conflate queer theory, politics, and postmodernism, showing that stories in defense of 1970s feminism can participate in the same dynamic of self-definition through overdrawn opposition, this time defining a feminism based on connection to the 1970s over against the queer-pomo-theory of the 1990s.

135. Ross, for example, inscribes a strong split on the issue of diversity between the 1970s and 1980s: "In the 1980s, women of colour and immigrant women, Jewish women, disabled women, and working-class women charged feminism, and lesbian feminism, with its white, Christian, able-bodied, middle-class character" (1995, 219).

136. The implication of Butler's theory is that the self is not the origin of morality in the Kantian sense of the "self-legislating" individual or moral agent who wills his own acts. Rather, according to Foucault, this sense of self-legislation is a mis-recognition of the effect of discourses as the cause. Thus, the human being as subject (of language and morality) is not the origin of the discourses it speaks or enacts, but is rather an effect of these discourses. The beauty of the self-legislating individual as the marker of freedom is that the individual has taken on the role of disciplining the self. As Foucault argues in *Discipline and Punish* (1977), through the panopticon the individual is impelled to impose on himself disciplinary practices that were once externally imposed on him (although Foucault at this point also undersells the on-going importance of physical violence as a disciplinary technique in conjunction with impelled self-discipline). Thus, self-discipline becomes a hallmark of the modern individual.

137. Dominant gender discourse is interstructured with discourses of race and class

dominance such that the claim to womanhood (or manhood) and hence to personhood is made tenuous for anyone outside dominant race and class communities. The gendered division of moral labor restricts white, middle-class women's activities in certain ways, by pinning them to the identity woman—the complementary partner of man—and proscribing activities outside the bounds of that role. Yet, African American women have often been denied their position as women, since their labor and activities have not necessarily been aligned with the roles prescribed by dominant gender. Narrow and exclusionary definitions of gender have led to important challenges to the category itself, such as Sojourner Truth's question "Ar'n't I a Woman?" or the slogan, "I am a Man, I am Somebody," used by striking Memphis Sanitation Workers and Martin Luther King, Jr., in 1968. Yet, African American women have also faced exclusions enacted by pinning them to the identity of women, as occurred when the Fifteenth Amendment to the Constitution barred denial of the right to vote on account of "race, color, or previous condition of servitude," but left African American women disenfranchised on account of sex. The definition of gender as two, and only two, complementary persons also reinforces compulsory heterosexuality. Those persons who do not accept the necessity of a partner who is their complementary opposite (whether they choose no partner, one who is not their opposite, or multiple partners) are also likely to labor and act outside the bounds of "appropriately" divided moral labor, and thus to lose their claim on moral personhood.

138. It is sedimentation which gives weight to traditions and which makes social constructions difficult to change. Initially, the theoretical move to the social construction of, for example, gender from a view of sex roles as biologically determined was a move to recognize the changeability of gender roles. If gender was socially "constructed" it could be deconstructed and/or re-constructed. Gender as a sedimented discourse, however, has in many ways proven resistant to change, even more so because one has to "assume" a gender in order to become a human being. Thus, social construction theory has not provided an easy path toward social change.

139. On the complexity and "invention" of relations between past and present see Hobsbawm and Ranger (1983).

140. Meaning exceeds the intention of the performer. Yet, as Butler argues, this excess and the instability it implies is not simply a failure: "The task will be to consider this threat and disruption not as a permanent contestation of social norms condemned to the pathos of perpetual failure, but rather as critical resources in the struggle to rearticulate the very terms of symbolic legitimacy and intelligibility" (3).

141. For Laclau and Mouffe (1985) it is ultimately articulatory chains, the connections among multiple meanings, that determine the meaning of a particular social field.

142. The two meanings of articulation are intertwined, because it is the surpluses and slippages of meaning in communication that allow or create the space for connections to be made. As Laclau and Mouffe argue with respect to the social: "Neither absolute fixity nor absolute non-fixity is possible" (111). Absolute fixity is not possible because of a "surplus of meaning" which is the "necessary terrain of every social practice." Communication is necessary precisely because persons are different from one another, but this difference also implies that meaning will never be exactly the same for all participants in communication. If meaning were completely transparent, this difference would be lost and all subject positions would ultimately merge. However, "the impossibility of an ultimate fixity of meaning implies that there have to be partial fixations—otherwise, the very flow of differences would be impossible" (112). Difference would be indistinguishable, and it would return to ultimate similarity. The impossibility of absolute non-fixity means that the space in-between fixity and non, what Laclau and Mouffe call a "no-man's-land [that makes] articulatory practice possible" (110–11), is not a normless vacuum but a space of articulation—of partially fixing

meanings and constructing connections. Thus, norms maintain partially fixed meanings and these meanings partially determine—they regulate—activity and the creation of value. The impossibility of absolute fixity means, however, that these norms are always open to change, to iterations which fix the meaning of the norms "differently."

143. Laclau and Mouffe (1985) argue that the creation of an alternative hegemony is necessary, because only an alternative hegemony can secure the productive power of a given social order. Because production, including norm productive activity, is always intertwined with regulation only an alternative hegemony can effectively empower an alternative social order. I take up the question of the relationship between alliance and hegemony in the next chapter. In this chapter I focus on the production of alternative articulations in both senses, the production or articulation of different norms and the articulations or connections that form alliances among normative activities.

144. Historical contextualization also challenges the division in ethics between modern reason as a site of agency and "traditions" as a site of determinism. Moral traditions are in Kantian terms "dogmatisms," to be overcome by modern reasoning which does not depend on the specificity of any particular culture, but is rather a capacity shared by all human beings. This distinction is currently maintained by theorists such as Habermas (1984–87, 2:329–30), yet the division between "modernity" and "traditions" often encodes a dominative practice (as I argue at length in Jakobsen 1995b). Mohanty has, for example, identified the problem of "First world" feminists reading "different" women as "a homogeneous, undifferentiated group leading truncated lives, victimized by the combined weight of 'their' traditions, cultures, and beliefs, and 'our' (Eurocentric) history" (1994, 145–46). In this configuration agency is ascribed to western women while "other" women are determined by their cultures. This modernity-traditions configuration also posits the relationship between agency and determinism as an opposition rather than asking how "traditions, cultures, and beliefs" are actively constructed in history. The modernity-traditions distinction uncritically accepts both the claims of modern reasoning to be outside of, different than, a tradition, and of traditions which claim to be unchanging through history rather than constructed in history. As Eric Hobsbawm and colleagues have argued in *The Invention of Tradition* (Hobsbawm and Ranger 1983), both a given tradition and its connection to the past may be as much "invented" as it is "real." Hobsbawm argues that the on-going invention of traditions in industrialized societies, such as the various ritual practices which surround and enact modern nationalism, imply that "such formalizations are not confined to so-called 'traditional' societies, but also have their place in modern ones" (5).

145. To emphasize boundaries through a practice of specification such as I undertake in this chapter does not vitiate the importance of concurrent strategies of inclusion. The complex and shifting nature of the boundaries which separate African American and white women implies that the recognition of womanist movement as a different undertaking than feminism does not remove imperatives for feminists to work for inclusivity, nor does it indicate an assumed connection between Black and white feminists.

146. On the relative autonomy of social differentiation in terms of race, see West (1988).

147. Hoagland states, "As I was coming to lesbian-feminist consciousness out of my earlier political consciousness, like many I came to believe that feminism was the theory and lesbianism the practice" (1988, 7). Hoagland notes the Atkinson formulation and then attributes the shift and conflation to Johnston: "In 1975 Jill Johnston said, 'Feminism is the complaint and lesbianism is the solution,' as cited by Sara Scott in *A Feminist Dictionary*, ed. Cheris Kramarae and Paula A. Treichler (Boston: Pandora Press, 1985), p. 229" (1988, 305–306, fn 12).

148. Cannon, in subsequent publication, directly challenges moves to "discipline"

womanist scholarship along this and other lines: "[W]e must disentangle the power relations within American society wherein certain people whether by accident, design, providence, or the most complicated means of academic currency exchange high-handedly dictate the specific disciplinary aims, setting the parameters as well as the agenda for each field of study" (1995, 24). She also argues against "Professors of religion [who] believe that they have the right to resist the expansion of the field by misinterpreting womanist scholarship as apolitical, inferior, and dangerously essentialist" (1995, 24). In this case the charge of "essentialism" works to exclude womanist scholarship and thus to reproduce the field of religious studies as "the same."

149. Both Cannon (1995, 24) and Hoagland (1988, 7) locate their work specifically as theoretical activity. Hoagland argues that lesbian work has been located as the practice of feminist theory, thereby subsuming lesbian movement under feminism. She argues that the difference of lesbian theory must be recognized in order to develop an adequate analysis of heterosexuality and its ties to gender relations. On the relationship between feminist theory and feminist theology see Davaney and Chopp (1997).

150. Throughout this section I will use the terminology "Black" or "African American" following the particular text which I am reading. I will also use the term "Black Church" as employed by Cannon and by Lincoln and Mamiya (1990) in *The Black Church in the African American Experience.*

151. Katie Cannon, personal communication, 1993.

152. Cannon criticizes the "conventional, often pretentious morality of middle-class American ideals" (76); "the parochialism of white culture which projects racist images upon the whole extent of the universe" (76); and "the white elitist attributes of passive gentleness and an enervative delicacy, considered particularly appropriate to womanhood" (125).

153. For a description of how whiteness developed as a racial category in conjunction with discourses of racism see Cornel West (1982), "A Genealogy of Modern Racism," chapter 2 in *Prophesy Deliverance! An Afro-American Revolutionary Christianity.*

154. "Black women have justly regarded survival against tyrannical systems of triple oppression as a true sphere of moral life" (1988, 3). Cannon specifically discusses free will as central to dominant understandings of responsibility on pages 144-45. It is important to recognize that Cannon is distancing herself from notions of freedom found in white ethics which emphasize individual freedom in the form of free will or free choice from the historical importance of freedom in the African American community. Lincoln and Mamiya (1990) state, "Throughout black history the term 'freedom' has found a deep religious resonance in the lives and hopes of African Americans" (4). They state the two understandings of freedom as "For whites freedom has bolstered the value of American individualism: to be free to pursue one's destiny without political or bureaucratic interference or restraint. But for African Americans freedom has always been communal in nature" (5). Cannon is specifically critical of the way in which emphasis on individual freedom in white ethics has reinforced capitalist social formation and of the assumption of free will or choice as the necessary *prerequisite* of moral agency, an assumption which excludes from agency those African Americans effectively denied freedom due to enslavement and white domination.

155. Cannon (1988, 12) quotes Barbara Christian regarding "the position the Black woman holds within her community, for she has, since its beginnings, been entrusted with its survival and enrichment" (Christian 1980, 60).

156. Cannon's specific understanding of community relatedness derives from her work on Howard Thurman, and the demand of responsibility to act for social reform or change is elaborated in her work on Martin Luther King, Jr. For more on these relations and responsibilities see Cannon's Chapter 6.

157. Bernice Johnson Reagon has stated that one of the dangers which this ethic carries

for Black women is a loss to the individual woman's health and well-being for the sake of communal survival. Bernice Johnson Reagon, "God's Gon' Trouble the Water," Emory University, March 18, 1992.

158. Drawing on Black women's literary traditions, particularly the life and work of Zora Neale Hurston, Cannon elaborates the structure of womanist responsibility by describing three sets of virtues taken from Mary Burgher's (1979) description of Black women writers, "the Black woman's daring act of remaking her lost innocence into invisible dignity, her never-practiced delicacy into quiet grace and her forced responsibility into unshouted courage" (Cannon 1988, 17). In her review of Cannon's book, Cheryl Sanders (1989), questions this particular description of womanist virtues: "However, the ethical norms that serve as a focus for Cannon's book—the 'invisible dignity,' 'quiet grace,' and 'unshouted courage' posited by Burgher—seem far removed from womanist criteria and much less credible as indicators of black women's moral wisdom. While dignity, grace, and courage are undeniably authentic features of black women's moral agency, adjectives such as 'invisible,' 'quiet,' and 'unshouted' hardly fit Hurston's life or work." I understand Cannon's use of the adjectives invisible, quiet and unshouted to refer to those ways in which Black women have often had to hide or mask their acts of resistance for the sake of survival.

159. For other constructive ethical texts by Black women see, for example, Marcia Riggs (1994), Emilie Townes (1993), and Emilie Townes, ed. (1993).

160. Cannon makes this connection in the context of considering how the theology of the Black community could have sustained Zora Neale Hurston in her life struggles, particularly through the difficult period of her life following social ostracization due to charges that she had been sexually involved with a ten-year-old boy (1988, 160–61). Cannon never specifically delineates how the Black Church in particular would have helped Hurston. Without such an explication, the question remains of whether it is possible that Black Churches would have participated in the community betrayal that Cannon understands to have undermined the continuing promise of Hurston's life and work. This question is important in light of Cannon's stated intent to test her methodology according to the criterion of "whether Black feminists who have given up on the community of faith will gain new insights concerning the reasonableness of theological ethics in deepening the Black woman's character, consciousness and capacity in the ongoing struggle for survival" (1988, 6). In addition, the fact that accusations of sexual misconduct were used to discredit an audacious woman like Hurston raises issues of the connections between racial and sexual oppression which are not addressed by Cannon in this text, although she does address these issues elsewhere (Cannon, 1989, 93). It should be clear that Cannon is not simply validating the Black Church tradition as if it has no problem with sexism. Cannon's claim to a "womanist" tradition effectively challenges the participation of the Black Church tradition in sexist domination. When describing her choice of specifically womanist methodology, Cannon states, "For too long the Black community's theological and ethical understandings have been written from a decidedly male bias" (1988, 6).

161. Cannon draws these universal claims from an analysis of the theology of Howard Thurman and Martin Luther King. She carefully analyzes distinctions between the two theologians while drawing out the "basic theological themes" underlying the ethics of both thinkers (1988, 174).

162. This claim for both specificity and universality is a "both/and" claim of the type described by Patricia Hill Collins (1990, 29).

163. Lincoln and Mamiya (1990, 12–13) argue for a dialectical understanding of the relationship between universalism and particularism as one of six major dialectics which form their sociological model of the Black Church. Marcia Riggs (1991) also emphasizes the

connection between the particular and the universal in developing her ethic for Black liberation (147, 151).

164. Appiah argues that some post-colonial Africans reject relativism so to prevent the possibility that the "horrifying new-old Africa of exploitation is to be understood, legitimated, in its own local terms." Persons in the post-colonial situation may instead appeal to universals in "a certain simple respect for human suffering," which prompts revolt against misery (353). While Appiah's argument against an imposition of relativism by Europeans onto Africans is convincing and his broadening of the modern/postmodern discursive field through the introduction of the non-(post)modern "neotraditional" is important, I doubt his implied argument that universals are either necessary or sufficient to prevent the legitimation of horror. Just as horror can be legitimated in local terms it can be de-legitimated in local terms; neither localism nor universalism is a sure guarantee against such horror. To claim such status for either is to claim the possibility of a moral guarantee.

165. For white feminists to respond to womanists changes the dominant division of moral labor by establishing Black women as primary norm producers to which white women might respond with labor for social change. The structures of racist relationship which separate (Black) womanist and (white) feminist movements cannot simply be discarded. Reading Cannon's text for the boundaries that it establishes between feminists and womanists through claims to specificity is critical at this point.

166. Hoagland (28–29) is extending the concepts of "compulsory heterosexuality," delineated by Adrienne Rich (1980) and "hetero-reality" delineated by Janice Raymond (1986, 3–4). Rich defines compulsory heterosexuality as a political institution which assures men's access to women physically, economically, and emotionally. Raymond defined hetero-reality as a hetero-relational society structured by the pervasive ideology that women exist for men.

167. Hoagland (1988, 256–58) counters the Kantian argument that acting from duty is morally superior to acting from caring for and about other persons. She does not recognize moral value in undertaking actions about which one does not care.

168. Hoagland creates the word "autokoenony," "from the greek 'auto' ('self') and 'koinonia' ('community, or any group whose members have something in common')" (1988, 145).

169. See Sedgwick (1990, 27–35) for an argument against the conflation of gender and sexuality.

170. In this sense Calhoun's (1994, 1995) project dovetails with Hoagland's.

171. This move is similar to the stance adopted by bell hooks (1989) in refusing to adopt the modified term "black feminist," in favor of fully claiming both black and feminist political stances.

172. The concept of moving through or across the fields of modernism and postmodernism was suggested to me by Maria Pramaggiore in her comments on an earlier draft of this chapter.

173. For example, in her response to Cheryl J. Sanders's discussion of the term "womanist," Cannon states, "a womanist liberation theological ethic rejects heuristic concepts such as 'heteropatriarchal familialist ideology,' and 'compulsory heterosexism,' but seeks instead heuristic models that explore sacred power and benevolent cohumanity" (Cannon, 1989, 93).

174. In formulating the question in this way "queer" is named as a site that is not co-extensive with, but neither does it supersede, "lesbian." Some women might undertake their work as queer and not lesbian, others as lesbian and not queer, and others as both lesbian and queer.

175. Diana Fuss (1991) questions whether the "inside/outside" dichotomy is a useful

focus for political intervention or whether such a focus submits to the terms of the dichotomy. The assertion of complexity is one method for intervening in the constraints of this dichotomy.

176. I also consider these issues at greater length in Jakobsen (1995b) and in my contribution to Davaney and Chopp (1997), which includes an initial reading of "Gay Rights, Special Rights."

177. Schematically, it is the norm in her triad "critique, norm, and utopia," which as the middle and mediating term does the work of providing these criteria, while the critique is directed against the dogmatic foundationalism of neo-Kantianism, and utopia provides the possibility for extending norms beyond the limits of modern rationalism.

178. In fact, Benhabib (1986) argues that through the process of rational interaction and social interpretation our particular needs can be transformed into common needs or generalizable interests.

179. See Eisenstein (1981) and Landes (1988) on the connections between a public-private split and the exclusion of women from the "public."

180. Ernesto Laclau and Chantal Mouffe (1985) have identified the mechanism at work in this type of stabilization as follows: "[I]t is known how the frontal opposition of many groups to a system can cease to be exterior to it and become simply a contradictory but internal location within that system—that is another difference. A hegemonic formation also embraces what opposes it, insofar as the opposing force accepts the system of basic articulations of that formation as something it negates, but the *place of negation* is defined by the internal parameters of the formation itself" (139, emphasis in original).

181. Benhabib here fails to acknowledge the complex relationships between the socially structured categories of identity which frequently inform oppression—such as race, ethnicity, and religion—and the communities and movements which resist this oppression.

182. The multi-cultural alliance is interesting, because the videotape later attacks multi-cultural curricula and because homophobia has been used, for example in New York State, to de-rail an entire multi-cultural curriculum.

183. This motif is shown perhaps most dramatically at the very end of the video when a Black child apparently is carried away by a white gay person.

184. I would like to thank Laura Levitt and Mary Hunt for pointing out the importance of this use of Kramer's body.

185. The issues of racial visibility and queer visibility are here brought together in the tokenized representation of Ru Paul as the non-threatening drag queen.

186. Kramer's use of this particular politics may be tied to his own distrust of (homo)-sexual desire as displayed in his 1987 novel *Faggots*.

187. For example, Kramer's identification with King appears also to be based on his status as a slain leader who died because the American public didn't care to protect his body, just as Kramer, a leader who has made visible his body as a carrier of HIV, is facing the possibility of death from AIDS because the American public has not cared to act more effectively in response to the pandemic.

188. For a full explanation of how Benhabib's configuration of universality grants recognition to non-western "others" while simultaneously effacing them, see Jakobsen (1995b).

189. I discuss the naturalization of the western "we" as a universal "we" in Benhabib's texts at length in Jakobsen (1995b). This naturalization depends on a naturalization of historical processes of modernization and rationalization which assumes that because these historical processes have become "global" processes they form the context for cross-cultural interaction. See Grewal and Kaplan (1994) for analysis of the unevenness of these "global processes."

190. For an explanation of cross-cultural moral interaction which does require a mutual entering into of each "other's" "worlds" see Lugones (1990b).

191. Perhaps most tellingly, Benhabib never engages with the question of universals which exceed this modern frame, such as Katie Cannon's (1988) *Black Womanist Ethics*. For example, at the end of the essay "Feminism and the Question of Postmodernism," (1992, 203–41), Benhabib states, "The fact that the view of Gilligan or Chodorow or Sarah [sic] Ruddick (or for that matter Julia Kristeva) only articulate the sensitivities of white, middle-class, affluent, first world, heterosexual women may be true (although I even have empirical doubts about this). Yet what are we ready to offer in their place: as a project of an ethics which should guide us in the future are we able to offer a better vision than the synthesis of autonomous justice thinking and empathetic care?" (230). In order to answer this question, Benhabib's task would be to engage those authors like Canon and Sarah Hoagland (1988) who have offered alternatives.

192. Benhabib also misses the full implications of articulatory practice by limiting articulation to the linguistic. Ernesto Laclau and Chantal Mouffe (1985) argue that "It is nevertheless important to understand the radical extent of the changes which are necessary in the political imaginary of the Left, if it wishes to succeed in founding a political practice fully located in the field of the democratic revolution and conscious of the depth and variety of hegemonic articulations which the present conjuncture requires. The fundamental obstacle to this task is . . . the conviction that the social is sutured at some point, from which it is possible to the meaning of any event independent of any articulatory practice" (176–77). Benhabib agrees that meaning can only be fixed through articulation, but this articulation is linguistic articulation. The "depth and variety" of articulatory practices is glossed over and, thereby, the diverse and complex ways in which connections among persons and groups might be made is undercut. Thus, Benhabib does not fully follow through on how the public as a space of solidarity as well as rights might be built up.

193. An example, here, would be the "sex wars" set off by attempts to unify feminism through the singular issue of an anti-pornography movement (Echols 1989, 289).

194. "[T]he approach that I am defending shows how social relations and identities are always constructed through asymmetrical forms of power. Since some social agents have more power than others, this will force the latter to establish some forms of alliances against them, and, in order to do so, they will have to construct their demands by articulating the demands of others. Hence the crucial role of categories such as 'hegemony' and 'articulation'" (Rajchman 1995, 40).

195. Several theorists have presented the possibility of multiple publics, questioning both whether a singular public sphere in relation to any given nation-state has ever existed historically and whether the idea of a single public should operate as an ethical or political ideal. Calhoun's (1993) anthology on *Habermas and the Public Sphere* includes a range of these positions. Calhoun suggests, however, that "It seems to me a loss simply to say that there are many public spheres, however, for that will leave us groping for a new term to describe the communicative relationships among them" (37). Note that Calhoun here reasserts communication as the primary site for theorizing relationships among publics. Various theorists have also presented a number of different ideas for how the relationships among publics should be conceptualized. Rather than locating the state as a strong public of decision making and a correlative civil society as the weak public of opinion formation and legitimation, Nancy Fraser (1990, reprinted in Calhoun 1993) has suggested the need for multiple strong publics and weak publics in reconfiguring relationships at a number of different sites including political, economic, social, and domestic spaces.

196. A primary difference between Benhabib and Foucault, for example, occurs with

regard to the role of legitimation in identifying domination and violence in the exercise of force. For Benhabib domination "suggests an *illegitimate* exercise of power bordering on force and perhaps even violence" (1986, 218, emphasis in original). Foucault, however, is not as concerned with the question of legitimacy in a power relation as with the possible resistances open to participants in the relationship. Even a legitimated exercise of power, as hierarchical gender relations historically have been legitimated, if it leaves little room for resistance may be dominative. Thus, Foucault uses the "traditional conjugal relationship in the eighteenth and nineteenth centuries" as the example of domination. Although the gender relations inscribed in this traditional relationship were at the time legitimated, they were also so constraining for women that the various resistances a wife might undertake were "finally no more than a certain number of tricks which never brought about a reversal of the situation" (1984b, 12).

197. As Chantal Mouffe (Rajchman 1995) argues, "To believe that a final resolution of conflicts is eventually possible—even if it is seen as an asymptomatic approaching to the regulative ideal of free unconstrained communication as in Habermas—is something that far from providing the necessary horizon of the democratic project, in fact, puts it at risk. . . . Any understanding of pluralism whose objective is to reach harmony is ultimately a negation of the positive value of diversity and difference" (44). Benhabib is also critical of the fact that Habermas sometimes appeals to consensus as the ideal outcome of intersubjective communication. She argues instead for intersubjective communication as a way of life, an on-going conversation (1992, 38). But, she also maintains the necessity of providing criteria for adjudicating conflict, and in the slippage in the relationship between the general and the particular lets slip the commitment to diversity to maintain the possibility of adjudication.

198. On some of the empowerments and constraints offered by technologies of imagination, see Anderson (1991 [1983]).

199. If Woman invoked only a single boundary then "gender" would refer only to the man-woman opposition, but as we have seen "gender" also invokes relations of race, class, religion, sexuality. . . .

200. It is important to note that modern, rational universalism is also criticized from perspectives which could be termed "conservative." Tronto, for example, lists among critics of modern universalism "Thomists" like Alasdair MacIntyre (1981, 1988), and "other assorted Aristotelians" (Tronto 1993, 149). Thus, advocacy of neither universalism nor pluralism is in and of itself politically progressive.

201. The anxiety about relativism is not simply reflective of ethical concerns. Rather, it points to two poles around which a number of issues in contemporary feminist and cultural theories have developed. For example, in her review essay, "Feminist Standpoint Theory and the Problems of Knowledge," Helen Longino (1993) describes two poles which mark contemporary feminist ethics and politics as well as epistemology: 1) an emphasis on pluralism in resistance to "hegemonic orthodoxy," expressing an important suspicion of attempts to replace one discredited (epistemological, ethical, or political) unity with another; and 2) because pluralism can easily slide into an uncritical valuing of heterogeneity or proliferation, a (re)turn to unity in diversity.

202. Tronto ultimately argues that the contemporary heightening of criticism of moral universalism is the result of historical shifts in economic and political conditions with the "result that the separation of public and private life [on which rational universalism depended] can no longer be sustained" (151). Tronto argues, however, that this shift does not "require that we abandon previous moral commitments, for example, to universalizability, or to a moral point of view that rejects special pleading to serve one's interests. What it also requires, though is that we recognize that humans are not only autonomous and equal, but

that they are also beings who require care" (152). In making this argument Tronto shifts back and forth between global economic conditions and "Western industrial societies," so that it is not finally clear to whom "we" refers, although the inference is those persons who have a previous moral commitment to universalism. She also does not specify a form of universalism. I have addressed the problems with this form of argument at length in Jakobsen (1995b).

203. It should be noted that Cortese (1990, 156) does not argue that rationalism should be abandoned, but rather that it does not suffice as a site for either emancipation or substantive moral life.

204. On the tensions between the individual as similarly equal to all other individuals and the individual as uniquely different from all others see Scott (1995).

205. Inderpal Grewal and Caren Kaplan (1994) in their Introduction to *Scattered Hegemonies: Postmodernity and Transnational Feminist Practices*, describe two poles in relation to pluralism which they hope to avoid: "In this collection of essays, we are interested in problematizing theory; more specifically, feminist theory. In many locations in the United States and Europe, theory often tends to be a homogenizing move by many First World women and men. That is, theory seems unable to deal with alterity at all or falls into a kind of relativism. Refusing either of these two moves, we would like to explore how we come to do feminist work across cultural divides" (2). Although Grewal and Kaplan never identify specifically what "kind" of relativism they wish to critique, it seems clear from their subsequent references that they are concerned about a kind of apolitical pluralism which cannot articulate a critique of dominative power relations. Grewal and Kaplan concur with Fred Pfeil's essay in the same volume that "ahistorical relativism is in danger of replacing historical specificity as well as feminist solidarity" (18), but they also argue that certain forms of postmodernism can be mobilized as "a critique of [postmodernism's] own approval of relativism" (7).

206. Specifically, Scott argues that the sexual difference between men and women, constituted through heterosexual desire, secured the boundaries of man as individual and different. The site of this differentiation was located in monogamous marriage which further differentiated man from the "primitive" (6). Thus, women's exclusion from the universal of human rights "was not an oversight, nor the result of the importation of old ideas about politics into the new regime. Rather, the equation of individuality and masculinity seemed to resolve an otherwise insoluble contradiction" (3). Scott goes on to argue that these contradictions of individualism "embraced two conflicting universalisms: the one the disembodied abstract individual, the other the so-called natural phenomenon of 'sexual difference'" (11). "Sexual difference" must be universal if the sameness of the individual is also to be universal. Thus, both identity and difference reside within the universal.

207. On the way in which Habermas establishes the relationship between "tradition" and "modernity" see Jakobsen (1995a, 340).

208. Zerilli is referring to, among others, Wittig's essay, "The Trojan Horse," (1984, reprinted in Wittig 1992, 68–75). Schor (1995), referring to Wittig's essay "Homo Sum" (1992, 46–58), similarly reads her as working to write lesbians into the universal. This reading is a significantly different appeal to the category of the universal than Schor's appeal to a feminist universal necessitated by and capable of consulting women's lack of freedom with regard to their bodies as specified by an equivalential list of violence done against women as discussed below.

209. Schor ultimately finds Wittig's work to be too tied to a structuralist "belief in the omnipotence of language in effecting social change" (1995, 38).

210. This claim is based in part on contemporary theories of dynamic systems (Hanneman 1988).

211. Young (1990, 190) argues that her conception of a heterogeneous public differs from interest group pluralism because its claim to status as a public implies that groups have to make accountable arguments for the justice of their position, rather than simply expressing their interests. She also argues for the representation of social groups rather than interest groups or ideological groups: "A social group is a collective of people who have affinity with one another because of a set of practices or way of life; they differentiate themselves from or are differentiated by at least one other group according to these cultural forms" (186). While her definition of a social group is based on shared practices and a way of life which differentiates it from interests, it also opens itself up to the type of policing for authenticity which dis-articulates complexity within groups.

212. In 1985, Laclau and Mouffe write similarly, "Between the logic of complete identity and that of pure difference, the experience of democracy should consist of the recognition of the multiplicity of social logics along with the necessity of their articulation. But this articulation should be constantly re-created and renegotiated, and there is no final point at which a balance is definitively achieved" (188).

213. Mouffe makes two steps in this argument which do not necessarily follow. First, throughout her article she tends to place the only possible site of a "we" as a common political identity:

> Nevertheless, the kind of pluralism I am advocating requires the establishment of a common bond, so that the multiplicity of democratic identities and differences do not explode into a separatism that would lead to the negation of the political community; for without any reference to the political community, democratic politics cannot exist. . . . A radical conception of citizenship could, I believe, provide that bond created through equivalence, that form of commonality that does not erase differences. It can play such a role because, as I have tried to show, it draws on an anti-essentialist framework according to which the commonality that is made possible by equivalence is not the expression of something positive, of a common essence, but of something purely negative. (1995, 44–45)

She does not clearly differentiate her invocation of a common bond as a horizon of meaning from those arguments she criticizes because they invoke the resolution of conflict as a horizon of meaning (1995, 44). I am suggesting alternatively that the space in-between the horizon of meaning of commonality and difference is a space of alliances, of building "we's" which are not defined by this opposition. The second problem is the assumption that chains of equivalence provide the only type of articulatory practice which can democratically constitute a "we." As with Benhabib's framework, the displacements which create "chains of equivalence" center the "west" and the norms of "western" democracy and undercut the radical potential of a democracy which can transfigure the western tradition. The contemporary theoretical project is to investigate those types of connections and relationships to analyze them in relation to diverse and complex norms. Thus, I am suggesting that the limits which are placed on pluralism are not necessarily those of a "common" identity, but the relationships (both connective and conflictual) among diverse and complex actors and their norms and values.

214. The meaning of "chains of equivalence" slips in *Hegemony and Socialist Strategy*. Sometimes equivalence is directly tied to the egalitarian imagination, as in the term "equivalential-egalitarian logic" (167). In this sense a chain of equivalence is a displacement of the egalitarian norm of democracy to a new group, for example, from equality among citizens to equality among genders. This displacement establishes equality at two sites: First it establishes the language of equality with reference to gender relations, persons of different genders should be equal; second, it establishes equality between the struggles for (egalitarian) citizenship rights and for (egalitarian) gender rights. Thus, feminist movement is a movement

for equal rights for women and as such it has equal claim to political space as do democratic movements for citizenship rights. Sometimes equivalence appears to refer simply to the links, the articulations, of hegemonic practice. So, for example, they refer to "the chain of equivalences equality = identity = totalitarianism," as a potentially hegemonic practice that does not necessarily participate in the "equivalential-egalitarian logic."

215. Thus, Laclau and Mouffe affirm the need for plurality in the face of the desire for transparency—a desire frequently activated in both progressive and conservative movements—whether in communication (the Habermasian utopia, the dream of a common language), in identity (the desire for a unified [woman] self and [women's] movement), or in the social (the desire to comprehend and reconcile the social in its totality).

216. I would also suggest that attention to this space would shift the potential meaning of the terms "equality" and "liberty" and further articulate the relationship between them. Laclau and Mouffe are making a strong and important political claim by holding equality and liberty together. In so doing, they resist the ways in which the two have been split apart either by Marxist movements which value equality while subordinating liberty or by neo-liberal movements which claim to value liberty and understand equality only in terms of an expression of liberty; thus, "equality" can mean only equality of opportunity, and democracy is subordinated to individual liberty. By arguing for a radically egalitarian and simultaneously plural society, Laclau and Mouffe challenge the binary which splits these terms. More importantly, it will also add more terms or norms to this process. Thus, the binary logic of equality split from liberty, or even the traces of the logic in equality limited by liberty as norms exterior to the (European) tradition of democratic revolution pull processes of democratization in new directions.

217. Thus, I am suggesting some possibilities for a complex theory of articulation (cf. Jameson 1995, 268–71).

218. An example of the shifts in identity which are necessary to alliance formation, but which do not necessarily produce "common" identity can be found in Jakobsen (1995a), a re-reading of Kobena Mercer's articulation of the complexities of position in relation to the controversies over Robert Mapplethorpe's photographs. Kobena Mercer argues like Laclau and Mouffe that it is the multiplicity of meaning, the ambi-valence, which allows him to undertake a practice of alliance formation in relation to the photographs of Robert Mapplethorpe in contemporary struggles over sexuality and art. Mercer initially reads Mapplethorpe's photographs of Black gay men as based on a racist split between Mapplethorpe as the subject of agency in creating the photographs and the Black male models as object. In light of Jesse Helms's homophobic attack on the photos, Mercer re-reads the photos in order to form an alliance in resistance to the Helmsian reading. Mercer is able to make an alliance with Mapplethorpe not because they share an identity as gay men, nor because anti-homophobic and anti-racist projects are equivalent, or can be made equivalent, rather it is precisely the space of ambi-valence between these struggles which allows the space for working to connect the anti-racist struggle within gay movement to the anti-homophobic struggle among various contestants in the battle over "art." Alliances in this sense are not simply amalgamations of given identities, but are rather constituted through the process of building new identities through relational work in the space in-between historically constituted identity. Mercer shifts his practices of identification in order to make an alliance with Mapplethorpe, and in so doing allows for the constitution of new forms of identity (new partially fixed nodes of identificatory practice). These shifts in practices of identification do not necessarily constitute a new *common* identity, but rather they constitute a new kind of relationship between Mercer and Mapplethorpe. Nor is common identity the telos or horizon of these practices, rather relationships and relational activities are the ground and horizon of activity. In order to be in movement together persons and groups need not share (or even

dream of sharing) a common identity, but rather we need to be able to work together and form on-going relationships.

219. At this point in the argument she does not make clear the evidence for the existence of this commonality, the limits of its particular application, or how it enables feminist gains.

220. On the complexity of claims and movements for women's bodily integrity in the contemporary United States see Jakobsen (1995c).

221. See Spivak (1988) on the ties between British opposition to sati and the extension of colonialism.

222. For an example of the contemporary critique of theories and practices of "community" see Joseph (1996).

223. The relational aspect of such a claim draws on the feminist insight that relationships are fundamental. What is often misunderstood when relationality is emphasized, particularly by the white, middle-class feminists whom Thistlethwaite criticizes for assuming connections, is that to claim relationships as fundamental does not imply that relationships are ontologically structured and necessarily good. Rather, social labor is necessary to establish relationships which are valuable to all parties concerned. Neither does a relational emphasis require that we all become friends before we can work together, nor that no boundaries be maintained across social divisions even if we do become friends. It is the process of negotiating boundaries which is critical to joint political action, not the process of reaching an understanding which transcends boundaries even if such a process is confined to the supposedly narrow limits of grounding rights in conflict resolution among different communities.

224. Drucilla Cornell (1993) provides an illustration through a contrast between a "Kantian understanding of the role of autonomy" and "Peirce's understanding of the self as 'habit'" (42) in the case of a man who thinks he should change his desires:

> Under the Kantian schema, he should try to control the desiring "me" through the reasoning, "I." Under the Peircian schema offered here, the same man will be *pulled* to transform his desires through the challenge to his habitual practice of desire inherent in his own conception of the ideal and in his contact with those he desires. He will not so much force himself to change as he will be forced to change. Yet he can also assess the changes in himself through the projection of hypothetical fantasies about himself, who he has been, and who he wants to become. He can *assess* as well as *accept* his habitual structure of desire as it inevitably breaks down in his contact with others. It is this process of assessment that allows him to intervene in what is happening to him. (1993 42–43, emphasis in original)

There are several important points in this description of change. First, in the Kantian formulation, the imperative to change is based in the opposition between reason and desire internal to a human subject (split between "me" and "I"), while in the Peircian formulation the imperative to change is instigated by interaction with others, but his own ideals are not lost in the space of interaction. Change always occurs in conjunction with assessment from the perspective of his ideals. Even in this description, however, the self appears to be an atomistic unit, influenced by interaction with others, whereas I am arguing that the self and his ideals or moral traditions are always relational and multiplicitous.

225. In Jakobsen (1995a) I consider a series of examples in contemporary public debates that demonstrate how the search for a clear and singular path of "agency" undercuts the effectiveness of feminist actions and attempts at alliance formation, for example, around the Anita Hill controversy.

226. The desire for unity can be enacted at various sites. Even when complex inter-relation is recognized as a starting point for subject formation, containment of diversity can still be enacted by positing an ideal of unity toward which we work. Thus, we begin from our various diverse and complexly interrelated moral traditions, but the purpose of inter-action, of dialogue, and of exchange will be to produce an ideal unity. The purpose of social movement is understood to be that of creating a not yet existent, but ideal, normative unity. Mullin argues that a site of unity could be an important part of the process of interrelation. Unity may lead her to "seek to understand the importance of her ties to multiple groups and to be sensitive to the working of power and privilege in all of those groups" (22). The site for unity that she suggests is a commitment to "understanding and fighting against the ef-fects of oppression on both persons and groups." It is important to note that she suggests that unity and homogeneity are not the same. Thus, she is articulating the possibility of simultaneously maintaining multiple identifications and a site of critique in relation to these various identifications. A focus on fighting oppression, however, places one in what Susan Gubar (1995) has identified as the "paradox of 'it takes one to know one,'" where identi-fications and activities are overdetermined by that which one is "fighting." In so doing, it unnecessarily narrows the connections and tensions among various identifications, failing to recognize that potential contradictions and critiques among and across sites may be about more than oppression, but also about different norms and traditions as shown by the differ-ences between, for example *Black Womanist Ethics,* built on the Black church tradition, and *Lesbian Ethics,* drawing on Greek philosophy (autokoenony) to describe ethical life in rela-tionships. A different method of configuring this relationship would be to locate critique of "oppression" as one part of various traditions of struggle, and in working in and between these traditions connections among struggles (which are not necessarily unities) can be pro-duced.

227. Diversity feels like loss if the only choices are a unity which is only sameness or a diversity which is only difference, where there are no relationships among differences, among diverse persons and communities. And so we flip back and forth in argument be-tween unity and difference, unable to articulate the various types of relationships between these two choices.

228. Mullin, like Pfeil and others, worries that the recognition of multiplicity can come "at the price of the exclusion of any commitment whatsoever" (17). She does not establish multiplicity as a good in and of itself, "neither heterogeneity nor its lack is inherently worth pursuing. Whether or not we should value diversity within the self depends on what the diverse elements are and how the diversity can be lived" (9). Mullin describes the ways in which Foucault, for example, "speaks of the plural self whose 'intoxication of abundance, which allows it to divide itself,' is preferred to 'dull constancy'" (Foucault 1984a, 84, quoted in Mullin 1995, 9). Alliance does not "exclude any commitment whatsoever," but rather engages and reworks the multiple commitments brought to the production of alliance. As Laclau and Mouffe (1985) suggest, agency is built through an alliance among subject positions which is a partial fixing of relational positioning. Because subject positions are constrained by the complex social relations which produce "subjectivity," the subject of agency is not completely dispersed among an infinite range of possible positions, nor is the subject a completely unified whole who is the sole author and ultimate ground of her actions. "[T]he category of the subject cannot be established either through the absolutization of a dispersion of 'subject positions,' or through the absolutist unification of these around a 'transcendental subject'" (Laclau and Mouffe 1985, 121). Moreover, neither absolute objec-tivity, nor absolute subjectivity is possible: "the moment of closure of a discursive totality, which is not given at the 'objective' level of that totality, cannot be established at the level of a 'meaning-giving subject.' . . . 'Objectivism' and 'subjectivism'; 'holism' and 'individualism'

are symmetrical expressions of the *desire* for a fullness that is permanently deferred" (121). It is, thus, articulations, the partial fixing of relationships which determines the effects of actions or activisms. Thus, making alliance the site of agency does not do away with, but rather engages, the complexity of interrelation.

229. Mullin also goes on to describe the limitations of analogies between persons and groups (18–21).

230. Kathy Davis and Sue Fisher, point out in the Introduction to *Negotiating the Margins: The Gendered Discourse of Power and Resistance*, "Similarly the longstanding assumption that a relationship exists between power and resistance has raised questions about how we simultaneously can hold onto the view that women construct their own lives *and* that they do so within determinant conditions" (1993, 3).

231. *Black Womanist Ethics* articulates womanist work in the moral tradition materialized through the history of the Black Church in the United States, while *Lesbian Ethics* articulates contemporary lesbian practices in relation to the normative labor of a philosopher. The differences between the two descriptions of self-in-relation of these two texts—womanist labor in the soul of the Black community and autokoenony—indicate the material(ized) differences between these two traditions. To merge or unify the two, even at their points of agreement or intersection, such as their common critique of "ethical freedom as control," would liquidate these differences and the different possibilities which they keep open. Nonetheless, the two can be connected as allies in struggles against multiple (diverse and complex) dominations.

232. Margaret Urban Walker (1989) developed this term to describe the ability to interrogate how traditional ethical systems such as justice can be employed to serve systems of domination.

> When we construct and consider representations of our moral situations we need to ask: what actual community of moral responsibility does this representation of moral thinking purport to represent? Who does it actually represent? What communicative strategies does it support? Who will be in a position (concretely, socially) to deploy these strategies? Who is in a position to transmit and enforce the rules which constrain them? In what forms of activity or endeavor will they have (or fail to have) an application, and who is served by these activities?

233. For more on the question of radical relationalism and response-ability see Jakobsen (1996).

References

Albrecht, Lisa, and Rose M. Brewer. 1990. *Bridges of Power: Women's Multicultural Alliances*. Philadelphia: New Society Publishers.

Allen, Robert. 1974. *Reluctant Reformers: Racism and Social Reform Movements in the United States*. With the Collaboration of Pamela P. Allen. Washington, D.C.: Howard University Press.

Anderson, Benedict. 1991 [1983]. *Imagined Communities*. London: Verso.

Andolsen, Barbara Hlikert. 1986. *"Daughters of Jefferson, Daughters of Bootblacks": Racism and American Feminism*. Macon, Ga.: Mercer University Press.

Andrews, William, ed. 1986. *Sisters of the Spirit: Three Black Women's Autobiographies of the Nineteenth Century*. Bloomington: Indiana University Press.

Appiah, Kwame Anthony. 1991. "Is the Post in Post-Modernism, the Post in Post-Colonial?" *Critical Inquiry* 17 (Winter): 336–57.

Aptheker, Bettina. 1989. *Tapestries of Life: Women's Work, Women's Consciousness and the Meaning of Daily Experience*. Amherst: University of Massachusetts Press.

Baldwin, James. 1962. *Another Country*. New York: Dial Press.

Bammer, Angelika. 1991. *Partial Visions: Feminism and Utopianism in the 1970s*. New York: Routledge.

Barnes, Gilbert H., and Dwight L. Dumond, eds. 1934. *Letters of Theodore Dwight Weld, Angelina Grimké Weld and Sarah Grimké, 1822–1844*, 2 vols. New York: D. Appleton Century Company.

Bartlett, Elizabeth Ann, ed. 1988. *Sarah Grimké: Letters on the Equality of the Sexes and Other Essays*. New Haven: Yale University Press.

Beal, Frances. 1981. "Slave of a Slave no More: Black Women in Struggle," *The Black Scholar* 12 (Nov/Dec): 16–17 (reprinted from) vol. 6 (March 1975).

Beauvoir, Simone de. 1972. *The Ethics of Ambiguity*, trans. Bernard Frechman. Secaucus, N.J.: The Citadel Press.

Beck, Evelyn Torton, ed. 1982. *Nice Jewish Girls: A Lesbian Anthology*. Watertown, Mass.: Persephone Press.

Beecher, Catharine. 1837. *An Essay on Slavery and Abolitionism with Reference to the Duty of American Women*. Philadelphia: Henry Perkins.

———. 1841. *Treatise on Domestic Economy for the Use of Young Ladies at Home and at School*. Boston: T. H. Webb & Co.

Beecher, Lyman. 1835. *A Plea for the West*. Cincinnati, Ohio: Truman & Smith.

———. 1961. *The Autobiography of Lyman Beecher*, ed. Barbara Cross, 2 vols. Cambridge, Mass.: Harvard University Press.

Bell, Catherine. 1992. *Ritual Theory, Ritual Practice*. New York: Oxford University Press.

Bellah, Robert, et. al. 1985. *Habits of the Heart: Individualism and Commitment in American Life*. San Francisco: Harper & Row.

Belsey, Catherine. 1980. *Critical Practice*. New York: Methuen.

Benhabib, Seyla. 1986. *Critique, Norm, and Utopia: A Study of the Foundations of Critical Theory*. New York: Columbia University Press.

———. 1987. "The Generalized and the Concrete Other: The Kohlberg-Gilligan Controversy and Moral Theory." In *Women and Moral Theory*, ed. Eva Feder Kittay and Diana T. Meyers, 154–177. Totowa, N.J.: Rowman & Littlefield.

———. 1992. *Situating the Self: Gender, Community and Postmodernism in Contemporary Ethics*. New York: Routledge.

Benhabib, Seyla, et al. 1995. *Feminist Contentions: A Philosophical Exchange*. New York: Routledge.

Blum, Lawrence. 1988. "Gilligan and Kohlberg: Implications for Moral Theory." *Ethics* 98 (April): 472–91.

Boydston, Jeanne, et al. 1988. *The Limits of Sisterhood: The Beecher Sisters on Women's Rights and Women's Sphere*. Chapel Hill: University of North Carolina Press.

Boylan, Anne. 1994. "Benevolence and Antislavery Activity among African American Women in New York and Boston, 1820–1840." In *The Abolitionist Sisterhood: Women's Political Culture in Antebellum America*, ed. Jean Fagan Yellin and John C. Van Horne, 119–38. Ithaca: Cornell University Press.

Brown, Elsa Barkley. 1989. "Womanist Consciousness: Maggie Lena Walker and the Independent Order of Saint Luke." *Signs: Journal of Women in Culture and Society* 14.3 (Spring): 610–34.

Brown, Wendy. 1992. *States of Injury: Power and Freedom in Late Modernity*. Princeton: Princeton University Press.

Bunch, Charlotte. 1987. *Passionate Politics: Essays 1968–1986, Feminist Theory in Action*. New York: St. Martin's Press.

Bunch, Charlotte, and Nancy Myron, eds. 1974. *Class and Feminism: A Collection of Essays from* The Furies. Baltimore: Diana Press.

Burgher, Mary. 1979. "Images of Self and Race in the Autobiographies of Black Women." In *Sturdy Black Bridges: Visions of Black Women in Literature*, ed. Roseann Bell et al., 107–22. New York: Anchor Books.

Butler, Judith. 1988. "Performative Acts and Gender Constitution: An Essay in Phenomenology and Feminist Theory." *Theater Journal* 40: 519–31.

———. 1990a. *Gender Trouble: Feminism and the Subversion of Identity*. New York: Routledge.

———. 1990b. "The Force of Fantasy: Feminism, Mapplethorpe, and Discursive Excess." *differences* 2.2 (Summer): 105–25.

———. 1993. *Bodies that Matter: On the Discursive Limits of "Sex"*. New York: Routledge.

Butler, Judith, and Joan W. Scott, eds. 1992. *Feminists Theorize the Political*. New York: Routledge.

Cade, Toni. 1970. *The Black Woman: An Anthology*. New York: New American Library.

Calhoun, Cheshire. 1994. "Separating Lesbian Theory from Feminist Theory." *Ethics* 104 (April): 558–81.

———. 1995. "The Gender Closet: Lesbian Disappearance Under the Sign 'Women.'" *Feminist Studies* 21.1 (Spring): 7–34.

Calhoun, Craig, ed. 1993. *Habermas and the Public Sphere*. Cambridge, Mass.: MIT Press.

Cannon, Katie Geneva. 1988. *Black Womanist Ethics*. Atlanta: Scholars Press.

———. 1989. "Roundtable Discussion: Christian Ethics and Theology in Womanist Perspective," a response to Cheryl Sanders. *The Journal of Feminist Studies in Religion* 5.2 (1989): 92–94.

———. 1995. *Katie's Canon: Womanism and the Soul of the Black Community*. New York: Continuum.

Caraway, Nancy. 1991. *Segregated Sisterhood: Racism and the Politics of American Feminism*. Knoxville: University of Tennessee Press.

Card, Claudia. 1995. *Lesbian Choices*. New York: Columbia University Press.

Ceplair, Larry, ed. and ann. 1989. *The Public Years of Sarah and Angelina Grimké: Selected Writings 1835–1839*. New York: Columbia University Press.

Childers, Mary, and bell hooks. 1990. "A Conversation about Race and Class." In *Conflicts in Feminism*, ed. Marianne Hirsch and Evelyn Fox Keller, 60–81. New York: Routledge.

Chopp, Rebecca. 1989. *The Power to Speak: Feminism, Language, God*. New York: Crossroad.

Chow, Rey. 1993. *Writing Diaspora: Tactics of Intervention in Contemporary Cultural Studies*. Bloomington: Indiana University Press.

Christian, Barbara. 1980. *Black Women Novelists: The Development of a Tradition, 1892–1976*. Westport, Conn.: Greenwood Press.

———. 1988. "Response to 'Black Women's Texts,'" *NWSA Journal* 1.1 (Autumn): 32–36.

Clarke, Cheryl. 1993. "'Living the Texts Out: Lesbians and the Uses of Black Women's Traditions." In *Theorizing Black Feminisms: The Visionary Pragmatism of Black Women*, ed. Stanlie M. James and Abena P. A. Busia, 214–27. New York: Routledge.

Cocks, Joan. 1989. *The Oppositional Imagination: Feminism, Critique and Political Theory*. New York: Routledge.

Collins, Patricia Hill. 1990. *Black Feminist Thought: Knowledge, Consciousness, and the Politics of Empowerment*. Boston: Unwin Hyman.

Combahee River Collective. 1983. "The Combahee River Collective Statement." In *Home Girls: A Black Feminist Anthology*, ed. Barbara Smith, 272–82. New York: Kitchen Table, Women of Color Press.

Cornell, Drucilla. 1993. *Transformations: Recollective Imagination and Sexual Difference*. New York: Routledge.

———. 1995. "What is Ethical Feminism?" in *Feminist Contentions*. Seyla Benhabib et al. New York: Routledge.

Cornillon, Susan Koppelman, ed. 1973. *Images of Women in Fiction: Feminist Perspectives*, Revised Edition. Bowling Green, Ohio: Bowling Green University Popular Press.

Cortese, Anthony. 1990. *Ethnic Ethics: The Restructuring of Moral Theory*. Albany: State University of New York Press.

Cott, Nancy. 1977. *The Bonds of Womanhood: "Woman's Sphere" in New England, 1780–1835*. New Haven: Yale University Press.

Cott, Nancy, and Elizabeth Pleck, eds. 1979. *A Heritage of Her Own: Toward a New Social History of American Women*. New York: Simon and Schuster.

Crawford, Vicki L., et al. 1990. *Women in the Civil Rights Movement: Trailblazers & Torchbearers, 1941–1965*. Bloomington: Indiana University Press.

Crenshaw, Kimberlé. 1989. "Demarginalizing the Intersection of Race and Sex: A Black Feminist Critique of Antidiscrimination Doctrine, Feminist Theory, and Antiracist Politics." *The University of Chicago Legal Forum*.

———. 1992. "Whose Story Is It Anyway? Feminist and Antiracist Appropriations of Anita Hill." In *Race-ing Justice, En-gendering Power*, ed. Toni Morrison, 402–20. New York: Pantheon Books.

Crosby, Christina. 1992. "Dealing with Differences." In *Feminists Theorize the Political*, ed. Judith Butler and Joan W. Scott, 130–43. New York: Routledge.

Däumer, Elisabeth. 1992. "Queer Ethics; Or, the Challenge of Bisexuality to Lesbian Ethics." *Hypatia* 7.4 (Fall): 91–105.

Davaney, Sheila, and Rebecca Chopp, eds. 1997. *Horizons in Feminist Theology: Identity, Tradition, and Norms*. Minneapolis: Fortress Press.

Davis, Angela. 1971. "Reflections on Black Women's Role in the Community of Slaves." *Black Scholar* 3: 3–13.

———. 1983. *Women, Race and Class*. New York: Random House.

Davis, Kathy, and Sue Fisher, eds. 1993. *Negotiating the Margins: The Gendered Discourse of Power and Resistance*. New Brunswick: Rutgers University Press.

de Lauretis, Teresa. 1986. "Feminist Studies/Critical Studies: Issues, Terms, and Contexts." In *Feminist Studies/Critical Studies*, ed. Teresa de Lauretis, 1–19. Bloomington: Indiana University Press.

D'Emilio, John. 1983. "Capitalism and Gay Identity." In *Powers of Desire*, ed. Ann Snitow et al., 100–13. New York: Monthly Review Press.

Dill, Bonnie Thorton. 1983. "Race, Class, and Gender: Prospects for an All-Inclusive Sisterhood." *Feminist Studies* 9: 131–50.

Diprose, Rosalyn. 1994. *The Bodies of Women: Ethics, Embodiment and Sexual Difference*. New York: Routledge.

Douglas, Carol Anne. 1990. *Love and Politics: Radical Feminist and Lesbian Theories*. San Francisco: Ism Press.

Douglas, Kelly Brown. 1994. *The Black Christ*. Maryknoll, N.Y.: Orbis Books.

Douglass, Frederick. 1895. "What I Found at the Northampton Association." In *History of Florence, Massachusetts. Including a Complete Account of the Northampton Association of Education and Industry*, ed. Charles A. Sheffeld. Florence, Mass., 131–32.

Drewal, Margaret Thompson. 1992. *Yoruba Ritual: Performers, Play, Agency*. Bloomington: Indiana University Press.

Duberman, Martin. 1993. *Stonewall*. New York: Plume Books.

DuBois, Ellen. 1978. *Feminism and Suffrage: The Emergence of an Independent Women's Movement in America, 1848–1869*. Ithaca: Cornell University Press.

DuBois, Ellen, and Vicki L. Ruiz, eds. 1990. *Unequal Sisters: A Multicultural Reader in U.S. Women's History*. New York: Routledge.

duCille, Ann. 1994. "The Occult of True Black Womanhood: Critical Demeanor and Black Feminist Studies." *Signs: Journal of Women in Culture and Society* 19.3 (Spring): 591–629.

Echols, Alice. 1989. *Daring to Be Bad: Radical Feminism in America 1967–1975*. Minneapolis: University of Minnesota Press.

Eiesland, Nancy. 1994. *The Disabled God: Toward a Liberatory Theology of Disability*. Nashville: Abingdon Press.

Eisenstein, Hester, and Alice Jardine, eds. 1985. *The Future of Difference*. New Brunswick: Rutgers University Press.

Eisenstein, Zillah. 1981. *The Radical Future of Liberal Feminism*. Boston: Northeastern University Press.

Eisenstein, Zillah, ed. 1978. *Capitalist Patriarchy: The Case for Socialist Feminism*. New York: Monthly Review Press.

Elam, Diane, and Robyn Wiegman, eds. 1995. *Feminism Beside Itself*. New York: Routledge.

Eugene, Toinette M. 1988. "Moral Values and Black Womanists," *The Journal of Religious Thought* 44.2 (Winter/Spring): 23–34.

Evans, James. 1990. "African-American Christianity and the Postmodern Condition." *Journal of the American Academy of Religion* 58.2 (Summer): 207–22.

Evans, Sara. 1979. *Personal Politics: The Roots of Women's Liberation in the Civil Rights Movement & the New Left*. New York: Vintage Books.

Feinberg, Leslie. 1993. *Stone Butch Blues*. Ithaca: Firebrand Books.

Firestone, Shulamith. 1970. *The Dialectic of Sex: The Case for Feminist Revolution*. New York: Bantam Books.

Fleischner, Jennifer. 1994. "Mothers and Sisters: The Family Romance of Antislavery Women Writers." In *Feminist Nightmares: Women at Odds*, ed. Susan Ostrov Weisser and Jennifer Fleischner, 125–41. New York: New York University Press.

Foucault, Michel. 1977. *Discipline and Punish: The Birth of the Prison*, trans. Alan Sheridan-Smith. New York: Pantheon Books.

———. 1984a. *The Foucault Reader*, ed. with an intro., Paul Rabinow. New York: Pantheon Books.

———. 1984b. "The Ethic of Care for the Self as a Practice of Freedom," interview by Paul Fornet-Betancourt, Helmut Becker, Alfredo Gomez-Müller, translated by J. D. Gauthier. In *The Final Foucault*, ed. James Bernauer and David Rasmussen, 1–20. Cambridge, Mass.: MIT Press.

Franke, Katherine. Forthcoming. "What's Wrong with Sexual Harassment?" *Stanford Law Review* 49.4.

Frankenberg, Ruth. 1993. *White Women, Race Matters: The Social Construction of Whiteness*. Minneapolis: University of Minnesota Press.

Fraser, Nancy. 1989. *Unruly Practices: Power, Discourse and Gender in Contemporary Social Theory*. Minneapolis: University of Minnesota Press.

———. 1990. "Rethinking the Public Sphere: A Contribution to the Critique of Actually Existing Democracy." *Social Text* 25/26: 56–80.

Frazer, Elizabeth, et al., eds. 1992. *Ethics: A Feminist Reader*. Oxford: Blackwell.

Friedman, Lawrence. 1982. *Gregarious Saints: Self and Community in American Abolitionism, 1830–1870*. Cambridge: Cambridge University Press.

Frye, Marilyn. 1990. "A Response to *Lesbian Ethics*," *Hypatia* 5.3 (Fall): 132–37.

Fuchs, Josef. 1983. *Personal Responsibility and Christian Morality*. Washington, D.C.: Georgetown University Press.

Fuss, Diana. 1989. *Essentially Speaking: Feminism, Nature, and Difference*. New York: Routledge.

———. 1991. "Inside/Out." In *Inside/Out: Lesbian Theories, Gay Theories*, ed. Diana Fuss, 1–12. New York: Routledge.

Gallop, Jane. 1992. *Around 1981: Academic Feminist Literary Theory*. New York: Routledge.

Garcia, Alma M. 1990. "The Development of Chicana Feminist Discourse, 1970–1980." In *Unequal Sisters: A Multicultural Reader in U.S. Women's History*, 418–31. New York: Routledge.

Gardiner, Judith Kegan, ed. 1995. *Provoking Agents: Gender and Agency in Theory and Practice*. Urbana: University of Illinois Press.

Gates, Henry Louis, ed. 1987. *The Classic Slave Narratives*. New York: New American Library.

Gert, Bernard. 1988. *Morality: A New Justification of the Moral Rules*. New York: Oxford University Press.

Giddings, Paula. 1984. *When and Where I Enter: The Impact of Black Women on Race and Sex in America*. New York: Bantam Books.

Gilbert, Olive. 1970. *Narrative of Sojourner Truth; A Bondswoman of Olden Time, With a History of Her Labors and Correspondence Drawn from Her "Book of Life."* Chicago: Johnson Publishing.

Gilligan, Carol. 1982. *In A Different Voice*. Cambridge, Mass.: Harvard University Press.

Ginzberg, Lori D. 1990. *Women and the Work of Benevolence: Morality, Politics, and Class in the 19th-Century United States*. New Haven: Yale University Press.

Grant, Jacquelyn. 1989. *White Women's Christ and Black Women's Jesus: Feminist Christology and Womanist Response*. Atlanta: Scholars Press.

Grewal, Inderpal, and Caren Kaplan, eds. 1994. *Scattered Hegemonies: Postmodernity and Transnational Feminist Practices*. Minneapolis: University of Minnesota Press.

Grimké, Angelina. 1838a. *An Appeal to the Women of the Nominally Free States*. Boston: Issac Knapp. Reprinted 1971. Freeport, N.Y.: Books for Libraries Press.

———. 1838b. *Letters to Catharine E. Beecher, In Reply to an Essay on Slavery and Abolitionism*. Boston: Issac Knapp.

Grosz, Elizabeth. 1989. *Sexual Subversions: Three French Feminisms*. St. Leonard's, Australia: Allen and Unwin.

Gubar, Susan. 1995. "Feminist Misogyny: Mary Wollstonecraft and the Paradox of 'It Takes One to Know One.'" In *Feminism Beside Itself*, ed. Diane Elam and Robyn Wiegman, 133–54. New York: Routledge.

Gutiérrez, Ramón A. 1993. "Community, Patriarchy and Individualism: The Politics of Chicano History and the Dream of Equality." *American Quarterly* 45.1 (March): 44–72.

Habermas, Jürgen. 1984–87. *The Theory of Communicative Action*, trans. Thomas McCarthy. 2 vols. Boston: Beacon Press.

Hanneman, Robert A. 1988. *Computer-Assisted Theory Building: Modeling Dynamic Social Systems*. Newbury Park, Calif.: Sage Publications.

Hansen, Debra Gold. 1993. *Strained Sisterhood: Gender and Class in the Boston Female Anti-Slavery Society*. Amherst: University of Massachusetts Press.

Harding, Sandra, ed. 1993. *The "Racial" Economy of Science: Toward a Democratic Future*. Bloomington: Indiana University Press.

Harley, Sharon, and Rosalyn Terborg-Penn. 1978. *The Afro-American Woman: Struggles and Images*. Port Washington, N.Y.: Kennikat Press.

Harrison, Beverly Wildung. 1985. *Making the Connections: Essays in Feminist Social Ethics*, ed. Carol S. Robb. Boston: Beacon Press.

Hayden, Dolores. 1981. *The Grand Domestic Revolution: A History of Feminist Designs for American Homes, Neighborhoods, and Cities*. Cambridge, Mass.: MIT Press.

Hermann and Stewart. 1994. *Theorizing Feminism: Parallel Trends in the Humanities and Social Sciences*. Boulder, Colo.: Westview Press.

Hersh, Blanche Glassman. 1978. *The Slavery of Sex: Feminist Abolitionists in America*. Urbana: University of Illinois Press.

Hewitt, Nancy A. 1984. *Women's Activism and Social Change, Rochester, New York 1922-1872*. Ithaca: Cornell University Press.

———. 1990. "Beyond the Search for Sisterhood: American Women's History in the 1980's." In *Unequal Sisters: A Multi-Cultural Reader in U.S. Women's History*, ed. Ellen Carol DuBois and Vicki L. Ruiz, 1-14. New York: Routledge.

Higginbotham, Evelyn Brooks. 1992. "African-American Women's History and the Metalanguage of Race." *Signs: Journal of Women in Culture and Society* 17.2 (Winter): 251-74.

———. 1993. *Righteous Discontent: The Women's Movement in the Black Baptist Church, 1880-1920*. Cambridge, Mass.: Harvard University Press.

Hirsch, Marianne, and Evelyn Fox Keller, eds. 1990. *Conflicts in Feminism*. New York: Routledge.

Hoagland, Sarah Lucia. 1988. *Lesbian Ethics: Toward New Value*. Palo Alto: Lesbian Studies Institute.

———. 1992. "Why Lesbian Ethics?" *Hypatia* 7.4 (Fall): 195-206.

Hobsbawm, Eric, and Terence Ranger, eds. 1983. *The Invention of Tradition*. Cambridge: Cambridge University Press.

Holloway, Karla F. C. 1995. *Codes of Conduct: Race, Ethics, and the Color of Our Character*. New Brunswick: Rutgers University Press.

hooks, bell. 1981. *Ain't I a Woman? Black Women and Feminism*. Boston: South End Press.

———. 1984. *Feminist Theory: From Margin to Center*. Boston: South End Press.

———. 1989. *Talking Back: Thinking Feminist, Thinking Black*. Boston: South End Press.

———. 1990. "Marginality as a Site of Resistance." In *Out There: Marginalization and Contemporary Cultures*, ed. Russell Ferguson et al., 341-43. Cambridge, Mass.: MIT Press.

Hull, Gloria, et al., eds. 1981. *All the Women Are White, All the Blacks Are Men, But Some of Us Are Brave*. Old Westbury, Conn.: The Feminist Press.

Irigaray, Luce. 1981a. "This Sex Which Is Not One," trans. Claudia Reeder. In *New French Feminisms: An Anthology*, ed. Elaine Marks and Isabelle de Courtivron, 99-106. New York: Schocken Books.

———. 1981b. "When the Goods Get Together," trans. Claudia Reeder. In *New French Feminisms: An Anthology*, ed. Elaine Marks and Isabelle de Courtivron, 107-10. New York: Schocken Books.

Isasi-Díaz, Ada María. 1993. En la Lucha, *In the Struggle: Elaborating a* Mujerista

Theology, A Hispanic Women's Liberation Theology. Minneapolis: Augsburg Fortress Publishers.

Jacobs, Harriet. 1987. *Incidents in the Life of a Slave Girl: Written by Herself*, ed. Jean Fagan Yellin. Cambridge, Mass.: Harvard University Press.

Jaggar, Alison. 1983. *Feminist Politics and Human Nature*. Totowa, N.J.: Rowman and Allenheld.

Jakobsen, Janet R. 1995a. "Agency and Alliance in Public Discourses about Sexuality." *Hypatia: Journal of Feminist Philosophy* 10.1 (Winter): 133–54.

———. 1995b. "Deconstructing the Paradox of Modernity: Feminism, Enlightenment and Cross-Cultural Moral Interactions." *Journal of Religious Ethics* 23.2 (Fall): 333–66.

———. 1995c. "Struggles for Women's Bodily Integrity in the United States and the Limits of Liberal Legal Theory." *Journal of Feminist Studies in Religion* 11.2 (Fall): 5–26.

———. 1996. "The Gendered Division of Moral Labor: Radical Relationalism and Feminist Ethics." In *Living Responsibly in Community: Essays in Honor of E. Clinton Gardner*, ed. Fred Glennon et al. Lanham, Md.: University Press of America.

James, Stanlie M., and Abena P. A. Busia, eds. 1993. *Theorizing Black Feminism: The Visionary Pragmatism of Black Women*. New York: Routledge.

Jameson, Fredric. 1995. "On Cultural Studies." In *The Identity in Question*, ed. John Rajchman, 251–95. Routledge: New York.

Johnston, Jill. 1973. *Lesbian Nation: The Feminist Solution*. New York: Simon and Schuster.

Jones, Jacqueline. 1985. *Labor of Love, Labor of Sorrow*. New York: Vintage Books.

Joseph, Gloria I. 1990. "Sojourner Truth: Archetypal Black Feminist." In *Wild Women in the Whirlwind: Afra-American Culture and the Contemporary Literary Renaissance*, ed. Joanne M. Braxton and Andrée Nicola McLaughlin, 35–47. New Brunswick: Rutgers University Press.

Joseph, Miranda. 1996. "If It's Community, It Must Be Correct." Women's Studies Colloquium, University of Arizona.

Keller, Catherine. 1986. *From a Broken Web: Separation, Sexism, and Self*. Boston: Beacon Press.

Kennedy, Elizabeth Lapovsky, and Madeline Davis. 1993. *Boots of Leather, Slippers of Gold: The History of a Lesbian Community*. New York: Routledge.

Kerber, Linda et al., eds. 1995. *U.S. History as Women's History: New Feminist Essays*. Chapel Hill: University of North Carolina Press.

King, Katie. 1986. "The Situation of Lesbianism as Feminism's Magical Sign: Contests for Meaning and the U.S. Women's Movement, 1968–1972." *Communication* 9: 65–92.

———. 1990. "Producing Sex, Theory, and Culture: Gay/Straight Remappings in Contemporary Feminism." In *Conflicts in Feminism*, ed. Marianne Hirsch and Evelyn Fox Keller, 82–101. New York: Routledge.

———. 1994. *Theory and Its Feminist Travels: Conversations in U.S. Women's Movements*. Bloomington: Indiana University Press.

Kittay, Eva Feder, and Diana T. Meyers, eds. 1987. *Women and Moral Theory*. Totowa, N.J.: Rowman and Littlefield.

Kramer, Larry. 1987. *Faggots*. New York: Plume Books.

Laclau, Ernesto. 1990. *New Reflections on the Revolution of Our Time.* New York: Routledge.

Laclau, Ernesto, and Chantal Mouffe. 1985. *Hegemony and Socialist Strategy: Towards a Radical Democratic Politics.* London: Verso.

Landes, Joan. 1988. *Women and the Public Sphere in the Age of the French Revolution.* Ithaca: Cornell University Press.

LaRue, Linda. 1970. "The Black Movement and Women's Liberation." *Black Scholar* 1: 36–42.

Lee-Lampshire, Wendy. 1995. "Decisions of Identity: Feminist Subjects and Grammars of Sexuality." *Hypatia: A Journal of Feminist Philosophy* 10.5 (Fall): 32–45.

Lerner, Gerda. 1971. *The Grimké Sisters from South Carolina: Pioneers for Women's Rights and Abolition.* New York: Schocken Books.

Lincoln, C. Eric, and Lawrence Mamiya. 1990. *The Black Church in the African American Experience.* Durham: Duke University Press.

Lippman, Walter. 1927. *The Phantom Public.* New York: Macmillan.

Longino, Helen E. 1993. "Feminist Standpoint Theory and the Problems of Knowledge." *Signs: Journal of Women in Culture and Society* 19.1 (Autumn): 201–12.

Lorde, Audre. 1982. *Zami: A New Spelling of My Name.* Freedom, Calif.: Crossing Press.

———. 1984. *Sister Outsider.* Trumansburg, N.Y.: Crossing Press.

Lovibond, Sabina. 1989. "Feminism and Postmodernism." *New Left Review* 178 (November-December): 5–28.

Lowenberg, Bert, and Ruth Bogin, eds. 1976. *Black Women in Nineteenth Century American Life: Their Words, Their Thoughts, Their Feelings.* University Park, Pa.: Pennsylvania State University Press.

Lugones, María. 1990a. "Playfulness, 'World'-Travelling, and Loving Perception." In *Making Face, Making Soul Haciendo Caras: Creative and Critical Perspectives by Women of Color*, ed. Gloria Anzaldúa, 390–402. San Francisco: Aunt Lute.

———. 1990b. "On the Logic of Pluralist Feminism." In *Feminist Ethics*, ed. Claudia Card, 35–44. Lawrence: University of Kansas Press.

———. 1990c. "*Hispaneando y Lesbiando*: On Sarah Hoagland's *Lesbian Ethics*," *Hypatia* 5. 3 (Fall): 138–46.

———. 1994. "Purity, Impurity, and Separation." *Signs: Journal of Women in Culture and Society* 19.2 (Winter): 458–79.

Lugones, María, and Elizabeth Spelman. 1983. "Have We Got a Theory for You!: Feminist Theory, Cultural Imperialism and the Demand for 'the Woman's Voice,' " *Women's Studies International Forum* 6.6: 573–81.

Lugones, María, in collaboration with Pat Alake Rosezelle. 1992. "Sisterhood and Friendship as Feminist Models." In *The Knowledge Explosion: Generation of Feminist Scholarship*, ed. Cheris Kramarae and Dale Spender. New York: Teachers College Press.

MacIntyre, Alasdair. 1981. *After Virtue: A Study in Moral Theory.* South Bend, Ind.: Notre Dame University Press.

———. *Whose Justice? Whose Rationality?* South Bend, Ind.: Notre Dame University Press.

Martin, Biddy. 1988. "Feminism, Criticism, and Foucault." In *Feminism and Foucault: Reflections on Resistance*, ed. Irene Diamond and Lee Quinby, 3–19. Boston: Northeastern University Press.

Martin, Joan M. 1996. "Work, Womanist." In *Dictionary of Feminist Theologies*, ed.

Letty M. Russell and J. Shannon Clarkson, 320–21. Louisville: Westminster John Knox Press.

McLaughlin, Andrée Nicola. 1990. "Black Women, Identity, and the Quest for Human Wholeness: Wild Women in the Whirlwind." In *Wild Women in the Whirlwind: Afra-American Culture and the Contemporary Literary Renaissance*, ed. Joanne M. Braxton and Andrée Nicola McLaughlin, 147–80. New Brunswick: Rutgers University Press.

Meese, Elizabeth. 1990. *(Ex)tensions: Re-Figuring Feminist Criticism*. Urbana: University of Illinois Press.

Mercer, Kobena. 1994. *Welcome to the Jungle: New Positions in Black Cultural Studies*. New York: Routledge.

Midgley, Clare. 1996. *Women Against Slavery: The British Campaigns 1780–1870*. New York: Routledge.

Millet, Kate. *Sexual Politics*. New York: Equinox Books.

Minow, Martha. 1990. *Making All the Difference: Inclusion, Exclusion, and American Law*. Ithaca: Cornell University Press.

Mohanty, Chandra Talpade. 1987. "Feminist Encounters: Locating the Politics of Experience." *Copyright*, I (Fall): 30–44.

———. 1994. "On Race and Voice: Challenges for Liberal Education in the 1990s." In *Between Borders: Pedagogy and the Politics of Cultural Studies*, ed. Henry Giroux and Peter McLaren, 145–66. New York: Routledge.

Mohanty, Chandra Talpade, et al., eds. 1991. *Third World Women and the Politics of Feminism*. Bloomington: Indiana University Press.

Moraga, Cherríe, and Gloria Anzaldúa. 1981. *This Bridge Called My Back: Writings by Radical Women of Color*. Watertown, Mass.: Persephone Press.

Morgan, Robin, ed. 1970. *Sisterhood is Powerful: An Anthology of Writings from the Women's Liberation Movement*. New York: Vintage Books.

Morton, Nelle. 1985. *The Journey is Home*. Boston: Beacon Press.

Mosse, George. 1985. *Nationalism and Sexuality: Middle-Class Morality and Sexual Norms in Modern Europe*. Madison: University of Wisconsin Press.

Mouffe, Chantal. 1992. "Feminism, Citizenship, and Radical Democratic Politics." In *Feminists Theorize the Political*, ed. Judith Butler and Joan Scott, 369. New York: Routledge.

———. 1993. *The Return of the Political*. London: Verso.

———. 1995. "Democratic Politics and the Question of Identity." In *The Identity in Question*, ed. John Rajchman, 32–45. New York: Routledge.

Mouffe, Chantal, ed. 1992. *Dimensions of Radical Democracy: Pluralism, Citizenship, Community*. London: Verso.

Mullin, Amy. 1995. "Selves, Diverse and Divided: Can Feminists Have Diversity without Multiplicity?" *Hypatia: A Journal of Feminist Philosophy* 10.5 (Fall): 1–31.

Myron, Nancy, and Charlotte Bunch, eds. 1975. *Lesbianism and the Women's Movement*. Baltimore: Diana Press.

Narayan, Uma. 1988. "Working Together across Differences: Some Considerations on Emotions and Political Practice." *Hypatia: Journal of Feminist Philosophy* 3.2 (Summer): 41–48.

Nestle, Joan. 1987. "Butch-Femme Relationships: Sexual Courage in the 1950s." In *A Restricted Country*, 100–109. Ithaca: Firebrand Books.

Nestle, Joan, ed. 1992. *The Persistent Desire: A Femme-Butch Reader*. Boston: Alyson Publications.

Omolade, Barbara. 1994. *The Rising Song of African American Women*. New York: Routledge.

Ong, Aihwa. 1988. "Colonialism and Modernity: Feminist Representations of Women in Non-Western Societies." *Inscriptions* 3/4: 79–93.

Painter, Nell Irvin. 1976. *Exodusters: Black Migration to Kansas after Reconstruction*. New York: W. W. Norton.

———. 1994. "Difference, Slavery, and Memory: Sojourner Truth in Feminist Abolitionism." In *The Abolitionist Sisterhood: Women's Political Culture in Antebellum America*, ed. Jean Fagan Yellin and John C. Van Horne, 139–58. Ithaca: Cornell University Press.

———. 1996a. "Representing Truth: Sojourner Truth's Knowing and Becoming Known." In *This Far by Faith: Readings in African-American Women's Religious Biography*, ed. Judith Weisenfeld and Richard Newman, 262–99. New York: Routledge.

———. 1996b. *Sojourner Truth: A Life, a Symbol*. New York: W. W. Norton.

Parker, Andrew, et al., eds. *Nationalisms and Sexualities*. New York: Routledge, 1992.

Pascoe, Peggy. 1990. *Relations of Rescue: The Search for Female Moral Authority in the American West, 1874–1939*. New York: Oxford University Press.

Pfeil, Fred. 1994. "No Basta Teorizar: In-Difference to Solidarity in Contemporary Fiction, Theory, and Practice." In *Scattered Hegemonies: Postmodernity and Transnational Feminist Practices*, ed. Inderpal Grewal and Caren Kaplan, 197–230. Minneapolis: University of Minnesota Press.

Phelan, Peggy. 1993. *Unmarked: The Politics of Performance*. New York: Routledge.

Phelan, Shane. 1989. *Identity Politics: Lesbian Feminism and the Limits of Community*. Philadelphia: Temple University Press.

———. 1994. *Getting Specific: Postmodern Lesbian Politics*. Minneapolis: University of Minnesota Press.

Pojman, Louis. 1989. *Ethical Theory: Classical and Contemporary Readings*. Belmont, Calif.: Wadsworth Publishing.

Pratt, Minnie Bruce. 1984. "Identity: Skin Blood Heart," in *Yours in Struggle: Three Feminist Perspectives on Anti-Semitism and Racism*, Elly Bulkin, Minnie Bruce Pratt, and Barbara Smith. Brooklyn, N.Y.: Long Haul Press.

Raboteau, Albert. *Slave Religion: The "Invisible Institution" in the Antebellum South*. New York: Oxford University Press, 1978.

Rajchman, John, ed. 1995. *The Identity in Question*. New York: Routledge.

Raymond, Janice G. 1986. *A Passion for Friends: Toward a Philosophy of Female Affection*. Boston: Beacon Press.

Reagon, Bernice Johnson. 1983. "Coalition Politics: Turning the Century." In *Home Girls: A Black Feminist Anthology*, ed. Barbara Smith, 356–68. New York: Kitchen Table, Women of Color Press.

Rich, Adrienne. 1980. "Compulsory Heterosexuality and Lesbian Existence." *Signs* 5.4 (Summer): 631–60.

Richard, Nelly. 1987/88. "Postmodernism and Periphery." *Third Text* 2 (Winter): 5–12.

Riggs, Marcia. 1991. "Toward a Mediating Ethic for Black Liberation: Ethical Insights

of Black Female Reformers of the Nineteenth Century." Ph.D. diss., Vanderbilt University.
———. 1994. *Awake, Arise, and Act: A Womanist Call for Black Liberation.* Cleveland: Pilgrim Press.
Rinehart, Jane A. 1994. "Roaming in the Margins: Speaking with Broken Tongues." *Frontiers* XIV.3: 19–48.
Robbins, Bruce, ed. 1993. *The Phantom Public Sphere.* Minneapolis: University of Minnesota Press.
Roof, Judith. 1995. "How to Satisfy a Woman Every Time." In *Feminism Beside Itself,* ed. Diane Elam and Robyn Wiegman, 55–70. New York: Routledge.
Ross, Becki L. 1995. *The House that Jill Built: A Lesbian Nation in Formation.* Toronto: University of Toronto Press.
Ryan, Mary P. 1981. *The Cradle of the Middle-Class: The Family in Oneida County, New York, 1780–1865.* Cambridge: Cambridge University Press.
Sacks, Karen Brodkin. 1989. "Toward a Unified Theory of Class, Race, and Gender." *American Ethnologist* 16.3 (August): 534–50.
Said, Edward. "Representing the Colonized: Anthropology's Interlocutors." *Critical Inquiry* 15, No. 2 (Winter 1989), 205–26.
Samantrai, Ranu. Forthcoming. *AlterNatives: Feminism and Postcolonialisms in Contemporary Britain.* Unpublished Manuscript.
Samois. 1987. *Coming to Power: Writings and Graphics on Lesbian S/M.* 3rd ed. Originally published 1981, reprinted 1982. Boston: Alyson Publications.
Sanders, Cheryl. 1989. Review of *Black Womanist Ethics* by Katie G. Cannon. In *Christianity and Crisis* 49 (December 11): 391–92.
Sanders, Cheryl, et al. 1989. "Roundtable Discussion: Christian Ethics and Theology in Womanist Perspective," *Journal of Feminist Studies in Religion* 5.2 (Fall): 83–112.
Sandoval, Chela. 1990. "Feminism and Racism: A Report on the 1981 National Women's Studies Association Conference." In *Making Face, Making Soul Haciendo Caras: Creative and Critical Perspectives by Women of Color,* ed. Gloria Anzaldúa, 55–71. San Francisco: Aunt Lute.
———. 1991. "U.S. Third World Feminism: The Theory and Method of Oppositional Consciousness in the Postmodern World." *Genders* 10 (Spring): 1–24.
Saxonhouse, Arlene W. 1992. *Fear of Diversity: The Birth of Political Science in Ancient Greek Thought.* Chicago: University of Chicago Press.
Schor, Naomi. 1995. "French Feminism Is a Universalism." *differences: A Journal of Feminist Cultural Studies* 7 (Spring): 15–47.
Schulman, Sarah. 1994. *My American History: Lesbian and Gay Life during the Reagan/Bush Years.* New York: Routledge.
Scott, Joan W. 1988. "Deconstructing Equality-Versus-Difference: Or, the Uses of Poststructuralist Theory for Feminism." *Feminist Studies* 14.2 (Spring): 33–50.
———. 1992. "Multiculturalism and the Politics of Identity." *October* 61: 12–19.
———. 1995. "Universalism and the History of Feminism." *differences: A Journal of Feminist Cultural Studies* 7 (Spring): 1–14.
Sedgwick, Eve Kosofsky. 1990. *Epistemology of the Closet.* Berkeley: University of California Press.
Shapiro, Susan. 1994. "*Écriture Judaïque*: Where Are the Jews in Western Discourse?"

In *Displacements: Cultural Identities in Question*, ed. Angelika Bammer, 182–201. Bloomington: Indiana University Press.

Signorile, Michelango. 1994. *Queer in America: Sex, the Media, and the Closets of Power*. New York: Anchor Books.

Simons, Margaret A. 1979. "Racism and Feminism: A Schism in the Sisterhood." *Feminist Studies* 5.2 (Summer): 384–401.

Singer, Peter, ed. 1994. *Ethics*. New York: Oxford University Press.

Sklar, Kathryn Kish. 1976. *Catharine Beecher: A Study in American Domesticity*. New York: W. W. Norton.

Smith, Barbara, ed. 1983. *Home Girls: A Black Feminist Anthology*. New York: Kitchen Table, Women of Color Press.

Spelman, Elizabeth. 1988. *Inessential Woman: Problems of Exclusion in Feminist Thought*. Boston: Beacon Press.

Spillers, Hortense J. 1992. "Interstices: A Small Drama of Words." In *Pleasure and Danger: Exploring Female Sexuality*, ed. Carole S. Vance, 3rd ed., 73–100. London: Pandora Press.

Spivak, Gayatri. 1988. "Can the Subaltern Speak?" In *Marxism and the Interpretation of Culture*, ed. Cary Nelson and Lawrence Grossberg, 271–313. Chicago: University of Illinois Press.

———. 1990. *The Post-Colonial Critic: Interviews Strategies, Dialogues*. New York: Routledge.

Stein, Arlene, ed. 1993. *Sisters, Sexperts, and Queers: Beyond the Lesbian Nation*. New York: Plume Books.

Sterling, Dorothy, ed. 1979. *Black Foremothers: Three Lives*. Old Westbury, N.Y.: The Feminist Press.

———, ed. 1984. *We Are Your Sisters: Black Women in the Nineteenth Century*. New York: W. W. Norton.

———, ed. 1987. *Turning the World Upside Down: The Anti-Slavery Convention of American Women Held in New York City May 9–12, 1837*. New York: The Feminist Press.

Stetson, Erlene, and Linda David. 1994. *Glorying in Tribulation: The Lifework of Sojourner Truth*. East Lansing: Michigan State University Press.

Stewart, Maria. 1987. *Maria W. Stewart, America's First Black Woman Political Writer: Essays and Speeches*, ed. Marilyn Richardson. Bloomington: Indiana University Press.

Strathern, Marilyn. 1987. "An Awkward Relationship: The Case of Feminism and Anthropology." *Signs: A Journal of Women in Culture and Society* 12.2 (Winter): 276–92.

Taylor, Verta, and Leila J. Rupp. 1993. "Women's Culture and Lesbian Feminist Activism: A Reconsideration of Cultural Feminism." *Signs: Journal of Women in Culture and Society* 19.1 (Autumn): 32–61.

Thistlethwaite, Susan. 1989. *Sex, Race, and God: Christian Feminism in Black and White*. New York: Crossroad.

Tocqueville, Alexis de. 1945. *Democracy in America*, ed. and trans. Phillips Bradley, 2 vols. New York: Vintage Books.

Townes, Emilie M. 1993. *Womanist Justice, Womanist Hope*. Atlanta: Scholars Press.

Townes, Emilie M., ed. 1993. *A Troubling in My Soul: Womanist Perspectives on Evil and Suffering.* Maryknoll, N.Y.: Orbis Books.

Tronto, Joan. 1993. *Moral Boundaries: A Political Argument for an Ethic of Care.* New York: Routledge.

Truth, Sojourner. 1991. *Narrative of Sojourner Truth; A Bondswoman of Olden Time, With a History of Her Labors and Correspondence Drawn from Her "Book of Life"*, intro. Jeffrey C. Stewart. Schomburg Library of Nineteenth-Century Black Women Writers, ed. Henry Louis Gates, Jr. New York: Oxford University Press.

Tsing, Anna Lowenhaupt. 1993. *In the Realm of the Diamond Queen: Marginality in an Out-of-the-Way Place.* Princeton: Princeton University Press.

United States Department of Labor. 1965. *The Negro Family: The Case for National Action.* Washington, D.C.: U.S. Government Printing Office.

Vaid, Urvashi. 1995. *Virtual Equality: The Mainstreaming of Gay & Lesbian Liberation.* New York: Anchor Books.

Vance, Carole, ed. 1992. *Pleasure and Danger: Exploring Female Sexuality.* 3rd ed. Originally published in 1984. New York: Routledge and Kegan Paul. Reprinted in 1989. London: Pandora Press.

Walker, Margaret Urban. 1989. "Moral Understanding: Alternative 'Epistemology' for a Feminist Ethics." *Hypatia* 4.2 (Summer): 14–28.

Walters, Suzanna Danuta. 1996. "From Here to Queer: Postmodernism, and the Lesbian Menace (Or, Why Can't a Woman Be More Like a Fag?)." *Signs: Journal of Women in Culture and Society* 21.4 (Summer): 830–69.

Walzer, Michael. 1983. *Spheres of Justice.* New York: Basic Books.

Warner, Michael, ed. 1993. *Fear of a Queer Planet: Queer Politics and Social Theory.* Minneapolis: University of Minnesota Press.

Weed, Elizabeth, and Naomi Schor, eds. 1989. "The Essential Difference: Another Look at Essentialism." Special Issue of *differences* 1.2 (Summer).

Weeks, Jeffrey. 1995. *Invented Moralities: Sexual Values in an Age of Uncertainty.* New York: Columbia University Press.

Welch, Sharon. 1985. *Communities of Resistance and Solidarity: A Feminist Theology of Liberation.* Maryknoll, N.Y.: Orbis Books.

———. 1990. *A Feminist Ethic of Risk.* Minneapolis: Augsburg/Fortress Press.

Welter, Barbara. 1966. "The Cult of True Womanhood: 1820, 1860." *American Quarterly* 18 (Summer): 151–74.

West, Cornel. 1982. *Prophesy Deliverance! An Afro-American Revolutionary Christianity.* Philadelphia: Westminster Press.

———. 1988. "Marxist Theory and the Specificity of African-American Oppression." In *Marxism and the Interpretation of Culture*, ed. Cary Nelson and Lawrence Grossberg, 17–33. Chicago: University of Chicago Press.

Whittier, Nancy. 1995. *Feminist Generations: The Persistence of the Radical Women's Movement.* Philadelphia: Temple University Press.

Williams, Delores. 1993a. *Sisters in the Wilderness: The Challenge of Womanist God-Talk.* Maryknoll, N.Y.: Orbis Books.

———. 1993b. "Visions, Inner Voices, Apparitions, and Defiance in Nineteenth-Century Black Women's Narratives." *Women's Studies Quarterly* 1 & 2: 81–89.

Winch, Julie. 1994. "'You Have Talents—Only Cultivate Them': Philadelphia's Black Female Literary Societies and the Abolitionist Crusade." In *The Abolitionist Sister-*

hood: Women's Political Culture in Antebellum America, ed. Jean Fagan Yellin and John C. Van Horne, 119–38. Ithaca: Cornell University Press.

Wittig, Monique. 1984. "The Trojan Horse." *Feminist Issues* 4.2 (Fall): 45–49.

———. 1992. *The Straight Mind and Other Essays*. Boston: Beacon Press.

Yellin, Jean Fagan. 1989. *Women and Sisters: The Antislavery Feminists in American Culture*. New Haven: Yale University Press.

Yellin, Jean Fagan, and John C. Van Horne, eds. 1994. *The Abolitionist Sisterhood: Women's Political Culture in Antebellum America*. Ithaca: Cornell University Press.

Young, Iris Marion. 1990. *Justice and the Politics of Difference*. Princeton: Princeton University Press.

———. 1994. "Gender as Seriality: Thinking about Women as a Social Collective." *Signs: Journal of Women in Culture and Society* 19.3 (Spring): 713–38.

Zandy, Janet, ed. 1990. *Calling Home: Working Class Women's Writings*. New Brunswick: Rutgers University Press.

Zerilli, Linda. 1993. "The Trojan Horse of Universalism: Language as a 'War Machine' in the Writings of Monique Wittig." In *The Phantom Public Sphere*, ed. Bruce Robbins, 142–72. Minneapolis: University of Minnesota Press.

Domination, 1, 4, 6-7, 142, 169-70, 204*n*232; relativist critique of, 152-53; resistance to, 143-44, 198*n*196; of white ethics, 106-107; of women's bodies, 122
Douglas, Carol Anne, 62-63
Douglass, Frederick, 51, 178*n*49, 182*n*80
Drewal, Margaret, 99
Duberman, Martin, 81, 187*n*114
DuBois, Ellen Carol, 190*n*133
Durkheim, Emile, 151

Echols, Alice, 189*n*125
Economies: of differentiation, 58, 101; domestic, 44-45, 180*n*61; moral, 18-19, 24, 31-33, 46, 56-57, 98, 169-70
Economies of the same, 26, 142, 187*n*111; in feminism, 77-78, 98, 101; in the normatively constituted "we," 128; as structuring the "public," 58-59, 95
Egalitarianism, 141
Eisenstein, Hester, 61-62, 196*n*179
Elaw, Zilpha, 48
Enlightenment, 4, 173*n*8
Equality: the dilemma of difference vs., 8-9, 174*n*13; labor theory of, 47; as a model of moral agency, 34, 35-41, 55; sameness implied in, 36, 40, 53
Equivalence, 74-77, 79-80, 93, 159-62, 185*n*105, 200*nn*213,214
Essentialism, critique of, 103-104, 193*n*148
Ethics, 15-19, 175*nn*23,24; and agency, 4, 20; of ambiguity, 21; and complexity, 21; "ethical feminism," 16; as individual, 23; and politics, 23-24, 124, 171; and the "problem" of relativism, 150
—Black womanist, 20, 170; and Christianity, 104, 108-109; as in the space outside of dominant society, 32, 102-103; specificity in the development of, 105, 106, 107-108; as stemming from traditions that precede modernity, 154; white ethics criticized, 106-107, 193*n*154
—lesbian, 16, 103, 110-17, 170-71; diversity of, 119; and lesbian agency, 112-13; and lesbian autonomy, 113, 116; as proceeding from modernity, 154; separatist stance of, 111, 113-14
Evans, James H., 109, 182*n*83
Evans, Sara, 61

Feminism: academic vs. movement, 62; "ampersand problem" for, 174*n*16; difference vs. equality debate in, 8-9, 174*n*13; difference vs. gender feminism, 174*n*13; diversity and complexity within, 1, 95-96; dominative, 85-87, 93-94; economy of the same in, 77-78, 98; lesbianism as a difference within, 84-85; lesbianism subsumed under, 103, 192*n*147; loss of commonality claimed in, 161-62, 202*n*219; norms disarticulated by, 124; and the queer movement, 122-24, 145-46. *See also* Lesbian-feminism
Feminist movement, 1, 173*n*2; alliances in, 25-26, 167; diversity and complexity in, 6; diversity unrecognized in, 59; liberal model of diversity in, 10-12; as a network constructed in and between differences, 102-103; and power relations, 6; reiterated norms in, 100. *See also* Abolition movements
—second-wave (1970s) movements, 26, 93-97, 165-66; academic vs. movement texts in, 62; autonomy and alliance in, 73-77, 80, 81, 93-96; and class, 60-61, 65, 88-93, 94; equivalence claims in, 74-77, 79-80, 93, 160, 200*n*214; and the gay liberation movement, 79, 81-88; as predominantly white, middle class and heterosexual, 60-66, 93-94, 183*n*94, 185*n*104; "problem of difference" in, 60-66, 95-96; and race, 60-61, 62-64, 66-73; and sexuality, 60, 64-65
Fisher, Sue, 204*n*230
Fleischner, Jennifer, 37
Foucault, Michel, 6, 182*n*84, 190*n*136, 197*n*196, 203*n*228
Frankenberg, Ruth, 63-64, 183*n*92
Fraser, Nancy, 197*n*195
Freedom, 107, 193*n*154
French Revolution, 153
Friedan, Betty, 84-85
Friedman, Lawrence, 37, 178*n*48
Frye, Marilyn, 16, 175*n*22
Fuchs, Josef, 177*n*39
The Furies, 61, 88-93, 182*n*88, 189*nn*127,130
Fuss, Diana, 195*n*175

Gage, Frances, 50, 51
Gallop, Jane, 62, 183*n*91
Garcia, Alma M., 61
Garrison, William, 178*n*49
"The Gay Agenda" (video), 129

Materialism, 71–73
Mathias, Robert, 180n64
Matriarchy, myth of Black, 68, 70
McLaughlin, Andrée Nicola, 153
Mediation, 143
Meese, Ed, 123, 129–34, 140–41, 158
Mercer, Kobena, 11, 71, 101, 201n218
Messer-Davidow, Ellen, 31, 174n11
Military, controversy over gays in, 129, 132
Miller, Nancy K., 62
"Minorities": construction of, 129–32, 135–
36, 168; containment of, 132–33, 134–35
Minow, Martha, 8, 29
Modernism, 104–105, 109, 113, 117, 153–
54, 192n144, 195n172
Mohanty, Chandra, 9–10, 173n7, 192n144
Moral agency, 3, 28, 33–34, 178n42; of Afri-
can American women, 34, 47–53, 105–10;
communitarian model of, 34, 42–46,
179n56; in complex power relations, 50–
51; contextualized, 152; equality model of,
34, 35–41, 55; lesbian separatist, 111–17;
and moral diversity, 53–57
Moral diversity, 4, 53–57
Moral economies, 18–19, 24, 31–33, 46, 56–
57, 98, 169–70
Morality: moral labor necessary for, 32–33,
177nn37,40; women's, 24, 29, 30–31,
177n35. *See also* Moral agency
Morgan, Robin. *See Sisterhood is Powerful*
Morton, Nelle, 165
Mosse, George, 181n72
Mouffe, Chantal, 143–44, 157–62, 192n143,
196n180; on agency, 203n228; on articulation, 197n192; on conflict resolution,
198n197; on democracy, 160, 200n212; on
desire for transparency, 201n215; on equality and liberty, 201n216; on equivalence,
159–60, 162, 185n105; on fixity and communication, 191n142; new common political identity called for by, 159, 161–62,
200n213
Mullin, Amy, 167–68, 203nn226,228,
204n229
Muteness, 37
Myron, Nancy, 91, 92. *See also Class and
Feminism*

National Gay and Lesbian Task Force, 135–
37, 140
Natural law theories, 177n39
Needs, true vs. false, 141

Negotiation, 167–68
Networks, 102–103
Norms, 98–99, 125–28; norm/difference
hierarchy, 8; dis-articulation of, 124; diverse and complex, 137; materialized by
communities, 127; and the operation of
power, 123–24; placed in the histories of
struggle, 101; and politics, 140–48; productive power of, 98; rearticulation of, 99–
100; reiteration of, 98–99; slave-produced,
30–31, 106; social matrix of, 18; space in-
between, 144; and values, 16–19, 24,
175n24; women-produced, 30–31, 33
Norquist, Grover, 133
Norton, Eleanor Homes, 78
Nunn, Sam, 132

Old Elizabeth, 48
One: and multiple others, 182n87
Ong, Aihwa, 80, 187n113
Oppressions: and alliance formation, 92–93;
equivalence claims among, 74–77, 94;
from the Other, 187n113; gay, 137–38; lesbian, 114–15; multiple simultaneous interlocking, 72; patriarchy as the base of, 90;
sexuality as the base of, 85
Osborne, Tori, 136–37
Other, 10, 187n113

Painter, Nell Irvin, 48, 50, 51, 53, 60,
181nn74,76
Particular(ity): slippage between the general
and, 140–42; particularity/universalism
binary, 109–10, 194n163. *See also*
Relativism, moral
Pascoe, Peggy, 176n30
Paternalism, 37–38, 111, 178n49
Patriarchy, 90; heteropatriarchy, 118
Peirce, Charles Sanders, 202n224
Petersen, Tasha, 90–91
Pfeil, Fred, 153, 166, 199n205, 203n228
Phelan, Shane, 174n16
Piaget, Jean, 151
Piercy, Marge, 79
Play, 169
Pluralism: complex, 27, 147, 152, 171; lib-
eral reductive pluralism, 10–12, 26, 173n9;
of particulars, 141; and the "problem" of
relativism, 151–52, 198n201
Politics: alliance politics, 156–64; difference
politics, 5, 21, 63–64, 83, 94, 98, 148,
173n9; and ethics, 23–24, 124, 171; iden-

JANET R. JAKOBSEN is Assistant Professor of Women's Studies and Religious Studies and Co-Coordinator of the Committee for Lesbian, Gay, and Bisexual Studies at the University of Arizona. She has worked as a policy analyst, lobbyist, and organizer in Washington, D.C. Her essays have appeared in such journals as *Hypatia*, the *Journal of Feminist Studies in Religion*, and the *Journal of Religious Ethics*.